# THE LITERAL IMAGINATION

# THE LITERAL IMAGINATION

## Selected Essays

---

Ian Watt

*Edited by Bruce Thompson*

The Society for the Promotion of Science and Scholarship
Palo Alto, California
*and*
The Stanford Humanities Center
Stanford University, Stanford, California

2002

The Society for the Promotion of Science and Scholarship, Inc.
Palo Alto, California
*and*
The Stanford Humanities Center
Stanford University, Stanford, California

The Society for the Promotion of Science and Scholarship is a nonprofit corpo-
ration established for the purposes of scholarly publishing, to benefit both academics and members of the general public. It has special interests in European
and British Studies.

Printed in the United States of America

Library of Congress Cataloging-in-Publication Data

Watt, Ian P.
  The literal imagination : selected essays / Ian Watt; edited by Bruce
Thompson.
     p. cm.
Includes index.
  ISBN 0-930664-24-8 (hardcover : alk. paper) -- ISBN 0-930664-25-6
(pbk. : alk. paper)
1. English literature--History and criticism. 2. World War,
1939-1945--Prisoners and prisons, Japanese. I. Thompson, Bruce. II.
Title.
  PR99.W36 2002
  820.9--dc21

                        2002005854

*In memory of Ruth Watt*

# TABLE OF CONTENTS

# FOREWORD

## Frederick Crews

Ian Watt's lasting fame as a literary analyst was secured in 1957 with the publication of *The Rise of the Novel*, which remains an indispensable text nearly half a century later. For countless academics who were then chafing under the dominance of New Critical formalism, Watt's book pointed a way out—not the only way, certainly, but the only one that wouldn't risk degenerating into a comfortable routine in its own right. The Wattian imperative was to take nothing for granted, to declare no subject matter off-limits in principle, and then to account for a literary work, career, or whole movement by reference to every factor—biographical, economic, social, cultural, philosophical—that appeared to resonate with the spirit of the text(s). The program was inexhaustible because it entailed no bias toward any given interpretative line. It was a model not of connect-the-dots "methodology" but of open-minded investigation.

I wish I could count myself among those who profited at once from *The Rise of the Novel*. It was, I realized much later, the perfect antidote to a more imposing book published in the same year, Northrop Frye's *Anatomy of Criticism*, which presumed to taxonomize all of literature within a few superordinate types. Here was no agenda for the historically curious inquirer but rather a *summa formalistica* declaring the range of possible imaginative expression to be already fully mapped. Recoiling from such an airless system, I soon found myself groping toward a mode of criticism that might do justice to the psychological immediacy of complex, self-divided works. Alas, another form of question-begging deductivism, the psychoanalytic kind, lay in ambush—obliging me, after a few years of rash theoretic enthusiasm, to spend decades trying to warn others against repeating my own error. How much better for all concerned if, from the outset, I had taken Watt's canny empiricism to heart![1]

As fate would have it, I soon became professionally associated with Watt and, in remarkably short order, found myself the beneficiary of his friendship. When, fresh out of graduate school, I joined Berkeley's English department in 1958, Watt was already one of its luminaries, along with Mark Schorer, Henry Nash Smith, Josephine Miles, Bertrand Bronson, and James D. Hart among others. There was no reason why the author of *The Rise of the Novel* should pay any regard to the greenest of recruits. But distinctions of rank never meant anything to Watt. More than any other senior colleague, he made me feel like an intellectual peer.[2]

The Ian Watt I came to know was ruggedly handsome, self-assured, and down-to-earth. He moved with athletic quickness, and his mind, too, was always a step ahead of you. Every form of sentimentality and sham amused him, and he typically punctuated his irreverent observations with a sharp sardonic laugh. As graduate chair of our department he was something of an autocrat, striking fear into students who sensed, correctly, that his personal judgment trumped the official rules. But later in the sixties, as Stanford's chair of English during a period of truly warlike turmoil, he would show himself capable of heroically restrained statesmanship.

There is, I am sure, no contradiction here; in both cases the same take-charge Ian was trying to keep his department focused on its intellectual mission. But the violence at Stanford, incited in part by a member of his own English faculty, brought to the fore a wisdom he had acquired in the 1940s when he had endured three-and-a-half years of harsh imprisonment at the hands of the Japanese military. As you can see from the final chapter below, that experience taught him that "the continuity of human affairs will not happen of itself." When the social fabric was tearing at Stanford, the former British army lieutenant put all

---

[1] Watt himself, it must be said, infrequently toyed with Freudian schemata, as manifested in Chapters 10 and 12 below. Even there, however, the reader will note a wealth of observational detail attesting to Watt's temperamental preference for anchoring his conclusions in facts.

[2] Indeed, the present book contains fossil evidence of that welcome. Watt's great essay "The First Paragraph of *The Ambassadors*," originally published in 1960, acknowledges advice offered by "Dorothea Krook, Frederick C. Crews, and Henry Nash Smith."

provocations and insults in abeyance and became a paragon of diplomacy, patience, and resolve.[3]

Watt's role as a successful administrator—he also served as the first dean of the University of East Anglia's School of English Studies and as founding director of the Stanford Humanities Center—bears fascinating connections with some of the other essays in this book. Now and again the reader will find Watt directly confronting the fallacies of unrestrained individualism, variously manifested in Romantic poets and radically negative modernists, in Hollywood's melodramatic clichés, in tenured anti-institutionalists, and in the contemporary intellectual's "image of himself as a passionate defender of the last citadels of human reason against the mounting tide of folly, vulgarity, and commercialism." For Watt, the missing ingredient was always the same: a properly humble consciousness of the way we are defined, supported, and rendered useful by those whose tasks and trials we share.

It is fitting, in this light, that the last of Watt's books to be published in his lifetime was called *Myths of Modern Individualism* (1994). So, too, it makes sense that the author to whom he would devote the most attention was Joseph Conrad—the subject of what many consider his finest work, *Conrad in the Nineteenth Century* (1980). That monograph casts a steady light on Conrad's themes and their multiple filiations with intellectual history; and typically, it neither idolizes the novelist nor succumbs to the faddish temptation of deploring his political benightedness. But beneath Watt's evenhandedness one detects a tacit endorsement of Conrad's core insight: that mundane solidarity is invaluable precisely because every other source of meaning is illusory.[4]

Watt, then, was a sophisticated student of a virtue that few thinkers today perceive as such: strategic compromise. That preoccupation is most subtly expressed below in the chapters touching on what he calls the Augustan empirical temper. Like Watt himself, the great Augustan authors were empiricists not in the sense of skeptically testing every

---

[3] In this regard, see William M. Chace, "Ian Watt: The Liberty of the Department," *Stanford Humanities Review* 8:1 (Spring 2000), 42-50. That entire special issue, entitled *Critical History: The Career of Ian Watt*, can be consulted with profit.

[4] Not surprisingly, some of Watt's finest shorter writings deal with Conrad. They can be found in his other posthumous collection, *Essays on Conrad* (Cambridge: Cambridge University Press, 2000).

proposition or of spurning all abstractions, but rather in their upholding of norms that spoke to common human experience. They were, in short, studiously anti-ideological.

Instead of fetishizing that posture, however, Watt recognizes it as yet another ideology, a quietistic one, and he shows how it emerged as an attitudinal truce after an epoch of exhausting wars and purges. Moreover, he lets us see that the Augustans, though perfectly sincere when invoking natural bonds and standards, were simultaneously advancing the interests of a propertied class. Likewise, he bares the elite assumptions behind their famous irony, which depended for its effect on a false show of deference to the democratic mob whose illusions would be scorned by the cognoscenti.

It would be a mistake, then, to assume that Augustan high irony struck a note that Watt himself was striving to emulate. "Isn't Swift a cook," he brilliantly asks, "who cares so much for cleanliness that all his dishes taste of soap?" Watt prefers the "open irony" of the last Augustan, Dr. Johnson, who considered himself no better or worse than the rest of the errant human race. And in his study of *The Ambassadors* Watt pauses to ask, "Is there really anything so wonderful about being distant and objective? Who wants to see life only or mainly in intellectual terms?"

The answer, of course, is that academics do. They were intellectualizing in 1960, when marmoreal verbal icons were all the rage, and they are still doing so today—but in an opposite mood, to literature's detriment rather than its worship. Neither mode can do justice to, say, the fertile messiness of a *Tristram Shandy* or to the complex temper of its age. Although ideology and history were familiar terrain for Watt, he would have endorsed neither an "identity politics" that aims to decertify the white-male classics nor an alleged historicism that caricatures our forebears as mere vessels of prejudice and oppression. Criticism, for him, was not a means of staking out turf or demonstrating one's radical bona fides; it was a jargon-free conversation among equals whose shared love of literature could be taken for granted.

The title Bruce Thompson has chosen for this collection is drawn from its final chapter, where Watt tells us that the humanities ought to uphold "a way of responding to experience which involves what I would call 'the literal imagination' entering as fully as possible in all the concrete particularities of a literary work or the lives of others or the lessons of history." That ideal is articulated at several other points below, but it would be just so much hot air if it weren't continually embodied in agile feats of analysis. Watt's own "concrete particularities" form the most telling, if implicit, critique of an academic practice that by now is humanistic in name only. Would it be too much to hope that, when the dust has mercifully settled over poststructuralism and postmodernism, critics will rediscover the kind of engagement from which Ian Watt never swerved?

# Acknowledgments

Publication of this volume of Ian Watt's essays would not have been possible without the generous financial support of the Stanford Humanities Center and the Department of History of the University of California, Santa Cruz. I am very grateful to Peter Stansky, Norris Pope, Ruth Watt, and Frederick Crews for their shrewd advice on the selection of essays; to Janet Gardiner of the Society for the Promotion of Science and Scholarship (SPOSS) for her patience and counsel during every phase of this project; and to the editors and publishers who have kindly granted permission to reprint Ian Watt's essays. Many thanks also to Candace Freiwald, Laura McShane, and Veronica Higoreda of UCSC's Stevenson Academic Services for their assistance in preparing the essays for republication. And it is a pleasure to salute Frederick Crew again for contributing the foreword to this collection of essays by his late friend and colleague.

Ruth Watt contributed to almost every phase of the preparation of this book, from the selection of the essays to the proofreading. She loved these essays and was delighted by the prospect of a collection that would make them accessible to a new generation of scholars and readers. Tragically, she did not live to see the publication of this volume. It is dedicated to her, with gratitude and affection.

Bruce Thompson

# THE LITERAL IMAGINATION

# 1

## Serious Reflections on *The Rise of the Novel*

Having, long ago, grimly refrained from posting sundry devastating retorts to a few of the original reviewers of *The Rise of the Novel*, I didn't at first find the attractions of contributing to the present series sufficient to warrant discomposing my posture of heroic abnegation.* It wasn't as though, stumbling gamely along towards my centenary, I couldn't any longer risk passing up one final opportunity to provoke incredulous outrage among those still elbowing their way up the professorial ladder: "'Sblood! Not buried yet?" Nor, certainly, had I any rankling sense that *The Rise of the Novel* had received less than its due—quite the contrary. However, I finally decided that a few rather miscellaneous reflections about the composition, the reception, and the shortcomings of the book, which had dimly glimmered in my mind from time to time, might have enough general interest to justify exposing myself to the charge of self-important anecdotage.

Retracing the stages of composition of *The Rise of the Novel* makes me realize how my operative, though largely unformulated, premises were intricately connected with the way the book was eventually received; and it also illustrates how academic writing, in its small way, is also subject to the processes of history.

Work on *The Rise of the Novel* began in 1938, when I held a Strathcona Research Fellowship at St. John's College, Cambridge. The war diverted me to other studies from 1939 to 1946; but when peace broke out I went back to work and finished a first draft early in 1947. I then

---

* "Serious Reflections on *The Rise of the Novel*" appeared originally in *NOVEL: A Forum on Fiction*, Vol. 1, No. 3, Spring 1968. Copyright NOVEL Corp. © 1968. Reprinted with permission.

laid the subject aside, and began various other more or less abortive projects; in 1951, however, I went back to the eighteenth-century novel, and the sixth revised draft was finally accepted for publication in 1956.

The main direction of the interminable and painful process of revision, forcibly stimulated in the last two years by the comments of various readers, stipendiary and otherwise, was towards making the book much shorter. This drastic reduction of scale primarily affected the beginning and the end.

Originally there was a long methodological first chapter. Having struggled through a good deal of Vaihinger, Wittgenstein, Carnap, Neurath, and other philosophers, I wanted not only to show it, but also to theorize about how literary history and criticism ought to be combined through what I then called the hypothetico-deductive method. Briefly, it seemed that the natural and social sciences had the advantage of beginning with objectively demonstrable data; and the equivalents of these data in literature—the written records—could also be made the starting point of inductive study along the lines of traditional biographical and bibliographical scholarship. But in the larger critical and historical area which interested me the case was quite different. Here my procedure would have to be largely deductive; and so the nearest I could get to objectivity would be to start from a hypothesis that was based, not on my own opinion, but on that of the majority of qualified observers.

That was the gist of my original thirty-five page heavily footnoted methodological introduction. Successive revisions eventually boiled it down to one word: the "if" in the opening paragraph which introduced the clauses "if we assume, as is commonly done, [that the novel is a new literary form], and that it was begun by Defoe, Richardson, and Fielding, how does it differ from the prose fiction of the past . . . and is there any reason why these differences appeared when and where they did?"

There is, I have since discovered, nothing exceptional about such drastic cutting; indeed it seems to be the rule rather than the exception that introductions begin by being infinitely expandable and end by proving equally expendable. But I probably wouldn't have cut quite so drastically for economy alone. Another reason was certainly a growing disenchantment with all theory, even my own. The decisive factor, however, was probably my slow-dawning realization that all those messy sheets of paper were in process of turning into that improbable object, a printed book. At once the question of my likely audience—even of my possible reviewers—became much more real; and this introduced all kinds of new considerations. One of them was the lurking (and unworthy) notion that it would be impolitic to affront the known prejudices of my main audience—students and teachers of literature—by flaunting the stigmata of my long fraternization with logical positivists and social scientists.

The deletion of the first chapter certainly made the book more palatable to publishers and readers; but it had an unexpected result—the whole of my cherished hypothetico-deductive method, which for me had continued to be immanent in that initial "if," passed quite unnoticed, and laid the book open to two general criticisms.

First, that its basic thesis was not original.[1] This, of course, was true; but originality would have been completely contrary to my chosen procedure.

Secondly, I was branded as a monocular modern, blind to the greatness of the ancients, and impervious to the legitimacy of other previous forms of fiction.[2] Here again, though the charge may be true, my methodological assumption had precluded any autonomous treatment of any forms of fiction other than those of early eighteenth-century England. The words "the rise of the novel," no doubt, looked as though I were making the much more unqualified assertion—that the only prose fiction which mattered began with Defoe; but such a supposition, I thought, was undercut not only by that initial "if," but also by my more modest and casual subtitle: "Studies in Defoe, Richardson, and Fielding."

What conclusions can be drawn from all this I'm not sure. Perhaps that one's methodological assumptions have to be repeated very frequently if they are to remain active in the minds of readers; perhaps that some form of typographical emphasis—a *Ulysses*-like giant "IF" occupying the whole first page—would have mediated my message better.

The second main cut during the process of revision was even larger in scale. It came at the end. There were originally three final chapters—a further one on *Tom Jones*, and one each on Smollett and Sterne. I cut out these chapters merely because they would have made the book much

---

[1] E.g., "Professor Watt *manages* [my italics] to challenge received opinion surprisingly little." J. Paul Hunter, *The Reluctant Pilgrim* (Baltimore: Johns Hopkins University Press, 1966), p. viii.

[2] E.g., "Ian Watt on the Novel Form," Appendix of E. M. Tillyard's *The Epic Strain in the English Novel* (London: Chatto & Windus, 1958).

too long; but although the omission helped me to see how to give what remained a much firmer organization, it also damaged the original proportions of the book. I had planned a structure in which the emphasis on "realism of presentation" in chapters two to eight was counterpoised by that on "realism of assessment" in the last five chapters. When this original structure was abandoned, the treatment of "realism of assessment" became so brief that, perhaps inevitably, the book was read as rather more simpleminded in its advocacy of "realism of presentation"[3] than it might have been otherwise. As a result I have had to grow accustomed to figuring in some minds as a permanent picketer for the Union Novel (International President H. James), carrying a sign which reads "Cervantes Go Home" on one side, and "Fielding is a Fink"[4] on the other.

Rereading *The Rise of the Novel*, I can certainly detect a good many unhappy relics of earlier drafts. Some are merely stylistic. The most masochistic reviser, I imagine, finds it difficult not to succumb to the enchantment of his own prose, especially when it comes to him with the Mosaic authority acquired when the tablets have been expensively retyped; much time, and a special frame of mind, and sometimes, alas, only the belated clarity of vision that comes when the words have been set up in type, are needed before one finally recognizes all those ancient anal succubi, and blushes with shame to think that one was so long pleasured by such graceless imbecilities. There are also residues of a more programmatic adhesion to my initial design than was wholly consistent with my final critical position. One of these can be seen in the chaptering. As the years passed I had chafed more and more under the restrictions of a positivist historical analysis of the elements of "newness" in the novel form. This finally led me to decompose the original chapters on Defoe and Richardson so that the social and historical approaches were separated from a more autonomous literary treatment of particular works. Thus, although *Robinson Crusoe* and *Pamela* were

---

[3] E.g., "Watt's all-pervasive assumption is that 'realism of presentation' is a good thing in itself," Wayne C. Booth, *The Rhetoric of Fiction* (Chicago: University of Chicago Press, 1961), p. 41.

[4] E.g., "Fielding is graduated without honors." *Modern Language Quarterly*, 21 (1960), 374. Here, and wherever else the need for brevity made it impossible to present a critic's judgment fairly, I have thought it more equitable to give the barest reference, omitting names.

used mainly for thematic and illustrative purposes, *Moll Flanders* and *Clarissa* were given independent critical essays.

As far as I can now guess at it, my guiding impulse when I worked on the later drafts was essentially rather simple—to write a book such as I myself would like to read. Such a book would certainly have what are usually called the scholarly virtues. I had long ago picked up the notion (I must not now speculate how or where) that one should be serious at least about what one had freely decided to do: in Conrad's terms, one should be concerned about the cut of one's clothes even in a community of blind men. My experience in the graduate schools of U.C.L.A. and Harvard had opened my eyes to what responsible professional research should be; and I had attempted to incorporate these standards in the substance of the manuscript. But now the main emphasis changed. I came to see more clearly that my aim also implied various difficult, and to some extent conflicting, compositional imperatives. As regards scale, it involved not treating any topic at exhaustive length. As regards prose, it involved a much more rapid pace, and even more important, a whole style of writing that was responsive to two other unformulated premises: that writing about literature should somehow convey its awareness of that honor; and that it should also embody, though without buttonholing intimacy, the notion that it is the product neither of a card index nor of a divine oracle, but of a putative human being communicating with other human beings.

I must hurry on past these peculiarly delicate pretensions, pausing only at one paradox they suggest: that in their extreme forms scholarly and literary considerations are diametrically opposed. At the scholarly pole we have a study which is in effect an organized collection of evidence, a meticulous concordance or catalogue of categorized citations, a corpus of texts with explanatory commentary. On some topics—as in Part III of H. T. Swedenberg's *The Theory of the Epic in England, 1650-1800* (1944), for example—this form can triumphantly justify itself; but for most subjects, quotations do not in fact speak for themselves; and if they are left to do so for very long, very few people keep on listening.

On the other hand, the more one departs from the exhaustive detailing of primary evidence, the more one is inevitably imposing one's own views and voice. For example, the literary need for prose of a reasonable pace requires much omission (a bore is a man who tells you everything) and, in particular, a severe pruning of quotations and qualifications. In

addition, stylistic genuflections towards the literary nature of the sub-
ject-matter, and towards the presumably exhaustible attention span of
the reader, obviously demand various kinds of departure from plain declarative statement to more multi-vocal, or in other respects more complex, kinds of prose.

At the scholarly extreme, then, one discourages readers; at the other,
one risks discouragement from the scholars. Omissions dictated by the
need for pace, for example, will run up against the all-but-universal presumption that if you don't mention a book, you haven't read it.[5] As regards prose style, every departure from plain declarative statement increases the chances of being misunderstood. Ironical modes of statement, for example, can be made to look very silly when they are quoted
as though they were meant literally;[6] fortunately one can always accuse
the critic of having missed one's irony.

In any case, whatever the undoubted difficulties involved in trying to
strike the right balance, and write both for the specialist and for what
must pass nowadays for the general reader, I am still persuaded that
there was—and is—nothing wrong with my basic compositional aim:
trying to increase the exceptions to the rule that "scholarly" usually
means "unreadable" and "readable" usually means "wrong."

---

[5] . . . to assure . . . readers . . . that Defoe was being consciously ironic [in *Moll
Flanders*] . . . the critic must have read a good part of the five hundred and
forty-seven items . . . in Professor John Robert Moore's *Checklist of the Writings of Daniel Defoe* . . . but this is precisely what none of the critics appear to
have done." (Maximillian E. Novak, "Conscious Irony in *Moll Flanders*: Facts
and Problems," *College English*, 26 [1964], 199). *Quippe peccavi*; but a good
many footnotes and references were dropped during my revisions; and later the
publishers asked for further drastic cuts. This horrified me at the time, but the
cuts helped bring about what I now regard as a satisfactory balance between
text and notes.

[6] Thus George Starr's objection (*Defoe and Spiritual Autobiography* [Princeton:
Princeton University Press, 1965], p. 120) to my writing, about the Friday-
Crusoe relationship: "A functional silence, broken only by an occasional 'No,
Friday,' or an abject 'Yes, Master,' is the golden music of Crusoe's *île joyeuse*,"
seems to me valid only if my statement is interpreted literally; and I had tried to
write the sentence in such a way that it wouldn't be.

## II

As far as the author is concerned, the reception of his book seems even slower and more painful than its gestation. First the elephantine parturition in publishing offices and printing houses. Next the onset of labor pains, usually announced by peremptory demands for collected galleys or the index not later than last Monday. After many more months that seem like years, a few advance copies eventually arrive. The first thing one sees is a misprint. With sinking feelings one puts the book away, and waits. With luck a friend writes a review for one of the weeklies, and it comes out only a few weeks after the official date of publication. Then a long deafening silence, only interrupted by a press-cutting agency that sends funny little yellow pasteups enshrining what the compositors of the *Brooklyn Daily* or the *Pomona Progress-Bulletin*[7] have made of the dust jacket, or of the notice sent out by Virginia Kirkus's Service. Finally, the numbing conviction that the grave will gape long before the learned journals allow themselves a majestically deliberate turn in your direction.

Whatever the delay, preparation for the majestic turn should begin much earlier than it usually does. If, for example, I had been advised to change my name at an early stage of authorship, and to adopt an intimidatingly sonorous nom de plume, it might have prevented my deep chagrin when the paronomastic insults to which my surname is so susceptible, and which had haunted me ever since first grade, relentlessly pursued my authorial reincarnation: the first printed notice of my work ended, with numbing irony, ". . . and now Watt."[8]

The century with which I coexist has instructed me that the only way to handle such traumatic experiences is to convince oneself that they are universal. It is with this therapeutic orientation that I now offer a brief analysis—from which other authors may incidentally benefit—of the institution of reviewing.

---

[7] "The novel has flourished in America since the growth of the lending library and the emancipation of women according to a study recently published by the University of California Press" (August 12, 1957). The *Lodi News-Sentinel* echoed this laconic interpretation *verbatim* the next day.

[8] *Philological Quarterly,* 31 (1952), 266.

Reviewing belongs to the large class of benevolent-aggressive dyadic relationships which are characterized, like dentistry, by an extreme asymmetry of roles. The transitive agent, the reviewer, is secure in the knowledge that his sitting duck can neither fly off nor hit back; despite this great freedom, however, reviewers seem to operate under a highly conventional set of institutionalized imperatives, all naturally directed towards producing the most pain with the least effort.

This expertise is highly valued whether it serves merely to maximize the personal pleasure of the reviewer, or, as more commonly, to equip him for the effective discharge of his primary professional obligation— to teach the universe some of the discipline it so sadly lacks. The first principle of reviewing, then, is the law of Maximal Offense; and its main applications can conveniently be memorized under the rubric of the three "P's": *Sprezzatura*; Unacknowledged Paraphrase; and Benevolent Patronage.

No review, of course, is complete without pointing out at least one error, but decorum requires that it be done with glancing casualness— the mandatory strategy is to suggest "I really don't have the time to go through more than one or two pages in search of this kind of thing." Quotation or misquotation follows. Note that too copious or specific a listing spoils the effect of habitual but careless contempt which is the hallmark of true *sprezzatura*. For instance, the comment "three of Defoe's titles are incorrectly given"[9] would lose much of its force if the errors were illustrated; and the whole effect would certainly be ruined if the reviewer should add "and there is a dangling participle on p. 201."

So much for tone. As regards content, Unacknowledged Paraphrase is the standard pattern. It begins with something to the effect that "What poor Professor W*** seems to have been trying to say," or "would have observed, had his maker endowed him with the wit, is . . . "—and there follows the required number of words in the form of a précis of the main point of the book with "immediacy of presentation," say, replacing the terms actually employed by the author—in this case "authenticity" or "realism of presentation."

The Unacknowledging Paraphrast usually employs Benevolent Patronage as his backstop. He is then in permanent possession of the useful option of being able to retort: "Why ever is that poor reviewee getting so bothered? After all, I went out of my way to make the handsome

---

[9] *Modern Language Quarterly* 21 (1960), 374.

concession that 'I imagine the book will be of considerable value to un-dergraduates' and may even 'remind [the specialist] of things he has for-gotten.'"[10]

So much for Maximal Offense. The second law of reviewing is mod-eled on the Enclosure Acts, and is usually called the "One Man One Field Principle." The reviewer's pastoral role, is, quite simply, to shoo writers back where they belong, if so dismal a pasture can be located. A simple example would be "If Mr. Watt had not attempted to combine literary history with criticism, his discussion . . . might have been of lasting value. . . . Unfortunately he has chosen a historico-philosophical approach, for which he seems less well equipped."[11] This is the egalitar-ian form of the law—"My Field—Keep Out"; but even after all fields have been equally allotted they must still be protected from dangerous pests; hence, the reviewer's pastoral role occasionally obliges him to put up a public notice for the protection of innocent wayfarers. One simple example of this "Beware the Dangerous Dog" posting is the reflection, "It seems to me that Mr. Watt gets a little 'Freudian' at the end."[12] "Seems," be it noted parenthetically, seems to be the reviewer's major lexical resource, possibly on legal grounds.

Some of the other established rituals of reviewing might at first seem to deserve the status of autonomous laws: the Law of Mandatory Regret (some always are); the "Quest for All the-Earmarks-of Law" (on which see the latest brand-book of dissertations, or search the author's ac-knowledgments for any signs of telltale indebtedness to not-in influ-ences); even the "Virtually Useless Index Law" (optional if there is no index). But further examination discloses that nearly all these are merely particular applications of the third basic principle of reviewing—the Law of Inevitable Disproportion. It can be put very simply: "If Not Too Many Then Too Few" (e.g., footnotes, quotations, jokes, ideas, friends, enemies, etc.).

Strictly speaking there is only one law for the intransitive agent, the reviewee: Forget it.

Unfortunately this law shares with most other forms of wisdom the sad truth that it is impossible to practice. It may, therefore, be useful to

---

[10] *Essays in Criticism*, 8 (1958), 433-37, 429, 437-38.

[11] *Birmingham Post*, Feb. 26, 1957.

[12] *Essays in Criticism*, 8 (1958), 438.

steel the patient for his ordeal by informing him of the main operative
procedures as they affect the reviewee. They are also three in number.

First, there is the Law of Absolute Irrelevance. There is nothing which
may not be introduced into public comment on any book. The author of
a work on eighteenth-century fiction, for example, must never imagine
himself safe from such no doubt well-founded, if not transparently ap-
posite, accusations as "Mr. Watt shows himself to be unaware of the
work of philosophers like Augustine, Anselm, and Bonaventura."[13]

Secondly, there is the Law of Inverse Qualification, which states that
the boiling point of malediction is inversely proportional to the age
and professional status of the reviewer. It is really a special case of the
universal law which states that the last acquired of Minerva's arts is
charity.

Finally we have the Law of Mistaken Identity. No reviewee can ever
recognize himself or his handiwork in the object which appears to have
come under the reviewer's purview. This is true, unfortunately, even of
laudatory reviews, for which the universally valid principle of Authorial
Insatiability must be invoked. One might expect a reviewee to be satisfied, for instance, if he is placed on a footing with Gibbon and Hume:[14]
actually he merely reads on, reflecting bitterly "Hm. He might at least
have taken the trouble to *elaborate* his only valuable insight"; and ex-
its muttering "*Not a word* about that witty thrust in footnote 397.
Criminal."

Lest any skeptical reader find this analysis lacking in objectivity, and
be led to surmise that I may be motivated by personal bias, I must also
add that none of the above principles and practices actually produces
the galloping *anomie* in the Republic of Academic Letters which might
be expected: for they are all subject to the ultimate truth about reviewing, the Statute of Amnesic Limitation. The reviewee will probably never
meet anyone who has read and remembers both the review and his
book; and the wounds received from reviews heal unimaginably rapidly
at the touch of time. The amnesia is equally functional for the reviewer:
perhaps fortunately, since if any of his blows proved as deadly as they
seem, they might sap his zest for battle.

---

[13] *Essays in Criticism*, 9 (1959), 206. Oddly enough there were in fact two references to the first, over-reverently indexed under St. Augustine.
[14] See Louis Kampf, "Review Essay" in *History and Theory*, 6 (1967), 88.

III

But I can no longer decently put off the only thing which may have been sustaining the interest of remaining readers—the always gratifying spectacle of public penitence. No prizes are offered for observing that a change of method and tone is called for. Anyone not utterly impervious to the possibilities of imitative form will be prepared for the logic which dictates that a first section which followed (admittedly at a great distance) Defoe's autobiographical mode, and a second which attempted to prove the writer not wholly deaf to Fielding's way of suggesting general principles by an ironic acceptance of their violation, should be succeeded by a third section which explores error and guilt in Richardson's copious manner.

What crows then shall I eat? How many have already been crammed down my recalcitrant gullet?

Professor J. C. Maxwell pointed out in charitable privacy a mistranslation of Aristotle on page 19 for which I can still find no explanation. As to the reviewers, some succeeded in convincing me that various confusions between British and American publishing styles had defaced the text with sundry reprehensible inconsistencies, while others demonstrated how I had misunderstood *Moll Flanders.*[15] But it seems better to use what space remains to confront, not my critics, but my own present sense of where my general intentions were mistaken, and how seriously my execution fell short of them.

The initial intention of the book is not, of course, unchallengeable. "Did the novel really rise?" To me, this question has the same kind of refrigerating generality as its much-mooted variant, "Is it now declining?"[16] Refrigerating because its meaning depends entirely on one's definition of the term "novel," and on the implications of the definite article which precedes it. My own title was really based on the current assumption in literary history, not on any personal or evaluative definition of

---

[15] I have discussed this elsewhere in an article, "The Recent Critical Fortunes of *Moll Flanders*," published in a new journal, *Eighteenth-Century Studies: A Journal of Literature and the Arts*, 1 (1967), 109-26.

[16] I except Alan Friedman's excellent *The Turn of the Novel* (New York: Oxford University Press, 1966) from this generalization, since its title is, I suppose, obliquely ironical as well as allusive; and its subject is a specific historical change.

"the novel"; and I take some modest comfort from the fact that the most widely accepted view today about the development of prose narrative forms still seems to be the one I began to investigate, impossible as it now seems, nearly thirty years ago, and at a time when special permission was needed before one could take works of English fiction out of the Cambridge University Library.

Granted the premise, then, that in some qualified sense what are usually called novels first began to be written on a considerable scale in England and in the early eighteenth century, there seems no pressing reason to believe that my basic intentions were mistaken. I am certainly more convinced than ever of the value of what I suppose were the more original emphases in my treatment of the problem—roughly the sociological and the philosophic. It still seems to me that the whole question of the historical, institutional, and social context of literature is very widely ignored, to the great detriment not only of much scholarly and critical writing, but of the general understanding of literature at every educational level. Secondly, though I can see more clearly now some of the inadequacies of logic and knowledge in the way I related philosophical ideas to the rise of the novel, the effort still seems to be preferable to the contrary, and still prevalent, tendency to write as though both ideas and novels existed independently of each other.

On the other hand I can see many ways in which my execution fell short of my intentions; and two of them, at least, seem worth considering in a little detail.

I've already alluded to the first—the truncation of my treatment of "realism of assessment." The omitted chapters on Fielding, Smollett and Sterne had attempted to show the various ways in which these later novelists got beyond "the tedious asseveration of literal authenticity" which characterized the formal realism of Defoe and Richardson, in order to bring the novel "into contact with the whole tradition of civilized values" (p. 288), which I took to be the ultimate aim of "realism of assessment." Something of the general range of these chapters can be surmised from the present concluding note (pp. 290-301): but many problems about the two realisms would have remained even if there had been no cuts.

To some extent the trouble was inherent in my method. I took over the commonest descriptive term applied to the novel—"realism"—and tried to clarify the issue by showing how the word was used to mean very different things. Nevertheless it seems clear to me now that I fell into the trap which awaits whoever employs the commonest of all Receipts to make an Academick Book—"Get yourself a couple of poles and turn'em loose."

There was, to begin with, an unavoidable asymmetry in the terms; for one thing "realism of assessment" implied an evaluative—and implicitly approbative—moral judgment by its user, whereas "realism of presentation" referred to narrower and more technical matters; and for another, "realism of presentation" was specifically related to my subject, the novel, whereas "realism of assessment" was obviously a concept which was equally applicable to all forms of literature. Quite apart from this, however, my treatment assumed it was somehow possible to separate the two kinds of realism in a novel's structural elements—from the single word to the plot as a whole: and though this separation may be legitimate as an analytic construct, it is much more problematic than I realized.

As regards the smallest units—words and phrases—there is always a tension between the literal meaning, the bare denotation, on the one hand, and the connotations of the word on the other, to say nothing of its larger reference to the narration and to the whole pattern of the reader's expectations. This is true of the simplest word, and even, unfortunately enough, of the word "real." Thus when Tolstoy writes that, while Prince Vassily was telling the rich Princess Marya that he had always loved her as a daughter, "a real tear appeared in his eye" (III, iv), it is not just a question of the lachrymal-gland product as opposed to glycerine. A whole host of larger distinctions and assessments crowd in. Most obviously, Tolstoy is reminding us of the emotional falsity of the whole Kuragin clan at the very moment Vassily seems to be expressing his first disinterested sentiment: we expected false tears. Yet if we ruminate further, we see that Tolstoy is checking an absolute judgment—the Kuragins are also, and alas, human.

But if Tolstoy is the supreme master of the total and natural simultaneity of realism of presentation and evaluation, some form of evaluation is always inextricably connected with any writer's presentation. Reading even the barest of Defoe's sentences in *Moll Flanders* we quite naturally go on from considering what is said to considering what is not said, and then to ask ourselves whether these conspicuous omissions are part of the picture of Moll's world or of Defoe's, or of both. That is, the reader finally concerns himself with Defoe's assessment of reality as it is implicit in words and phrases and sentences just as much as he does with

Fielding. The difference is only that Fielding's words and phrases intentionally invoke not only the actual narrative event, but the whole literary, historical, and philosophical perspective in which character or action should be placed by the reader.

There is also a similar continual interplay of presentation and assessment—explicit or tacit—in the larger compositional elements of all narrative. This interplay can be briefly considered in relation to two of the larger compositional elements—the narrative episode and the plot as a whole.

The reader's impulse to make some kind of larger interpretation is quite independent of the author's wishes: it is a habit we have picked up from life. In every episode of *Moll Flanders* we develop our continuing judgment of the heroine as a criminal, as a woman, as a penitent, as an individual. Defoe, it is true, makes no very consistent effort to guide us as to what norms he intends to use; but this merely makes the problem more difficult. There is a similar difficulty as regards Defoe's plot: we observe various elements of randomness and contradiction; and these finally become part of our final estimate of Defoe's view of life—we may decide, for instance, that the plot as a whole means something like: "If there is a pattern in human life it must be based on the single constant of individual biography and nothing else."

Here again Fielding is at the opposite pole; he really tells us that *Tom Jones* means what we can deduce from it: "This is the way I judge youth and goodness in general to be: and the general direction of life is towards the ordering of social groups, which are the supreme constants of the world as I see it." So with each of Fielding's narrative episodes: they are clearly responsible for whatever we can intelligently deduce from them.

My treatment did not go very far in this kind of analysis, perhaps because of my conceptual scheme. One major aspect of this problem has since been resolutely faced by Sheldon Sacks in his *Fiction and the Shape of Belief* (Berkeley and Los Angeles, 1964). But there are others: and a treatment of two of them, it now seems to me, might have clarified some of the larger connections of my subject.

"Realism of presentation" implies a narrative surface that is more or less identical with its meaning. But Fielding's novelistic technique is not primarily expressive in this sense. In his day the word "artificial" was still an approbative term though it was becoming obsolete (="skilfully made"—1738; ="according to the rules of art"—1753, *OED*); and the elements of repetition, parallelism, and antithesis in Fielding's narrative pattern are intended to have an autonomous aesthetic appeal for their own sake—an appeal which is in its way similar to that of the combination of repetition and variation in sonata form, or to the sort of baroque narrative artifice which Casalduero has described in *Don Quixote*.[17]

Obtrusive patterning of this kind may do violence to the criteria of formal realism; but it is one way of solving another perennial problem for the novelist—that of detachment. Just as overtly as his generalized names or the multiple references of his diction, Fielding's plot invites the reader to detachment, and thence to conscious assessment.

In this and in many other ways, then, the relationship between the two realisms is more complicated than I thought. It was easy to show how realism of assessment, achieved through explicit authorial commentary, militated against realism of presentation; it was equally true, although less obvious, that emphasis on authenticity in itself makes it more difficult both for the reader and the author to achieve the aesthetic distance which encourages realism of assessment.

The second of the problems arising from the relationship between the two kinds of realism involves a rather different issue. If one goes a little further into the relationship between individual lives and actions and the social and moral norms by which they are judged, the relation between one aspect of eighteenth-century fiction and the later tradition of the novel becomes much clearer. Richardson and Fielding are alike in the sense that—in *Pamela* as in *Tom Jones*—the as-yet-undifferentiated ego of the protagonist is brought into contact with the various psychological, moral, and social norms of the author and his period. The very form of their basic plots enacts their normative assessment: and this helps one to see why the *Bildungsroman* has been one of the classic patterns in the tradition of the novel: the reader watches the individual being introduced to the general.

The insistence of Fielding and Richardson on normative standards was something they shared with their age. And it now seems to me that my failure to focus on evaluative fictional procedures which bore no di-

---

[17] Joaquín Casalduero, "The Composition of *Don Quixote*," *Cervantes Across the Centuries*, ed. Angel Flores and M. J. Bernadete (New York: Dryden Press, 1947), pp. 56-93. See also my "Afterword" *to Joseph Andrews* (New York: Harper and Row, "Perennial Classics," 1966). [Reprinted as Chapter 8 in this volume.]

rect relationship to later technical developments in the genre, was connected with my grossest substantive failure of execution. Briefly, through diffuse implication and assumption, rather than through explicit statement, I presented the "rise of the novel" as though it had been achieved in collusion with various changes in philosophical, moral, and psychological outlook, and with something called the rising middle class (that restless bunch). In so doing I tended to make it look as though the novel had emerged in consistent, though largely unconscious, opposition to the traditional social and literary establishment of the time.

Insofar as the main literary tendencies of the eighteenth century in England are labeled neoclassical, the contradiction is largely real: there was no convenient or prestigious place for prose fiction in the critical tradition that stemmed from Aristotle, Horace, and the Italian Renaissance critics; and most neoclassical critical theory was inimical to the particularizing, vernacular, and domestic kind of writing characteristic of the novel.

But for the writers of the time this contradiction was probably theoretical rather than operative; and in my concentration on "new" factors to account for a "new" form, I overlooked another set of common tendencies and traditions in eighteenth-century English life and literature, much more powerful than neoclassical theory, and only uneasily connected with it. These tendencies, which were reflected in many, though not all, of the features of the fiction of the period, are those which, for want of a better term, we call Augustan.

The term is admittedly vague, and can be misleading.[18] I use "Augustan" to denote the very substantial measure of general cultural continuity in England from 1660 to 1800, a continuity which seems to me to outweigh the period's admittedly enormous division of opinion. In this sense, Augustan, like Georgian, is virtually a synonym for an elite outlook based on the defense of a civilized social order; and, quite as much as the card-carrying Augustans, all the major eighteenth-century novelists seem to me to belong to this movement, as did their successors, Jane Austen and Scott. They made stringent and wide-ranging criticisms of

---

[18] See James William Johnson, in his valuable article "The Meaning of Augustan": "it is the first four decades of the eighteenth century which are properly called 'Augustan,'" *Journal of the History of Ideas*, 19 (1958), 507-22; and Paul Fussell, *The Rhetorical World of Augustan Humanism: Ethics and Imagery from Swift to Burke* (Oxford: The Clarendon Press, 1965).

their age, but in ways and with accents which suggest that the Augustan norms seemed to them to have universal validity;[19] and these norms surely encouraged some of the special literary features which their novels had in common.

The political and religious settlements of 1660, 1689, and 1714 had brought about a very drastic reduction of the spectrum of literary attention: kings and courts, the military and heroic virtues, the intervention of God in human affairs—all these traditional components of classical literature, and especially of its chief narrative form, the epic, disappeared or at least occupied a much less prominent place. In *The Rise of the Novel* I related these changes to various aspects of individualism; but I should have added that much of the literary climate of the Augustan Age was determined by this drastic and pervasive reduction in the scale of human concerns. One result was to leave English literature free for a more intensive and undisturbed cultivation of what was left—the social, personal, and domestic life, and the application to it of what remained of traditional norms.

Of course we think of Augustan as denoting a primarily public demeanor; but the importance which the Augustans attached to private and social interests is actually very striking in contrast with France, where religious, political, and intellectual divisions were so much more acute and imperative; and the assumption that the private life is man's major concern, which seems to me to be a characteristic Augustan attitude, in Temple and Congreve and Addison as well as in Pope, Johnson, and Hume, points directly to the subject matter of the novel.

In two main ways: to the novel's relatively detailed description of domestic life; and to the novel's interest in individual self-definition.

Minuteness of description was in some respects contrary to the neoclassical emphasis on generality and *la belle nature*. But although Swift and Johnson, for instance, mock detailed verisimilitude, and protest against numbering the streaks of the tulip, their own practice shows

---

[19] The fairly common view that Defoe and Fielding were in some sense radical dissenters from the class system of their day is only now being dispelled by such studies as Malvin R. Zirker's excellent *Fielding's Social Pamphlets* (Berkeley and Los Angeles: University of California Press, 1966). It is surely a move in the right direction to look at the similarities between the works of Richardson and Fielding, as William Park has recently done in "Fielding and Richardson," *PMLA*, 26 (1966), 381-88.

them to have been continually and successfully interested in the detailed presentation of the domestic scene. They did this mainly, it is true, in such peripheral literary forms as the journal and the private letter; but these are agreed to be modes of writing in which the Augustans were supreme. One could, indeed, reasonably argue that in the eighteenth century the most minute—and the most triumphant—descriptions of individual character in action against a fully presented environment are to be found, not in fiction, but in the various miscellaneous modes of the literature of experience. Thus Fanny Burney's novels hardly match the vividness of Horace Walpole's letters about social visits or parties of pleasure to Vauxhall, although her diaries almost do. Nor, I think, does even Richardson take us quite as close to the flux and reflux of consciousness as Boswell often does in his journals.

The question of individual self-definition is somewhat more difficult, since it is less characteristic of the English eighteenth-century novelists than it was to become later in France and Germany with Rousseau, Goethe, and their successors. Still, one can certainly find the concern in many of the English novels of the period, from Defoe to Sterne, and it is central in Richardson. The identity crisis of Pamela,[20] for example, to say nothing of Clarissa's or Lovelace's, surely belongs to the same spiritual and psychological world as James Boswell's hectic pursuit of James Boswell.

There are, however, two general features of the Augustan attitude which seem to me to have been considerably less favorable to the emergence of what was later to be characteristic of the novel: the Augustan stresses on masculine and adult values. The two are, of course, functionally related; as when Chesterfield told his son that "Women . . . are only children of a larger growth" (September 5th, 1748). The pervasive importance of the Augustan attitude in the eighteenth-century novel suggests why it characteristically places much less emphasis on adolescent and feminine values than did later fiction.

When John Barth speaks of *Roderick Random* as a "healthy, hard-nosed counteragent to the cult of Love,"[21] his engaging truculence, supported by the example of his own later fiction, helps us to see how alien

---

[20] For one treatment of this, see my "Samuel Richardson," *The Listener*, February 4, 1965, reprinted in *The Novelist as Innovator*, ed. Walter Allen (London: British Broadcasting Company, 1965). [Reprinted as Chapter 7 in this volume.]
[21] "Afterword," *Roderick Random* (New York: Signet Classics, 1964).

to Smollett is the novel's standard assumption that its moral and social norms can be generated purely out of the presentation of personal relationships. That particular assumption, of course, belongs to a very limited phase of historical development. It is primarily middle-class, leisured, and secular; it is also mainly adolescent and feminine; and one need not argue that Smollett's contemptuous misogyny is typically Augustan to see the emphasis on feminine sensibility in Richardson, and later in Fanny Burney and the women novelists, as contrary to the predominant Augustan emphasis.

Of course the opposition isn't absolute. If we venture so far as the second part of *Pamela*, for instance, the novel's Augustan quality becomes much more obtrusive: it is an important part of Richardson's general ideological commitment that his servant girl should eventually develop into someone who speaks with the voice of a man, and a very grown-up one at that—an Addison or even a Locke.

The contradiction between Augustan values on the one hand, and feminine and youthful attitudes on the other, comes to the fore most revealingly in Jane Austen. As has often been observed, her young heroines finally marry older men—comprehensive epitomes of the Augustan norms such as Mr. Darcy and Mr. Knightley. Her novels in fact dramatize the process whereby feminine and adolescent values are painfully educated in the norms of the mature, rational, and educated male world.

Here, no doubt, is the essence of some contemporary objections to the Augustan attitude and to eighteenth-century fiction: that it's conformist, cautious, cold; too much superego and too little id. Perhaps that's why today the most popular eighteenth-century novel is the one which is least committed to disciplined and adult values. *Fanny Hill* is the delicious exception that proves the rule; if there's anything more anomalous than a young Augustan, it's surely an ancient Venus.

# 2

# THE AUGUSTAN AGE

Such general literary terms as *Renaissance* or *Romanticism* create at least as much confusion as enlightenment; and one could certainly make the same objection to the word *Augustan.** There is probably no other literary term that is applied quite so loosely. When people talk about "The Augustans," they are most likely to mean the writers of the age of Queen Anne—Addison, Pope, Swift, and so on; here the Augustan period means 1702-1714. But actually it is often stretched as far back as 1660, the year of the Restoration of Charles II, and as far forwards as either 1760, presumably to give a neat 100-year span, or even the end of the eighteenth century, presumably so that Johnson and Gibbon can be included.[1]

However, no one has ever succeeded in destroying a word by showing that its usages are very inconsistent, or that the phenomena it is sup-

* This essay appeared originally as the introduction to *The Augustan Age: Approaches to Its Literature, Life, and Thought*, ed. Ian Watt (Greenwich, Conn.: Fawcett Publications, 1968), pp. 11-29, and is reprinted by assent of Ruth Watt and by agreement with Random House, Inc. Three paragraphs of the conclusion, which refer to the contents of the anthology, have been omitted here. Portions of this introduction were originally given at the David Nichol Smith Memorial Seminar in Eighteenth-Century Studies held at the Australian National University at Canberra, August 15-19, 1966, and as broadcasts on the Third Program of the British Broadcasting Company, reprinted in *The Listener*, April 6 and 13, 1967.
[1] For some recent discussions of the term, see Paul Fussell, *The Rhetorical World of Augustan Humanism* (Oxford: The Clarendon Press, 1965), and James William Johnson, *The Formation of English Neo-Classical Thought* (Princeton: Princeton University Press, 1967).

posed to denote are much more diverse than people realize. The opposite approach—trying to see why the confusion or, to put it more kindly, the word's rich variety of connotation—should have arisen—at least has the practical advantage of doing something to elucidate an existent problem.

I

The most obvious point of departure is the implied analogy with the general literary and cultural situation under the Emperor Caesar Augustus in ancient Rome.

One of the many things that used to puzzle me in *Gulliver's Travels* was an episode in Book 3, when Gulliver is on the Island of Sorcerers, Glubdubdrib. As the chief illustration of how "great services done to princes and states" are never justly rewarded, a Roman naval hero is called up from the dead. At the battle of Actium he had been "the sole cause of Antony's flight," and therefore of Augustus's final triumph. Afterwards, "on the confidence of some merit . . . " Swift relates, "he went to Rome and solicited at the court of Augustus to be preferred to a greater ship . . . but without any regard to his pretensions, it was given to a youth who had never seen the sea, the son of Libertina, who waited on one of the Emperor's mistresses." Eventually the hero retired from Rome and died in complete neglect.

Why, I wondered, should Swift have selected Augustus, of all people, as his symbol of the corruption and injustice of monarchs? Didn't Swift know that he was supposed to be an Augustan himself?

The probable answer is: he didn't know and he wouldn't have liked it. We can see one reason why in the previous chapter. There Caesar and Brutus are conjured up from the dead at Gulliver's request, but it is Brutus he wants to see most. Gulliver is "struck with a profound veneration at the sight" and "could easily discover the most consummate virtue, the greatest intrepidity and firmness of mind, the truest love of his country, and general benevolence for mankind, in every lineament of his countenance." Gulliver's—and Swift's—"profound veneration" for Brutus reminds us that there were two quite opposite ways of looking at Augustus.

On one side there were the various partisans of absolute authority in Church and State. Augustus had ended the Civil War and brought Rome peace, worldwide dominion, and an unprecedented flourishing of the arts; and so it was natural that after all the wars of religion during the sixteenth and seventeenth centuries, the new autocratic nation-states of Europe should take Augustan Rome as their model. In France, as soon as Louis XIV began to rule, the poets, led by Boileau, hailed him as a new Augustus. Later the military, architectural, and literary triumphs under the reign of *le Roi Soleil* set the pattern for other European monarchies.

At about the same time Edmund Waller initiated the tradition in England by addressing Oliver Cromwell as Augustus in his "Panegyric to my Lord Protector" (1655). But it was only after the end of the Civil War and the Restoration of Charles II that the Augustan analogy became at all plausible. John Dryden called Charles II "Augustus" in several poems; and he often compared his own situation as a poet to that of Virgil and Horace in Augustan Rome. Later on, indeed, some writers, including Atterbury and Oldmixon, thought that the reign of Charles II had really been England's Augustan Age. Thus Bishop Atterbury in 1690 wrote that Waller "undoubtedly stands first in the list of refiners, and for aught I know, the last, too; for I question whether in Charles II's reign English did not come into its full perfection; and whether it has not had its Augustan Age as well as the Latin." Atterbury was thinking of the perfection of the English language rather than of its literature; but a generation later John Oldmixon had literature especially in mind when he wrote, in his *Reflections on Dr. Swift's Letter to the Earl of Oxford about the English Tongue* (1712), that the reign of Charles II "probably may be the Augustan Age of English Poetry." This view of the Restoration period, though never generally adopted, has the implicit support of Dr. Johnson, in his famous encomium on Dryden: "What was said of Rome, adorned by Augustus, may be applied by an easy metaphor to English poetry embellished by Dryden, '*lateritiam invenit, marmoriam relinquit,*' he found it brick and left it marble."

The other and opposite attitude towards the political aspect of the Augustan analogy came to the fore in England among Dryden's immediate successors. But it had a much older history.

Medieval tradition had converted Julius Caesar, and therefore his successor Augustus, into the divinely sanctioned founders of the Holy Roman Empire. This is why, in *The Inferno*, Dante had placed Brutus next to Judas Iscariot. The habit of seeing Caesar as a hero, and Brutus as a traitor, was hardly challenged until the Renaissance. But during the struggles of the Florentine republic against Milan early in the fifteenth century, the civic humanists, such as Leonardo Bruni, Poggio, and Salutati, took a completely different view of Roman history and argued that Julius Caesar had really been a tyrant who had destroyed the ancient democratic liberties of republican Rome.

This division in political perspectives continued during the next two centuries; all those who stood or claimed to stand for political liberty took Cato and Brutus as their heroes. In England, Swift, like Addison and Cato, was in the libertarian tradition. In the *Drapier's Letters* he satirically called George I "Caesar" because he really believed that the Hanoverians were tyrants like Augustus, who had brought about an "entire subversion of the Roman Liberty and Constitution" and set up "the vilest tyranny that Heaven, in its anger, ever inflicted."

There was yet another reason why any parallel between contemporary England and Augustan Rome seemed historically ominous. Many classical historians—Polybius, Livy, Plutarch, and Florus—had seen the reign of Augustus as the beginning of an irreversible process of historical decline. This pessimistic form of the cyclical view of history was the standard one in English histories of Rome, from Polydore Vergil's to Laurence Eachard's; and the Augustan parallel therefore tended to reinforce Pope and Swift in their gloomy political outlook. Swift, for instance, wrote that "The *Epicureans* began to spread at *Rome* in the Empire of Augustus, as the *Socinians*, and even the *Epicureans* too, did in England towards the End of King *Charles* the Second's Reign; which is reckoned, though very absurdly, our *Augustan* Age."

There's yet another complexity in English attitudes towards the Augustan analogy: whatever their political views, all writers couldn't help but envy one aspect of the Augustan Age—the enlightened patronage for which Augustus's minister Maecenas had long been the symbol. The trade-union view of the poets was expressed in Martial's *Sint Maecenates, non deerunt, Flacce, Marones* ("If there are great patrons, great poets will not be lacking").

The climax of this aspect of the analogy comes in Goldsmith's "Account of the Augustan Age of England" (1759), the first explicit treatment of the subject. Goldsmith wrote that although the English were "yet undetermined" when their Augustan Age had actually been, some favoring the "writers in the times of Queen Elizabeth . . . others . . . the reign of James I, and others . . . Charles II," he himself "would readily give [his] vote for the reign of Queen Anne, or some years before that period."

The reasons for Goldsmith's choice are interesting: under the ministries of Somers and later of Harley, that is between 1697 and 1714, "patronage was fashionable among our nobility," and there was "a just balance between patronage and the press." Before then, according to Goldsmith, subservience to the court had been necessary for writers to make their living. Since then, on the other hand, "writers who can be content prudently to catch the public" by catering to their low tastes can get on without the approval of more discriminating readers and patrons.

Even after making allowance for Goldsmith's retrospective envy, one must agree that the times when Somers was a member of the Kit-Cat Club, and later when Swift, Prior, Pope, and Gay were the intimates of another chief minister, Lord Treasurer Harley, had certainly been the closest English parallel to the Augustan Age of Rome, when Augustus and Maecenas had favored Virgil, Horace, and Livy with their patronage and friendship. And one important reason why there is such a dramatic break in literary history at the death of Queen Anne, and why Pope and Swift were so bitter in their later works, is that to them the Hanoverians and Walpole not only seemed to threaten an inglorious end to England's historical greatness but had in fact brought the great era of literary patronage to an end.

In 1727 George II came to the throne, and, as ill luck would have it, his second name was Augustus. Pope wrote to Swift: "Horace might keep his coach in Augustus's time, if he pleased, but I won't in the time of our Augustus." Ten years later Pope's "Epistle to Augustus" (1737) provided the climax to the concern of the English Augustans with the Roman parallel. Pope's poem was an imitation of Horace's "Epistle to Augustus." But Horace had written his poem in answer to Augustus's friendly invitation; and he was confident enough both about Augustus's virtues as a ruler and about the greatness of the literature of his own time to make his poem a proclamation of the poet's lofty traditional role as *utilis urbi*, as the conscience of the state.

Pope's version of Horace is based on totally different beliefs and attitudes. Pope can't see the development of English poetry and drama as one of continuous improvement and refinement, although he does his best with the poetic reforms of Waller and Dryden, and the moral purity of Roscommon and Addison. Nor can Pope share Horace's easy solidarity with the social, political, and literary life of his own time. Instead, Pope's poem is primarily destructive, and it succeeds only when it is animated by the energy of contemptuous exasperation.

For instance, where Horace had affirmed the social value of poetry and given as one example the traditional hymns of rural piety, Pope's version ironically mocks Hopkins and Sternhold's popular version of the psalms:

> How could Devotion touch the country pews,
> Unless the Gods bestow'd a proper Muse?
> Verse cheers their leisure, Verse assists their work,
> Verse prays for Peace, or sings down Pope and Turk.
> The silenced Preacher yields to potent strain,
> And feels that grace his prayer besought in vain;
> The blessing thrills through all the labouring throng,
> And Heaven is won by violence of Song.

There's the same derogatory reversal in political matters. Where Horace had jokingly opened with his fear of intruding on the Emperor's more important state concerns, Pope opens with an ironical thrust at George's absence abroad in the arms of his mistress, Madame Walmoden, while Spanish privateers are allowed to roam the seas cutting off Jenkins's ear:

> While You, great Patron of Mankind! Sustain
> The balanced World, and open all the Main;
> Your Country, chief, in Arms abroad defend,
> At home, with Morals, Arts, and Laws amend;
> How shall the Muse, from such a Monarch, steal
> An hour, and not defraud the Public Weal?

The terms of Pope's preliminary advertisement also reveal a wholly ironical set of attitudes towards the society of his time:

The Reflections of Horace, and the Judgments past in his Epistle to Augustus, seem'd so seasonable to the present Times, that I could not help applying them to the use of my own country. The Author thought them considerable enough to address them to his Prince; whom he paints with the great and good qualities of a Monarch, upon whom the Romans depended for the Encrease of an Absolute Empire. But to make the poem entirely English, I was willing to add one or two of those which contribute to the Happiness of a Free People, and are more consistent with the Welfare of our Neighbours.

Logically, Pope's irony about "consistency with the welfare of our neighbours" achieves its derogatory parallel with Rome only at the price of reproving George II and Walpole for being insufficiently belligerent;

and we may well reflect that though the *Pax Augusta* was no doubt no-
bler, it was also much bloodier and more oppressive. Similarly Pope's
joke about the "happiness of a free people" glosses over the awkward
fact that Pope himself owed his independence as a writer to conditions
which were equally inconceivable either in Augustan Rome or in the
France of Louis XIV. As is made clear by the sequel, where Pope goes
on to reprove George II for the indiscriminate nature of his patronage
by an ironically exaggerated allusion to Augustus, who "not only pro-
hibited all but the best Writers to name him, but recommended that
Care to the Civil Magistrate." It was just because the Stuarts had finally
lost most of the royal prerogatives that George's magistrates couldn't
send Pope to join Ovid in exile on the Black Sea for his calculated *lèse-
majesté*. On this, one imagines, Pope and his readers were equally ambivalent: as long as they were securely possessed of the advantages of
peace, prosperity, and *habeas corpus*, they were quite willing to enjoy
the ironic denunciations that the parallel with a more absolutist political
and social structure made possible.

Of course, on the essential issue of the monarch's traditional responsibility for civilization as a whole, Pope's ironic contrast between the
two Augustuses was wholly justified, as was made abundantly clear by
King George Augustus's own comment: "Who is this Pope that I hear so
much about? I cannot discover what is her merit. Why will not my subjects write in prose?"

In the last analysis, then, both the similarities and the differences between eighteenth-century England and Augustan Rome only served to
sharpen Pope's and Swift's awareness of how unheroic and disordered
their own world was. History had moved beyond them, chaos really
threatened, and the only possible posture was public denunciation and
an unremitting rearguard action. Embattled and embittered, Pope and
Swift became that very un-Horatian thing, an intransigent minority.
One may doubt the judgments that underlie the absolute pessimism of
their historical perspective; but one must admit that it gave them an advantage denied to their less gloomy contemporaries: their sense of the
unreality of the Augustan analogy freed them from its inhibiting mod-
eration. In fact it did more than free them; it impelled them, in such
works as *The Dunciad* and *Gulliver's Travels*, to create negative fictions
of the highest order of imaginative intensity and conviction.

Yet if the English Augustan writers saw the parallel in a mainly negative and ironic light, this is itself a tribute to the pervasive force of the

cultural ideal of the Roman Augustans. Virgil and Horace provided English intellectual life with a pattern by which contemporary realities could be measured; and most of the writers of the period confronted the tension between aspiration and actuality much less intransigently than Pope and Swift. In fact it is hardly too much to say that the Augustan model became the main cultural pattern for the English educated classes throughout the period between the Civil War and the French Revolution; and it was a pattern not only for literature and the arts but for a very wide range of psychological, moral, social, and national attitudes.

It's in this sense, probably, that the period between 1660 and 1800 is best thought of as classical. I myself very much doubt whether any system of literary criticism ever does more to control, or even explain, the writing actually produced than, say, the legal system either controls or explains most of our actual behavior. I therefore doubt whether the neoclassical critical system, as it was elaborated in England on the basis of Aristotle, Horace, and the Italian and French critics, had very much unifying or directing influence on the writers of the period between Dryden and Dr. Johnson. But the actual literature of Augustan Rome— and particularly the works of Cicero, Horace, and Virgil—certainly did.

Horace especially. He was taught in the grammar schools and universities; quoted constantly in the periodicals and in Parliament; translated and imitated by everyone who aspired to the muses: more than anyone else he provided a common standard of thought and feeling and diction for almost the whole of literate society. After 1660 there was to be no more enthusiasm, no more quarrelling about religious or political extremes: here Horace's attitudes provided a suitable model. In religion the tolerant Anglicanism of the English religious Establishment welcomed Horace's *parcus deorum cultor et infrequens*, his sparing but decorous support of public religious rituals. In politics Horace's discreet quietism, combined with a strong patriotic and civic sense, was equally appropriate for the new age. One could go further: the famous motto *nil admirari*—"marvel at nothing"—which Bolingbroke adopted for his own, seems to sum up a whole ideal of personal character that came to dominate English life: a tradition that combines a relaxed indifference to emotional or imaginative experience with an equable, independent, and wide-eyed self-command.

It would hardly make sense to say that the English character is Shakespearean or Miltonic; it makes a little more sense, I think, to say that it is—or was until recently—Horatian. What the French call *le phlègme*

*anglais* only came into being during the eighteenth century, largely under the influence of Roman stoicism. One observes the character-type
coming into being in such early Augustan writers as Halifax and Congreve; by the end of the eighteenth century it is the established social
ideal, as we can see in the stiff upper lips of Jane Austen's heroes. This
kind of English character, the product of classical education and the
English public schools, was, as Matthew Arnold never tired of saying,
insufficiently Hellenic. One wouldn't say that the Elizabethans were particularly Roman; but one certainly recognizes that quality in the first
English ruler whom a poet addressed as Augustus—Oliver Cromwell.
Since then—for good and ill—the prevailing quality of English national
life has been Roman rather than Greek.

In the eighteenth century the two most distinguished writers of Latin
verse, Addison and Johnson, were also two of the most influential mor-
alists. That we know what we mean by an Addisonian or a Johnsonian
kind of person shows how deeply we identify them with characteristic
models of conduct in ordinary life. They were two of the chief writers,
among a great many, who played an indispensable part in shaping that
special, celebrated, and enduring concept, the English gentleman; if one
had to sum up that concept in a word, Augustan would probably fit as
well as any.

II

No one, I think, has used the phrase "Hanoverian Literature," and
when Thackeray wrote of *The Four Georges*, his quaternion was con-
temptuously jocular; yet the word *Georgian*, which came into use at
about the same time (1855), has always been one of unqualified approval.

Why? Surely because we recognize that the period from 1660-1800
set a uniquely high standard of civilized achievement in all the applied
arts—from the great mansions of the nobility to the modest brick
houses of the middle class, from the high-style silver and glassware and
furniture made by famous craftsmen to the ordinary doorknobs and
crockery of everyday domestic use. Of course the chronological period
covered by the word *Georgian* is largely the same as that described by
the word *Augustan* in its larger sense; and this, combined with the
rather separate usages of the two terms, draws attention to an interesting duality in our present attitudes to the eighteenth century.

On the one hand we think of the lost Georgian world as the pinnacle of England's achievement in all the arts of life. Our own age, which has made the landscape a parking lot for houses, the house a parking lot for people, and the city just a parking lot, cannot but envy an age that discovered the secret of building human houses, and making them harmonize with their natural surroundings in the country or with each other in city squares and terraces. The word *Augustan*, on the other hand, evokes a very different response. Pope and Swift support the modern intellectual's image of himself as a passionate defender of the last citadels of human reason against the mounting tide of folly, vulgarity, and commercialism. *The Dunciad* has become a prophetic book in the academy, and the fate of Gulliver among the Houyhnhnms has been interpreted as a prophetic enactment of the process of human alienation. So our dual terminology helps us to have it both ways. The great Augustan writers of Queen Anne prefigure the modern writer as the righteous voice of radical dissent from an ignominious world; while Georgian culture embodies our nostalgia for reasonable and aesthetic and widely shared solutions to the ordinary problems of living in society.

But if, as I believe, Swift and Pope are essentially intransigent deviations from the norm, there may be a closer connection between the terms *Augustan* and *Georgian* than the distinction in usage suggests. *Georgian* may be merely the visual and domestic aspect, and *Augustan* the literary and intellectual one, of what is essentially a single and relatively unified style of life.

The causes of this degree of uniformity are largely political and social. If we ask what common features of English society between 1660 and 1800 made it different from the periods before and after, the answer is very simple: before 1660, and especially before 1641, what mattered most in civilization were kings, courts, and clerics; after 1800, industry, commerce, and the gradually emergent common people became the dominant forces; but in between these periods it was the landowning classes who mattered most; their power and wealth go straight up from about 1640 until near the end of the eighteenth century.

The Civil War had been largely caused by the struggles of the landowners against Stuart economic and judicial encroachment; and many of the peers and the gentry took the Puritan side. Very soon, however, the nobility and the gentry found they had even more cause to fear the dangers of religious and political equality, and so by the time of the Restoration they had largely shed their Puritan and revolutionary alle-

giances. In the words of Clarendon in 1661, they united to avoid any re-
currence of "that accursed dose . . . a commonwealth" whose first ingredient had been "the confounding the Commons of England . . . with
the common people of England." The landowners certainly got the most
out of the Restoration Settlement. Almost the whole political and legal
*status quo* of before the Civil War was restored but not the conditions
of land tenure, for, whereas the monarchy lost all its feudal prerogatives
as head of the landholding system, the landowners, freed of their obligations to the crown, continued to exercise their old rights in the manorial
courts.

Thus strengthened, the landed interest held the balance of political
power from 1660 till the end of the next century. Not, of course, that
they were in opposition to the rapidly growing power of trade and industry centered in London; they were allied with it, for the joint defense
of property both against the weakened power of Church and State, and
against the mass of propertyless laborers in town and country; it was
only very late in the eighteenth century that this alliance was threatened
by the growing power and independence of commerce and industry,
manifested in the reform movements associated with such Londoners as
Beckford and Wilkes, and later Pitt the Younger. Even so, it was only
with the Reform Bill of 1832 and the subsequent abolition of the Corn
Laws that trade and industry gained a controlling political and economic voice, and thus ended the period in which England was dominated, as never before or since, by the landed interest.

As far as I know, the only scholar to attempt a general connection between this historical fact and the nature of Augustan literature is F. W.
Bateson. His "A Word for Waller" argues that there is a central contradiction between the "community of sense" that was ideally supposed to
comprise the whole of literate Augustan society, and the "rigid social
stratification" that gave decisive power to a landed aristocracy.[2]

We must surely agree that our sense of both Augustan literature and
of its society is very much dominated by an impression of a powerful
and pervasive class stratification. This emphasis on class may itself be
regarded as one aspect of the general strategy of the landed interest: a

---

[2] See F.W. Bateson, *English Poetry: A Critical Introduction* (London: Longmans
Green, 1950), pp. 165-74. Reprinted in *The Augustan Age: Approaches to Its
Literature, Life, and Thought*, ed. Ian Watt (New York: Fawcett Publications,
1968), pp. 189-96.

conservative defense of the *status quo* and, above all, of the rights of property, against interference from above or below.

To some extent conservatism is probably a general characteristic of all agricultural societies where most of the land is held by a very small minority of the people; but the particular historical circumstances of the Civil War must have had a good deal to do with the special attitude of the landed interest during the period that followed; and I think this special attitude helps us to understand some of the general traits of Augustan literature.

This special attitude is the one Bateson describes as the Augustan ideal—the effort to encompass in a system of basic agreement the whole "community of sense," that is, the property-owners.

How far this kind of accommodation went can be seen by a comparison with France. In England there was none of that tessellated structure of different degrees of nobility, all with special legal, political, social, and economic prerogatives, which made the French aristocracy so hateful to outsiders and yet so divided within itself. In comparison, the dealings of the English aristocracy with other classes show a very striking tolerance and lack of exclusiveness.

This conciliatory attempt to include the whole propertied part of society in the general cultural consensus is closely allied to the empirical temper so evident in the political and intellectual life of the period. When people had got too excited about political and religious theory, Civil War had ensued; apparently ideological principles were in themselves dangerous. These principles continued to divide men under both Charles II and James II; but then Locke and the Glorious Revolution provided what were widely thought to be permanent solutions. The quiet skill with which the ruling class turned against the successive threats of Monmouth, of James II, and of the Stuart Pretenders, shows a very remarkable subordination of theoretical to practical considerations.

The Augustan writers present, most characteristically, an equally practical and untheoretical attitude to life; and the effort at consensus is also very evident, especially in the prevailing critical assumptions of the period. When Johnson, for example, defined taste as "an intuitive perception of consonance and propriety," it was because he believed "consonance and propriety" to be something all sensible men would immediately perceive. A similar assumption underlies the work of Addison and Steele, in *The Tatler* and *The Spectator*: they were overt propagandists for the cause of increasing the consensus of taste. Party differences, it is true, are loud and obtrusive in many of the pamphlets and satires of the period; and yet these political divisions are largely irrelevant to most of the main works of Augustan literature. One would hardly know from *An Essay on Man* that Pope was a Tory, or from *Tom Jones* that Fielding was a Whig; both works appeal—like *The Spectator* and *The Rambler*—to the same kind of audience—skeptical, observant, worldly-wise, widely read, and essentially conservative; they have a similar tone of voice—rational, polite, controlled; and their common aim is to remind man of his proper place in the total scheme of things.

The writing of the period is also pervaded by a predominantly practical attitude to life. In Swift's Brobdingnag, we observe, science is confined "to what may be useful in life, to the improvement of agriculture and all mechanic arts"; and Johnson's outlook was equally pragmatic: "As gold which he cannot spend will make no man rich, so knowledge which he cannot apply will make no man wise."

One result of this empirical humanism was to break down the usual separation between imaginative and other kinds of writing. Johnson is a good example—his output is extraordinarily miscellaneous, from plays and poetry, to scholarship, lexicography, political pamphlets, books of travel, and even *An Account of An Attempt to Ascertain the Longitude at Sea* (1755). On the other hand, the great works of learning in the eighteenth century are also among its greatest literature. Berkeley and Hume in philosophy; Gibbon in history; Adam Smith in economics; Gilbert White in natural history; Arthur Young in agriculture—one could go on. The reason for this is presumably that the period's basic operative assumptions about literature were much more empirical than ever before or since.

This essentially practical and constructive concern for the common interests of mankind, which characterizes both the landowning classes and the main writers of the Augustan period, had much to do with creating what we call Georgian England.

One of the ways in which the eighteenth-century English aristocracy differed from the French was the degree to which their own estates absorbed their interests and energies. The English peers and great landowners were leaders in the improvements of farming methods that brought about the agricultural revolution; and their political power enabled them to push through the innumerable Enclosure Acts, which were an indispensable part not only of a more efficient use of the land but of the formation of the English countryside of lanes and hedges and parklands that we know today. By the middle of the eighteenth century the whole countryside was being transformed. As Horace Walpole wrote: "Every journey is made through a succession of pictures. . . . If no lapse to barbarism, formality and seclusion is made, what landscapes will dignify every quarter of our island, when the daily plantations that are making have attained venerable maturity."

This, certainly, was one of the supreme aesthetic successes of the eighteenth century; and it arose from one of the most pervasive general concerns of Augustan literature—the idea that man should pattern his daily life in accord with taste, nature, and reason. This kind of emphasis isn't one that is very likely to dominate an age where people still dream of heroic achievements on the battlefield, or of achieving salvation in the next world. One reason why Pope and Shenstone and Horace Walpole were all so interested in creating a truly civilized indoor and outdoor context for human living is that they weren't more interested in anything else. As a result we think of them in connection with their houses and their gardens, which is not, I think, true of most earlier or later English writers.

Arthur Humphreys's essay on Sharawadgi traces some of the history of the Georgian concern with landscape.[3] It was one major example of the interpenetration of painting, aesthetic theory, agricultural change, and literature that was very characteristic of the period. Thus the most successful of the professional landscapers, Capability Brown, according to Hannah More, "illustrate[d] everything he says about gardening with some literary or grammatical allusion. He told me he compared his art to literary composition. 'Now there,' he said, pointing his finger, 'I make a comma, and there,' pointing to another part '. . .a parenthesis.'"

The landscape movement was itself largely the result of some of the most distinctive literary interests of the eighteenth century. Thus the greatest single landmark in the establishment of the Augustan heroic couplet, Sir John Denham's "Cooper's Hill" (1642), also set the pattern for the innumerable topographical poems of the period. There were many other popular genres that dealt with country life: the agricultural Georgic, such as John Philip's "Cyder" (1708), Gay's "Wine" (1708),

---

[3] A.R. Humphreys, "The Quest of the Sharawadgi: A Digression," in *The Augustan Age: Approaches to Its Literature, Life, and Thought*, ed. Ian Watt (New York: Fawcett Publications, 1968), pp. 77-96.

and John Dyer's "The Fleece" (1757); the pastoral, of which those of Gay and Pope are the best known; and the poems of retirement to the countryside, of which all the poets of the period offer versions, and of which John Pomfret's "The Choice" (1700) was perhaps the most famous at the time.

If one moves from the popular poetic genres to the great poems of the period, two, at least, embody the essential Georgian program for the countryside. Goldsmith's "The Deserted Village" (1770) is perhaps the best known; but Pope's "Epistle to Burlington" (1731) is probably the most complete expression of the complementary nature of the Georgian and the Augustan ideals. It moves from the details of style in daily living to a larger view of the moral values of civilization itself. The ostentatious palace and the vast formal garden were typical of the baroque style, but only kings, great princes, or a few millionaires could afford them. The humbler Georgian ideal was much more widely accessible. Pope presents the baroque splendor of Timon's villa as equally offensive to practical convenience, moral perception, and aesthetic judgment; and he contrasts it with the perfect appropriateness of the ideal Palladian house set in an informal garden that modulates naturally into pasture and woodland.

To pass a day in Timon's villa is to be affronted by pride and ostentation. In the vast banqueting hall the visitor is forced to ask:

> Is this a dinner? this a Genial room?
> No 'tis a Temple, and a Hecatomb.
> A solemn Sacrifice, perform'd in state,
> You drink by measure, and to minutes eat ...
> Between each Act the trembling salvers ring,
> From soup to sweet-wine, and God bless the King.
> In plenty starving, tantaliz'd in state,
> And complaisantly help'd to all I hate,
> Treated, caress'd, and tir'd, I take my leave,
> Sick of his civil Pride from Morn to Eve;
> I curse such lavish cost, and little skill,
> And swear no Day was ever past so ill.
> Yet hence the Poor are cloath'd, the Hungry fed;
> Health to himself, and to his Infants bread
> The Lab'rer bears: What his hard Heart denies,
> His charitable Vanity supplies.
> Another age shall see the golden Ear
> Imbrown the Slope, and nod on the Parterre,

> Deep Harvests bury all his pride has plann'd,
> And laughing Ceres re-assume the land.

But if pride must fall, and rightly so, the gardens of Lord Bathurst's two county seats, and the Palladian houses of Richard Boyle, Lord Burlington on Piccadilly, and at Chiswick, will endure, because they are socially, morally, and aesthetically valid.

> Who then shall grace, or who improve the Soil?
> Who plants like BATHURST, or who builds like BOYLE,
> 'Tis Use alone that sanctifies Expense
> And Splendour borrows all her rays from Sense.

> His Father's Acres who enjoys in peace,
> Or makes his Neighbours glad, if he encrease;
> Whose chearful Tenants bless their yearly toil,
> Yet to their Lord owe more than to the soil;
> Whose ample Lawns are not asham'd to feed
> The milky heifer and deserving steed;
> Whose rising Forests, not for pride or show,
> But future Buildings, future Navies grow:
> Let his plantations stretch from down to down,
> First shade a Country, and then raise a Town.

In Pope's perspective here all contradictions are resolved—between rich and poor, between town and country, between a rural "Little England" and an imperial Britannia ruling the waves. The ideal is specifically Georgian; but it is also Augustan. Horace had told the man of taste to flee from grandeur (*fuge magna*) and the falseness of city life, into a modest rural villa; and Virgil had given the motif a kind of religious justification in the Fourth Eclogue, where he promises—and Pope here echoes—a return to the Golden Age, to Saturnian times, to an idyllic rural plenitude.

The political implications of this program were no doubt both unreal and unjust. Unreal because Pope's London, like Augustan Rome, was the largest city of the western world, and the center of an industrial, commercial, and imperial economy on which the writers were in no obscure fashion directly dependent. Unjust because, in the same way that the comfortable Horatian and Virgilian retreats presupposed slavery as their economic basis, so the elegance of Georgian life was depend-

ent on a laboring peasantry who—in the literature and the social reality
of the period—were complacently treated as barely human.

Yet the unreality of the Georgian myth is ultimately irrelevant. Goldsmith's "Deserted Village" may never have existed; but his legendary
"Sweet Auburn" stands today as an image of England as many of us
would still like it to be. The England of travel posters, with its picturesque village streets and country houses, is essentially Georgian. Indeed
much of what is most admirable about England today is really a nostal-
gic survival of the Georgian scene and its Augustan patterns of behavior:
universities like country houses; the weekend gardeners; and the unique
national passion for parks and preservation.

Perhaps it is an exaggeration to say that the Georgian Myth is still
alive today. It would be truer to say that it has not yet been replaced;
that we still hardly know whether it's possible to have a valid civilization without the rural economy and the rigid class system under which
the last intellectually respectable English example arose.

### III

In a general sense, then, the Augustan tradition is really for good and
ill, the main tradition of European civilization. One reason why its literature is not very popular today is that it belonged so intensely to the
immediate and practical life of its time: it was largely an occasional literature. Another reason is that we are opposed to many of its basic values: it was commonsensical and elitist and social where we want to be
original and egalitarian and individualist. Again, Freud and modern de-
mocracy have made us aware of how deeply traditional civilization
arose from psychological and social repression: and so we imagine that
the Augustan attitude arose from a complacent blindness to man's real
nature.

Actually one of the constants in Augustan writing is a sense of the
cost of preserving civilization. Deeply committed to social order, the
Augustans made the necessary sacrifices with open eyes. Johnson and
Pope would have agreed with William Law when he wrote that "our
*Imaginations* and *Desires* . . . are the greatest Reality we have." The
public good, in their view, required man to discipline the impulses of his
imagination and his passions.

# 3

# THE IRONIC VOICE

The adjective Augustan surely evokes a special way of speaking—precise in syntax, elegant in diction, and very detached in its attitude to the subject, to the audience, and even to the self and its feelings. In its most characteristic mode the Augustan voice is ironic.*

In no other period, certainly, are so many of the acknowledged masterpieces ironic both in their basic strategy and in their local style: "Absalom and Achitophel," *The Tale of a Tub, Gulliver's Travels, The Rape of the Lock, The Dunciad, The Way of the World, The Beggar's Opera.* Nor can we read for very long in many others before finding an important ironical element: the indulgent mockery of Addison in *The Spectator;* or of Goldsmith in *The Citizen of the World;* the lofty awareness of the narrow limits placed on man's endeavor in "The Vanity of Human Wishes" and *The Decline and Fall of the Roman Empire;* the comic counterpoint of action and comment in *Tom Jones* and *Tristram Shandy.* From 1660 to the end of the eighteenth century the ironical voice pervades the scene, from the philosophical heights of Berkeley and Hume to the polemic abysses of Grub Street.

---

* This essay is reprinted here by assent of Ruth Watt and agreement with Random House, Inc. It appeared originally as a chapter in *The Augustan Age: Approaches to Its Literature, Life, and Thought,* ed. Ian Watt (Greenwich, Conn.: Fawcett Publications, 1968), pp. 101-14—a revised and expanded version of a talk with the same title broadcast on the BBC Third Program and later reprinted in *The Listener* (April 27, 1967). This version also incorporates parts of a talk titled "The Ironic Tradition in Augustan Prose from Swift to Johnson" at the Third Clark Literary Seminar, July 14, 1956, published in *Restoration and Augustan Prose* (Los Angeles: William Andrews Clark Memorial Library, 1956).

I

Why is the ironic way of speaking so essential a part of the Augustan attitude?

In the *Verses* on his own death Swift claims that he inaugurates the ironic tradition in eighteenth-century literature:

> Arbuthnot is no more my Friend,
> Who dares to Irony pretend;
> Which I was born to introduce,
> Refin'd it first, and shew'd its Use.

Swift also gives a clue to the social function of irony in his letter to *The Tatler* on "the continual corruptions of our English tongue," where he singles out two of his favorite lexical *bêtes noires* and writes: "I have done my Utmost for some Years to stop the Progress of *Mobb* and *Banter*, but have been plainly borne down by Numbers."

"Mob" and "Banter" are being singled out as vulgar new coinages; but the reason for their being invented, and for Swift's disgust at them, is also significant.

"Mob" was the modish abbreviation of *mobile vulgus*; and Swift objected as much to the thing as he did to the abbreviation. The word first appeared in the place of "rabble," when the London crowd, under Shaftesbury's direction, rioted against Charles II in favor of Monmouth. "Mob" was naturalized, according to the *Oxford English Dictionary*, in 1688, the year of the Glorious Revolution; and for the following century most of the great men of letters remained on guard against the mob, against all those who threatened to subvert the established order, whether in politics or in literature or in manners.

To say that the Augustans invented the dichotomy of the elite and the mob would obviously be exaggerated; but they certainly conceptualized the distinction and applied it more unremittingly than ever before. The distinction almost defines the way they looked at themselves as writers. They were a righteous minority battling for true standards against every kind of deviation from the norm: against the Dunces and the Foplings and the Virtuosos and the pedants and the false wits.

Out of this there arose a vision of a double, a divided audience that made irony, in the elementary sense of speaking by contraries, an appropriate, and almost an obligatory, mode of discourse.

To the chosen few—the men of wit and judgment and learning—you could speak as subtly and elliptically as you wished. But to the many—the mob—you obviously couldn't, and in any case wouldn't, use the same language; in Dr. Johnson's telling phrase, they had "no claim to the honour of serious confutation." The Augustan writer's sense of his audience, therefore, resulted in a continual pressure toward shaping every element of discourse, from the single word to the total work, with two opposite categories of people in mind. In *Gulliver's Travels*, for example, the mob was provided with the most elementary kind of travel and narrative interest—if you played the ironic game as well as Swift, you might even take in an Irish bishop and persuade him that Lemuel Gulliver was a real man writing about real voyages. Meanwhile Swift's intellectual peers could savor simultaneously not only their own satiric applications of the fable, which were the book's true purpose, but also the literary skill with which the mob was being hoodwinked. This double interpretation is typical of the writer's ironic posture in general: it is both a formal expression of the qualitative division in the reading public and a flattering reinforcement of the sense of superiority that animates the more sophisticated part of it.

Separating the true wits from the mob was an infinitely adaptable strategy. If, for example, the Hanoverian boors and the vulgar new millionaires, along with their political toadies and their poets laureate, seemed to most people to be the great ones of their time, Pope could put a brave face on the situation and announce that "Scribblers or peers alike are mob to me"; and Fielding could continue the tradition by attacking what he called the "mobility," and explaining in *Tom Jones* that "wherever this word [mob] occurs in our writings, it intends persons without virtue or sense, in all stations; and many of the highest rank are often meant by it."

The moral and intellectual qualities of the mob, then, were the complete antithesis of what the Augustans wanted; and so were its natural modes of speech, including banter.

In *A Tale of a Tub*, after promising us a treatise entitled "A Modest Defense of the Proceedings of the *Rabble* in all Ages," Swift turns briefly, in the prefatory "Apology," to the subject of banter. "This Polite Word," he tells us, "was first borrowed from the Bullies in *White-Fryars*, then fell among the Footmen, and at last retired to the Pedants." Swift goes on to attack banter as openly rude personal abuse, cast in the vulgar dialect of the marketplace. Its rhetorical aim, perhaps, is the same as irony's—to expose your enemy to shame and ridicule—but the ironic game is played in much more seemly fashion. Irony tends to well-bred understatement, to meiosis; and while the gentleman is disposing of his foe by irony, he need never discompose the serenity of his features either by anger or laughter. The true gentleman, like Fontenelle, *"n'a jamais fait ha ha ha."* Whether Swift, as reported, never laughed, we do not know; I think he probably did, but not often and certainly not in his prose. Puttenham had defined irony as "the dry mock." Swift's prose rigidly obeys the code of irony that, like the code of behaviour officially prescribed for Prussian officers, allows no more than *"ein kurzes militärische Lachen"*—a single chilling "Ha!"

Irony is better suited to the gentleman and the wit than banter in many other ways: it's rude to stick our tongue out in public, but it's the very pink of politeness to praise your enemy with your tongue in your cheek. Moreover, the obliquity of the insult makes it much more difficult to counter. As Max Beerbohm said long ago of the father of irony, the Socratic method is not a game at which two can play. Which, presumably, is why it has always appealed both to those social classes and to those individuals who think of themselves as an elite.

## II

One function of the Augustan ironic posture, then, was to differentiate the speech, especially the aggressive speech, of the elite from that of the mob. The need for this distinction was itself the result of the enormous importance that Augustan society gave to talk. Dennis asked what he thought was a purely rhetorical question when he wrote: "What indeed can anyone mean, when he speaks of a fine gentleman, but one who is qualified in conversation, to please the best company of either sex?" This emphasis on conversation as an expression of social and intellectual fastidiousness inevitably affected the most basic elements of speech, diction, and syntax. The new preoccupation with correctness obviously also served to separate educated speakers from the vulgarity of the mob. So it is wholly consistent that Swift should also have been deeply concerned, both in *The Tatler* essay and elsewhere, with the reform of language, and that he tried to persuade Harley to set up an English equivalent to the *Académie française*, which would codify and make permanent the meanings and correct uses of words.

Uneducated speech—the banter of the mob—tends towards repetition, concreteness, and hyperbole; the direction of Augustan diction was towards economy, abstraction, and understatement. How this direction prepares the way for the ironic voice can be illustrated in the famous line from Swift's *A Tale of a Tub*, in the "Digression of Madness": "Last week I saw a Woman *flay'd*, and you will hardly believe, how much it altered her Person for the worse."

The ominous modulations of "you will hardly believe" and "for the worse" would lose their effect if Swift's prose were not so beautifully concise; our attention would be too occupied by the difficulty of making out the sentence's bare meaning to take in the double range of implication—the author's mock obtuseness about human suffering and Swift's actual intention of shocking us into realizing it.

The effect in the passage also depends on understatement and on abstractness of diction.

Understatement was not likely to be effective in most earlier kinds of English prose. In Jacobean prose, for example, the competition for our attention would usually be much too energetic for the simple meiosis of "how much her person was altered for the worse" to stand out as an effective climax.

Swift's perfectly controlled simplicity, combined with his habit of understatement, probably did much to attune the ears of succeeding generations of readers to similar ironic effects in later writers: also to the opposite duplicities of calculated hyperbole. This ironic technique is typical of the style of David Hume, for instance, who also "abhorred . . . *Waggery* and *Banter*." When Hume writes of the "hideous hypothesis . . . for which *Spinoza* is so universally infamous," his vocabulary is normally so rational and unemphatic that such words as "hideous" and "infamous" can only be intentionally ironic hyperboles. The Deist minority among his readers would delightedly recognize them as such and at the same time find their pleasure increased by Hume's straight-faced parody of the zealous indignation of the orthodox mob.

Perhaps the most significant characteristic of the ironic Augustan style, however, is that exemplified in the cool, distant generality of Swift's "how much it altered her person." A degree of abstraction seems to be necessary for ironic diction—partly because very few nonabstract terms have an opposite: there is no antonym, so far as I know, for *Ian Watt*; and partly because the use of abstract words in itself often creates an ironical effect: if anyone who knows my proper name calls me "Professor," I at once suspect—and resent—a certain ironical distancing; the speaker is making an implicit claim to elite status by mocking mine.

Sometimes, of course, the use of general and abstract terms may generate irony unintentionally. When Dr. Johnson, for example, gave us his immortal definition of gin as "a compendious mode of drunkenness," the context—a serious attack in the *Literary Magazine* (No. 13) on the "enormous and insupportable mischiefs" arising from intemperance— proves that he did not mean to be ironical. The abstract modifier *compendious*, taken in conjunction with its concrete referent *gin*, arouses a suspicion of irony merely because of the absence of the expected moral connotation: *compendiousness*, which Johnson defined in the *Dictionary* as that "by which time is saved and circuition cut off," normally has an approbative connotation that, in the context, is contrary to expectation. But the main reason for our surprise is the mere generality of the diction, whose lack of connotation is so conspicuous as to generate irony.

The analytic generalizing tendency of the eighteenth-century vocabulary may itself, then, be regarded as tending to produce irony whether intended or not, partly because it excludes the normally attendant feelings and evaluations with which its concrete referent is usually associated; and partly because generalized diction has its own kind of connotation, always suggesting a cool, unemotional, and hence skeptical evaluation of what it describes. This in itself expresses the characteristic posture of the Augustan writers—a lofty, analytic, and slightly supercilious command of the entire human scene. Shaftesbury, for example, proclaimed the great benefits of "raillery"—the banter of the elite—for composing differences among educated gentlemen; as for what he called "the mere Vulgar of Mankind," much more drastic disciplinary measures were obviously called for. The mob, he wrote, "often stand in need of such a rectifying Object as the *Gallows* before their Eyes." In this comment there's surely an implicit social and literary alignment of Shaftesbury, the Whig Deist, with his ideological opposite, the Tory churchman Swift. Both give us a vision conspicuously removed from the ordinary man's concrete apprehensions. Just as in the case of Swift's use of "person" for the bleeding flesh of the flayed woman, Shaftesbury's abstract diction dissolves the physical horror of the gallows into the metaphysical air; the witty abstract understatement of "rectifying object" is a whole world away from the concrete experience of the gallows, and the sweating blood lust of the crowds watching the public hanging of criminals on Tyburn Hill. In short, generality of diction combines with economy and understatement to express the vast distance between the wit and the mob, between the philosopher and the human animal.

Careful and concise use of words, together with a highly developed mastery of the language of abstraction and generalization, hardly suffice in themselves for effective irony; they require to be set in a perfectly controlled syntax. The normal syntax of earlier prose, of the Elizabethans and Jacobeans, for instance, doesn't immediately strike one as an effective instrument of polite literary discussion, dispassionate philosophical analysis, or subtly restrained irony. As clause follows clause, in Hooker or Donne or Milton, we're aware, not so much of the sentence as the unified expression of a single and distinct idea, but of an unlimited flow of eloquence that expresses the richness and variety of the flux of experience. An emphasis on sentence structure as an instrument whereby one mind abstracts a finite element of meaning from the infinite possibilities offered by reality, and then shapes that finite element so that another mind can recognize it as a separate unit of meaning, seems to be a fairly recent, and in the main, an Augustan, achievement in the history of English prose.

As one would expect, the classical mind of Ben Jonson early led him towards the ease and simplicity of Augustan prose; but one notices that his irony still tends to be expressed through sensory metaphor rather than through logical structure.

Here, for instance, is Ben Jonson on the typical Augustan theme of the quotidian littleness of life: "What a deal of cold business doth a man spend the better part of life in! in scattering compliment, tendering visits, gathering and venting news, following feasts and plays, making a little winter love in a dark corner."

Jonson's ironic effect comes through ending an accumulation of phrases with a climax—"a little winter love in a dark corner"—where love, widely reported to be the peak of mankind's emotional experience, is placed in the perspective of littleness, winter, and darkness; rhetorically the climax is only a matter of making the final phrase echo the opening metaphor: "What a deal of cold business . . . "

Sir William Temple, Swift's early patron, is much closer to the normal Augustan syntax in his famous aphorism: "When all is done, human life is, at the greatest and the best, but like a froward child, that must be played with and humoured a little to keep it quiet till it falls asleep, and then the care is over."

The separation of the subject—"human life"—from the long predicate focuses the reader's attention on the sentence as a unit; the prepared climax on "till it falls asleep, and then the care is over" is syntactical as well as verbal and metaphorical. Here Temple comes close to the most typical pattern of the Augustan syntax, especially in its ironical form— the periodic sentence. In Swift's "You will hardly believe, how much it altered her Person for the worse," it's the suspended predication of "for the worse" which gives the sentence its rhetorical effectiveness as irony; and we meet a more elaborate version of the periodic sentence in many of the great Augustan ironists. In Hume's essay "Of Miracles," for instance: "So that upon the whole, we may conclude, that the Christian Religion not only was at first attended with miracles, but even at this day cannot be believed by any reasonable person without one."

Hume's stylistic effect depends on the reader's capacity to hold the whole sentence in his mind, waiting for the predicate "cannot be believed by any reasonable person" to be completed by the last two words, "without one," and remembering that the artfully unemphatic pronoun "one" stands for "miracle."

The periodic sentence is the extreme example of the sentence as the intellectual imposition of order upon the items of experience. In this sense it is as characteristic of the Augustan attitude in prose as the closed heroic couplet is in poetry, although the periodic sentence only reached its full development late in the period, with Johnson and Gibbon. In both the heroic couplet and the periodic sentence, broadly speaking, the effort is for the speaker or writer to contain or stabilize order, in some way impose a pattern, on the miscellaneous multifariousness of experience and individual attitudes. Both are standardized modes of speech that invite the writer and the reader alike to the posture of balanced assessment: the posture that is essential if we are to be attentive to irony.

III

This brings us to one instinctive modern objection to Augustan prose: it's too public in manner and too logical to express the unstructured diversity of reality, and therefore strikes us as impersonal, contrived, and false.

It's probably true, I think, that to a writer wholly given over to the cultivated complicity in human pettiness that the consciously ironic perspective requires, the subjective world of feeling—and also of what Wordsworth called "the primary affections and duties"—will seem meager and unimportant. Such a writer will tend to see himself and his emotional life ironically, and write—with Gibbon—"I sighed as a lover, I obeyed as a son." The abstractions, the conventional roles, the mighty framework for the eternal littleness of man—they surely damp our resolution to live our own lives; and we're reminded of the words of the Russian poet Alexander Blok: "In the vodka of irony the mocker drowns his hope along with his despair." Gibbon won't let himself look very hard either at his hope or at his despair; and one imagines that Mr. and Mrs. Gibbon found little more emotional satisfaction in their son than Mademoiselle Susan Curchod in her lover. Incidentally, most of the greatest eighteenth-century ironists—Swift, Pope, Hume, and Gibbon— were bachelors.

On the other hand, irony and the periodic sentence need not necessarily isolate the speaker from his own personal life and the rest of struggling humanity. Henry Fielding and Laurence Sterne among the novelists, Thomas Gray and Horace Walpole among the letter writers, are obvious examples; and so is Dr. Johnson at his best.

In irony, as in so much else, Swift and Johnson are the mighty opposites. Both start from similar intellectual positions—from Christianity and a deep pessimism about human life. After a discussion of man's natural goodness, Lady McLeod accused Dr. Johnson of being "worse than Swift"; and if in the *Tale of a Tub* Swift had called happiness "the sublime and refined Point of Felicity, called *the Possession of being well deceived*; The Serene Peaceful State of being a Fool among Knaves," Johnson so little liked "any one who said they were happy" that when on one occasion his judgment was challenged, he thundered: "I tell you, the woman is ugly, and sickly, and foolish, and poor; and would it not make a man hang himself to hear such a creature say, it was happy?"

The tone of Johnson's retort points to the distinguishing feature of his irony. The rhetoric usually operates through fairly conscious hyperbole, and this in itself humanizes by breaking down the decorous impersonality that was normally a part of Augustan irony. Johnson brings himself—his own anger, not to say unhappiness—into the irony; he is not outside the ironic contradiction of attitudes but within it; he knows and relishes the folly of his own hyperbolic impatience, and this drastically qualifies what might otherwise appear to be an assertion of his own superiority to the wishful deceptions of fallible humanity.

Bringing himself into the ironic contradiction of attitudes was easy enough for Johnson—was indeed inevitable—when he was merely being reported by Boswell, or, as in the present case, by Mrs. Thrale; but Johnson locates himself within his ironic vision almost as consistently in his writings for publication. The letter to Lord Chesterfield one might call half public; and there we notice how the brilliance of Johnson's ironies at Chesterfield's expense is qualified and humanized by the confession of his own earlier personal humiliation: "no man is well pleased to have his all neglected, be it ever so little."

In Johnson's published works, in the *Lives of the Poets* and *The Rambler*, for instance, we have the same refusal to locate himself permanently on the Parnassian eminence, above and beyond the mob, from which Swift and Pope had looked down. This, I know, is contrary to the opinions of those who see Johnson's magniloquence as arrogant and impersonal. Johnson's style is, in a sense, both. But we may perhaps change T. S. Eliot's phrase about Donne and say that Johnson could be as personal as he pleased because he could be as impersonal as he pleased; he could introduce his own experience and his own mixed and fallible human nature into his public prose without any violation of neoclassical decorum, because his perspective on himself and on the world was broad enough and impersonal enough to avoid any deflection of our attention from the subject to the personality involved in it.

As an example of this, perhaps the famous passage about Shenstone's gardening will serve:

> Whether to plant a walk in undulating curves, and to place a bench at every turn where there is an object to catch the view; to make water run where it will be heard, and to stagnate where it will be seen; to leave intervals where the eye will be pleased, and to thicken the plantation where there is something to be hidden demands any great powers of mind, I will not enquire; perhaps a sullen and surly speculator may think such performances rather the sport than the business of human reason. But it must be at least confessed, that to embellish the form of Nature is an innocent amusement; and some praise must be allowed by the most supercilious observer to him, who does best what such multitudes are contending to do well.

Johnson's rhetorically effective devotion to justice prevents him from ranging the full force of his mind against Shenstone and the multitudes who are contending in the sports of human reason. Those who mock must remind themselves that they may be sullen, surly, or supercilious and that to set the just bounds of speculation is not easy. Johnson does not see the situation as an elite versus a mob, but rather as a very specific contrast of particular and equally human attitudes; in the present case, a degree of folly on the part of the doers is at least free of the charge of malignity that might be leveled at the critics; and so Johnson "rejoices to concur with the common reader"—with the mob—as far as he honestly can.

The Shenstone passage illustrates many other distinguishing features of Johnson's irony. The complication of the periodic syntax is necessary to enable Johnson to reenact for us all the gradations of attitude in the judging mind, and at the same time to allow of such incidental ironic felicities as "stagnate where it will be seen," where Johnson's formidable analytic power is shown easily constrained to a suitably comic antithesis—"stagnate" and "seen." Later we have the more outright jeer of "thicken the plantation where there is something to be hidden" archly prepared for by the earlier portion of the antithesis, to "leave intervals where the eye will be pleased"—we're already primed to congratulate ourselves at the trickery whereby Shenstone avoids "displeasing" the eye. The whole conception of prose, indeed, allows for the complex organization of a wider range of feeling and attitude than that of Swift, and its final ironical surprise—the placing of Shenstone above the multitudes—is in the direction of magnanimous allowance rather than of direct climactic derision.

The passage can, perhaps, not unfairly be compared with an equally famous passage in Swift—the judgment of the King of Brobdingnag: "I cannot but conclude the Bulk of your Natives to be the most pernicious Race of little odious Vermin that Nature ever suffered to crawl upon the Surface of the Earth." Swift here allows himself more latitude than usual for adjectival qualification, but it is only for steadier bringing home of the single rational judgment: the taxonomist, at first completely baffled, has at last found proper words; man is pernicious—harmful, but harmful, not as lions or natural catastrophes are, but as cockroaches are, or bedbugs. No complication of the verdict is allowed. I must confess that I find something obtrusive about the intense delimitation of intention in Swift's prose: the tone, the words, the syntax, the logic—all are aseptic; all bespeak what Johnson characteristically called Swift's "oriental scrupulosity" about his ablutions. Isn't Swift a cook who cares so much for cleanliness that all his dishes taste of soap?

Several other general points about Johnson's irony must be made very briefly. First, he was a true skeptic: "prodigies are always seen in proportion as they are expected" surely rivals Hume in its serene repudiation of popular credulity. In a sense Johnson was even more skeptical about reason than the romantic ironists; after all, they assumed in their heart of hearts that reason was truer than feeling, even if it wasn't so nice. Johnson made no such *a priori* assumptions and therefore avoided letting the dichotomizing habit, whether in the Swiftian or the romantic way, become his master: "I hope . . . that I have lived long enough in the world, to prevent me from expecting to find any action of which both the original motive and all the parts were good." All is mixed; one cannot merely present a system of erroneous or inadequate ideas and leave the reader to elicit the truth by working out the opposite *per contrarium* in the obvious ironical manner. The universe is not logical; it is certainly not disposed in an endless series of exact linear contradictions; and so to discern what is false or foolish will not in itself give us any grip on reality. Johnson never forgot this; if he uses antithetical polarities, their status is provisional, exploratory, pragmatic, and his irony in general is the product of a continually fresh attempt to perceive and express the total setting of any perception. Perhaps we can call it an open irony, as opposed to the more predetermined and closed dichotomies within which Swift tends to work.

For this open irony Johnson had the full, indeed the unequalled, possession of a truly philosophical analytic power that could embody itself in the unexpected but logically convincing metaphor as easily as in the intricately appropriate abstraction. Consider, for the first, the famous epigram on Gray: "He has a kind of strutting dignity and is tall by walking on tiptoe"; and for the second—the manipulation of the intricately appropriate abstraction—the passage of the "Life" where Johnson considers Swift's treatment of his domestics: "That he was disposed to do his servants good on important occasions is no great mitigation; benefaction can be but rare, and tyrannick peevishness is perpetual." Johnson enlists the full weight of abstraction and impersonality in his wounding judgment; but there is—to use Bertrand Bronson's fine phrase—a "yeast of insobriety" behind "tyrannick peevishness" that makes us marvel at the power that could both observe the phenomenon and make the expression fit the crime. The judgment, of course, is contrary to the apparent, the commonly accepted scale of values; but its subversive paradox gains total authority from the fine balance of the phrasing: "benefaction can be but rare, and tyrannick peevishness is perpetual."

Here, perhaps, we have the major ironical characteristic of Johnson's style—the almost continual contrast between the poised, philosophical assurance of the manner and the "yeast of insobriety" that informs the matter: while the grand generality of the manner functions as the hallmark of Johnson's public *persona*, the matter reveals a deep commitment to the particularities of a personal experience of reality; and somewhere within the dichotomy reason and passion are made one.

## IV

But if Johnson is in some respects the opposite of Swift, he shares with him, and perhaps only with him, the highest position among those who contributed to the development of what, not altogether correctly, Matthew Arnold called the "age of prose and reason." This development—the Augustan drive to precise, rational, and polished discourse—was wholly consonant with the attitude of being above the vulgar tumult, which was equally characteristic of Augustan Rome and of the English landed elite of the eighteenth century. The particular emphasis on irony is also a necessary part of this attitude. Caesar Augustus himself thought it appropriate to see his own glorious existence in an ironic perspective when, on his deathbed, he asked, "Have I played my part creditably in the comedy of life?" Irony, essentially, is a way of putting individual thoughts and feelings and observation into a wider context; and the realistic, skeptical, and detached temper of the Augustan attitude required a mode of speech in which the norms of society and history were always present.

The other most obvious feature of Augustan prose, the periodic style, survived in a more mechanical form to become the basis of the common prose of public address from Macaulay to the editorialists of the *Times*. All that accumulated "load of educated and official assumptions," as V. S. Pritchett has said, takes the mandarin style, "the Big Bow Wow," further and further away from the expressive needs and habits of speech and writing today. Whether the opposite modern tendency—which so often leads merely to discourse that is merely "little Bow Wow talking to himself"—is preferable to the pomp of debased Augustan prose when it has lost its positive qualities, its precise and elegant analytic power, is not easy to decide. But it seems clear that no other equally effective style of public discourse has been developed to take the place of the style that was developed in the Augustan period.

This style also made possible some of the greatest writing in the language. At its best the ironic voice of the eighteenth century can set before us the infinite disparities and discontinuities of an individual life, and then place them in a larger context of generalization; in Johnson, especially, it continually moves us to a rapture of assent because its irony enlists all the resources of experience, understanding, and art to create a dispassionate image of the endless incongruities that beset us in this vale of tears, inconguities that are, no doubt, the most truly universal norms to be discovered in what the Augustans called Nature.

4

# PUBLISHERS AND SINNERS: THE AUGUSTAN VIEW

One fairly widespread feature of Augustan literature is the idea that the temple of the Muses was being profaned by sinful and arrogant booksellers and that the true wit, therefore, should miss no opportunity of cutting them down to size.[*] Hostility to publishers is not, of course, peculiar to the eighteenth century, but it does seem uniquely powerful and pervasive in the literature of the period from Dryden to Goldsmith; their iniquities seem to meet us everywhere, not only in verse and prose satire, but in fiction and drama, to say nothing of private letters and parliamentary debates. It's usually only a matter of incidental jeers, but there is also something of a special literary tradition in which the bookseller figures as comic villain; in poetry, of course, there's the *Dunciad*, with Lintot and Curll given leading roles and a dozen or so other booksellers in the cast; there are prose pamphlets like Richard Savage's (and probably in part Pope's) *An Author to be Let* (1729), plays like Fielding's *The Author's Farce* (1730) and Samuel Foote's *The Author* (1757), Archibald Campbell's Lucianic dialogue *The Sale of Authors* (1767), and a host of novels including most notably, *Amelia* and *Roderick Random*. The period is also characterized by the amount of personal friction between authors and booksellers: David Hume brandishing his sword at Jacob Robinson, Dr. Johnson knocking Thomas Osborne down, Goldsmith trying to do the same to Evans, and Pope, determined to make the punishment fit the crime, choosing the emetic as his weapon and applying it to the bowels of that gross feeder at the table of the Muses, Edmund Curll.

[*] "Publishers and Sinners: The Augustan View" appeared originally in *Studies in Bibliography* 12 (1959), 3-20, published by the University of Virginia Press. Reprinted with permission.

Why do the booksellers loom so large on the literary scene? Was their bad eminence peculiar to England? What literary consequences did it have? And to what extent was the hostility which the booksellers provoked—in Pope, for instance—justified? I must preface my necessarily cursory and speculative attempt to indicate answers to these inherently difficult problems with a note of scholarly caution. We must remember that despite the many additions to our picture of the institutional structure of the Augustan literary world since the two main monographs on the subject, Alexandre Beljame's *Le public et les hommes de lettres en Angleterre au dix-huitème siècle* (1881), and A. S. Collins's *Authorship in the Days of Johnson* (1927), the limits to our knowledge are still numerous and in some respects crippling; nor can much be done about them until the short-title catalogue finally wings its way into the eighteenth century, and until we are then supplied with an Augustan equivalent to Paul Morrison's *Index of Printers, Publishers and Booksellers* (1955).

I

When, in the early seventeenth century, leadership in all the activities connected with the printing press passed from Germany and Italy to France and the Netherlands, England was still very far behind. It produced very little paper, for instance, and all its type was imported or of foreign design. In the next hundred years, however, the picture changed dramatically: in 1686 the many efforts to manufacture good white paper for printing had succeeded sufficiently for the White Paper Makers to be incorporated, and by 1713 two-thirds of the country's requirements were being produced at home; as for type, Caslon set up his foundry in 1720, and from then onwards his ideas, and later Baskerville's, turned England into an exporter of type and a leader in typographical design.[1]

---

[1] In addition to Beljame and Collins I am particularly indebted to: Ellic Howe, *The London Compositor* (London: Bibliographical Society, 1947); Frank A. Mumby, *Publishing and Bookselling*, 3d ed. (London: Jonathan Cape, 1954); Marjorie Plant, *The English Book Trade: An Economic History* (New York: R. R. Bowker, 1939); William M. Sale, Jr., *Samuel Richardson: Master Printer* (Ithaca: Cornell University Press, 1950); H. R. Plomer's three Dictionaries of Booksellers and Printers; James Sutherland's edition of the *Dunciad* in the Twickenham Pope; George F. Papali's unpublished doctoral dissertation "The Life and Work of Jacob Tonson" (London 1933); and Peter Murray Hill, who

We find very similar contrasts when we turn from methods of production to types of publication. In the early seventeenth century, for example, Holland and then France led in the field of the newspaper, but the world's first daily, the *Daily Courant*, came out in England in 1702. The foundation of the *Journal des Savants* in 1665 exemplifies France's earlier prominence in another kind of periodical, the learned review; but the foundation of the *Tatler* and *Spectator* shows the England of Queen Anne initiating quite a new periodical genre which became very popular abroad; and Cave's *Gentlemen's Magazine*, founded in 1731, was equally novel and influential. Among the many other signs of England's increasing prominence two other important innovations in the world of letters may be cited: in England the effective development of the circulating library began in 1740, whereas the spread of the *cabinet de lecture* in France came later, in about 1763; and there is a similar twenty-year priority in the matter of encyclopedias—that of Diderot published between 1751 and 1776 followed the example set in England by the printer Ephraim Chambers in 1728.

I make these contrasts only to underline the fact that the appearance of the *Dunciad* in 1728 coincides with England's very recently achieved leadership in a great number of publishing activities, activities which set the pattern for future developments both there and elsewhere. The main causes of these developments, I suppose, are the same as those which had brought about England's commercial expansion in general; but one of them seems to be of special importance: the ending of Stuart absolutism, with all its traditional and restrictive social and economic attitudes, by the Glorious and Protestant Revolution of 1688, with its encouragement of free individual enterprise in every field. The importance of this changed commercial and ideological background can be estimated either by looking at how the Stuarts had earlier attempted in innumerable ways to control and restrict the development of printing and bookselling, or at how in France authors, printers, and publishers alike remained subject to every kind of harassment at the hands of autocratic and clerical power until the French Revolution.

In the eighteenth century, then, the English book trade in general flourished as never before; it remains to inquire why it was the booksellers rather than the printers who held the dominating position; and, first

---

lent me his unpublished paper "Two Augustan Booksellers: John Dunton and Edmund Curll."

of all, therefore, to inquire what the division of functions actually was. For, in the present context, the term "bookseller" is itself very confusing; there was no real eighteenth-century equivalent to our booksellers today, men exclusively devoted to the retailing of books; and on the other hand, the convenient practice of equating the "bookseller" of the eighteenth century with the "publisher" of today is also misleading, since at that time no one was exclusively engaged in the publishing business either.

There are really five main roles in the business of getting a book into the purchaser's hands: first, of course, the writing of it; second, the transfer of the manuscript to the printer; third, the printing itself (in which category I include, as the eighteenth century did not, folding, tying and binding the printed sheets); fourth, the storage and distribution of the finished product; and fifth, the retailing of it to the buyer in a shop or through some other channel. Today, we usually think of the publisher as one who undertakes or controls the middle three of these operations: getting the copy from the author, arranging for the printing, and lastly, storing the book and sending it out to the retail booksellers. From the Elizabethan period until quite late in the nineteenth century, however, almost any permutation or combination of any of the five functions was possible, although the increasingly common practice in the eighteenth century was for the booksellers to perform not only the three functions we now expect of a publisher, but also the final one, that of selling the book to the public.

The 1757 edition of Campbell's *The London Tradesman* makes the position reasonably clear: the bookseller's function is "to purchase original copies from authors, to employ printers to print them, and publish and sell them on their own account, or at auctions, and sell them at an advanced price: but," the writer adds, significantly, "their chief riches and profit is in the property of valuable copies." It is the "property of valuable copies" which occasioned not only the many legal battles of the booksellers in the eighteenth century, but also most of the public attacks against them; and it is this control of copies which I shall have primarily in mind when I refer, as I normally shall, to booksellers or publishers without distinction as far as the eighteenth century is concerned. I should perhaps add that contemporary usage of the term "publisher" was itself confusing: normally, as in Swift and Pope, it refers to whoever is responsible for making a book available to the public, under whatever conditions, but later a more technical sense also appears, confined to the wholesaling, and perhaps the retailing, of the finished book, and specifically excluding responsibility either for printing or for ownership of the copy.

The division of labor in the book trade in the eighteenth century, then, had not yet crystalized into its present form, although we must remember that it has not done so universally even today, especially in backward areas: University Presses, for example, often both print and act as publishers. Compared with the earliest days of printing, however, when Caxton had personally written the text, set it up, printed it, and sold it, the division of labor had gone fairly far by the time of Pope; in fact it is not a gross oversimplification to say that the big London booksellers, the Tonsons, the Lintots, Andrew Millar, and Robert Dodsley, carried on their business very much as publishers do today, except that they also happened to run bookstores.

In the general history of the book trade the crucial separation was that between printer and bookseller, usually said to have begun with Anthony Koberger as early as the end of the fifteenth century. By the end of the sixteenth century the English printers were already loudly complaining that they could hardly make a living because the booksellers, through their complete control of the retail market, were able to dictate their own terms and had forced printing prices down very severely. The main reason for the economic advantage of the bookseller, I suppose, is that by its nature printing requires both a large initial capital outlay, for the press, type, and so on, and a considerable regular volume of business to meet costs and wages. Bookselling, on the other hand, needs no staff, and very little in the way of premises or equipment; while in the seventeenth and eighteenth centuries, at least, it was very easy to acquire a stock. John Dunton, one of the Dunces attacked by Swift and Pope, describes in his *Life and Errors* how, in 1681, he merely "took up with half a shop [and] a warehouse," published one religious work, Thomas Doolittle's *The Sufferings of Christ*, and then, "exchanging it through the whole trade" of booksellers "furnished my shop with all sorts of books saleable at that time."

It was easy, then, to become a bookseller. To trade with any security, however, also involved being a member of the Stationers' Company and this normally required a good deal of capital: the commonest way of becoming free of the Company was by serving a seven-year apprenticeship, and the average premium charged by master printers, for example, during the eighteenth century was about twenty pounds, a very consid-

erable sum in those days. But that was the only hurdle, at least after
1695 when the Licensing Act of 1662 had lapsed, and with it the restrictive powers both of the Stationers' Company and of the "Surveyor of
the Imprimery and Printing Presses," a post created by the 1662 Act and
long filled by the notorious Sir Roger L'Estrange.

The end of licensing had even more important indirect implications
for the development of bookselling, since it terminated the many government efforts to hold the number of printers down to the theoretical
legal limit of twenty which had been set by the Tudors and reaffirmed
by a Star Chamber decree of 1627. By 1724 there were seventy-five
printers active in London, and by 1785 the number had risen to 124.
Nor does this alone fully indicate the scale of the increase after 1695:
the number of presses in an individual printing office, which had previously been limited to two in most cases, was now free to go up, sometimes to as many as nine; and even more important, perhaps, printing in
the provinces, which had been forbidden by a Star Chamber decree of
1586, spread rapidly—in 1724 there were already at least twenty-eight
provincial printers at work.

The development of the provincial market no doubt helped to foster
the spread of the reading habit on which the prosperity of eighteenth-
century booksellers was partly based; and so did the increase in newspapers, which was much stimulated by the ending of effective censor-
ship. Whatever the reasons, there is no doubt that, compared either with
their former condition or with that of their French counterparts, the
booksellers of the Augustan period were extremely well-off. The bookseller Thomas Guy, helped it is true by a variety of speculative enter-
prises, was the most eminent charitable endower of the time—Guy's
Hospital is but one of many benefactions; Jacob Tonson paid over
twenty thousand pounds for his country estate, Hazel; and a generation
later both Andrew Millar and William Strahan left fortunes of nearly a
hundred thousand pounds. They and a good many others, booksellers
such as the elder Thomas Osborne, Awnsham Churchill, and Bernard
Lintot, printer-publishers such as Samuel Buckley, John Barber, and
Samuel Richardson, were as wealthy as all but the biggest London merchants and financiers. The improved social and economic status of the
paper, printing, and bookselling trades in general is further suggested by
the fact that the Stationers' Company, which had produced no Lord
Mayor of London during its first hundred years, produced no less than

five of them during the eighteenth century.[2] The solid prosperity of the bookselling trade in particular is attested by the fact that several publishing houses were founded which continue today—Charles Rivington set up shop, for example, in 1711, Thomas Longman in 1724, and John Murray in 1768; while John Brindley, in 1728, started a bookshop in New Bond Street which still survives, under the name of Ellis's.

The contrast with the position in France is striking. The greatest of the booksellers there, Charles-Joseph Pancoucke, made only a very modest fortune—"une honnête aisance"—and that right at the end of the eighteenth century. Until then the chief authorities[3] agree that the very dark picture of French eighteenth-century bookselling painted by Diderot in his *Lettre sur le commerce de la librairie* (1767) is in the main justified. It is true that Paris had always had many more booksellers than London, some 235 in 1600 apparently, a figure which was certainly not equaled in London until the eighteenth century; and also that in the early decades of the seventeenth century publishing flourished, with Scarron earning as much as a thousand livres—some fifty pounds, perhaps—for one book of his *Virgile travesti,* and with the bookseller Claude Barbin occupying a privileged position among literary men somewhat like Tonson's in England half a century later. But from the time of Louis XIV onward printers, publishers, and authors alike were increasingly subject to a crippling interference and persecution from church, state, and nobility: most of the great French writers of the eighteenth century knew imprisonment or exile, and many of their works—perhaps the majority—were published abroad, banned, or only issued posthumously. As for the booksellers, they were, for example, forbidden to set up shop anywhere except in two of the quarters of Paris, so that the police could keep their eye on them more easily; further, they needed official approval before any book could be published; and even so the royal imprimatur was always liable to be suddenly revoked—as happened in the famous battle between Diderot and the Jesuits over the *Encyclopédie.*

---

[2] Alfred B. Beaven, *The Aldermen of the City of London* (London: E. Fisher & Co., 1908-1913), II, 101, 125, 130, 131.

[3] E.g. Edmond Werdet, *Histoire du livre en France*, 5 vols. (Paris, 1861-2); André Brulé, *Les Gens de lettres* ("La Vie au dix-huitième siècle," Paris: M. Seheur, 1928); Jean-Alexis Néret, *Histoire illustré de la librairie* (Paris: Lemarne, 1953). David T. Pottinger's excellent *The French Book Trade in the Ancien Regime 1500-1791* (Cambridge: Harvard University Press, 1958) appeared too late to be used in this paper.

II

For many reasons, then, French booksellers were neither so free nor so prosperous as their English counterparts in the eighteenth century; and this had many important literary consequences. Most important of all, perhaps, is the fact that in France patronage remained the chief way for writers to earn a living, and this prevented the degree of what one may call the democratization of literature which, for good or evil, occurred in England: both materially and spiritually the home of the French eighteenth-century writer remained the court and the aristocratic salon, whereas in England it was fast becoming the coffeehouse and the bookseller's backroom—Tom Davies's, for example, where Boswell met Johnson.

The eventual literary effect of the changed economic and social orientation of the author in England has a close bearing on our answer to the question of whether the widespread hostility of Augustan writers to the booksellers, a hostility which has no genuine parallel in France, was really justified.

The mere fact that in England the booksellers were much more prominent and prosperous than they had been before or were elsewhere, would no doubt be enough to explain most of the attacks against them in Pope's time: since it was a new situation in the world of letters it was bound to excite envy. In any case, as far as the Augustan writers were concerned the increasing power and prestige of the booksellers was a particularly striking example of the current changes in the class structure which threatened the hierarchical social tradition which had their ideological allegiance.

Quite apart from these historical considerations it also must be remembered that the very nature of the relationship between publisher and author in general tends to breed animosity, like that between landlord and tenant. The letters of Dryden to his publisher, Jacob Tonson, for instance, reveal how rich in possibilities of friction is the situation where the writer is wholly dependent on a man whose ultimate concern is only to get the right kind of copy at the right time for the agreed price, and how this friction is exacerbated by the fact that the writer typically comes to what is essentially an economic transaction with a not wholly material view of his role. So in the end history remembers, not that Dryden got more from Tonson than any poet had got from a bookseller before, but only that Dryden blamed Tonson's meanness for the cursory nature of the annotation to his Virgil; that he sent him a messenger with the ominous triplet:

> With leering looks, bull-faced and freckled fair,
> With two left legs, and Judas colour'd hair
> And frowzy pores that taint the ambient air.

And that he accompanied it with the verbal message—"Tell the dog that he who wrote these can write more."

It is a pity that he didn't, but of course Tonson wouldn't have paid him for them, and a *Dunciad* is only possible to a poet who, like Pope, is well beyond the reach of immediate financial necessity. But by an irony he must have relished, Pope himself was only in this fortunate position as a result of the very considerable increase in the scale of payments to authors from the days of Dryden onwards. It was Tonson, apparently, who was mainly responsible for the change: he lured Dryden away from his earlier publisher, Herringman, by offering twenty pounds for his version of *Troilus and Cressida*, in 1679; for the *Fables* we have the contract between them for the payment of 250 guineas for 10,000 lines—a shilling a couplet; and according to Pope, Dryden made 1,200 pounds for the Virgil. Less than a generation later, however, Pope was able to play Tonson off against his aspiring rivals, notably Bernard Lintot, to much greater effect, so that, partly through the sale of subscription copies given him free, and partly through Lintot's payment of 200 pounds for the copy of each of the six volumes, Pope probably cleared about five thousand pounds for the *Iliad*, and not much less for the *Odyssey*. To attempt some assessment of this in terms of income level, it might be fair to say that, since interest rates of 5 and 6 per cent were common, the two works alone could have given Pope an income of 500 pounds a year; an income which was more than that of some of the lesser bishoprics, which was over twice the average income Gregory King assigned to "lesser merchants," and which fell short of Johnson's estimate of "splendour" only by a hundred pounds.

Pope, of course, was exceptional, but there are many other indications of the very high prices paid to authors, especially later in the century; sums of a thousand pounds or more for a substantial work, were not uncommon—for Mrs. Carter's *Epictetus* for example or Fielding's *Amelia*. Indeed there is perhaps no other period where so many of the acknowledged masterpieces received such immediate and handsome monetary reward—one thinks of 700 pounds for *Tom Jones*, of over 1,000 pounds for *The Sentimental Journey*, of 6,000 pounds for the *Decline and Fall*, of 500 pounds for the first edition alone of *The Wealth of Nations*. Johnson's *Lives of the Poets*, it is true, brought Johnson only 300 guineas, but that was more than the 200 he had asked, and Malone thought that if he had gone as high as 1,000 or even 1,500 guineas the booksellers would have accepted: similarly, the mere 200 pounds which Swift received for *Gulliver's Travels* was the figure he had named.

One of the two main exceptions to this tendency for increasingly high scales of literary payment by booksellers does a good deal to explain Pope's generally unfavorable attitude: poetry rarely commanded a high price, except for collected editions after the author had made his name. The reason for this relatively low scale of payments for poetry is probably that the booksellers tended to value copy mainly by the two criteria of the known demand for the subject and the probable size, and therefore price, of the book. Any work in several quarto volumes which was either a survey of some important field of knowledge or was of such established literary status that it could be regarded as indispensable to a gentleman's library, constituted a likely investment; and for this reason large works by indifferent writers often received huge rewards—John Hawkesworth, for instance, made 6,000 pounds in 1773 for his three-volume account of Cook's voyages. The usual payment for poetry, on the other hand, was very small: a poem that was less than book length, as most are, averaged from five to twenty pounds: Johnson received ten pounds for *London*, Pope seven for *The Rape of the Lock*, and fifteen for the *Essay on Criticism*; on longer poems the highest rates of payment seem to have been the 200 pounds which Pope received for a one-year copyright on the *Essay on Man*, and the 220 guineas which Young received for his very lengthy *Night Thoughts*.

Insofar as the market price of payment influenced what the author wrote, the system, then, discouraged poetry and favored whatever literary genres enabled the author to fill the most sheets the most quickly. This conclusion was in fact drawn by many writers, including Goldsmith. Typically he began with poetry, but having received only twenty guineas for *The Traveller*, and perhaps not much more for *The Deserted Village*, despite its five editions in three months, he came to the conclusion that "by pursuing plain prose I can make shift to eat, drink and wear good clothes." The fact is that Griffin, Goldsmith's publisher, could hardly expect to make a great deal out of *The Deserted Village* at only two shillings a copy. The relative brevity of poetry, combined with the longer time it takes to write, would in general seem to make it peculiarly unsuited to payment by the sheet, and peculiarly suited to a system of patronage, if only because many patrons may be presumed to be even more chary of their time than of their money.

The other main exception to the tendency for high scales of literary remuneration occurred when a work proved unexpectedly successful; *Robinson Crusoe*, for example, is said to have brought Defoe very little, but to have laid the basis of William Taylor's publishing fortune. The reason for this exception is that although the booksellers may in the main have deserved Johnson's praise as generous, liberal-minded men, they still tended to treat literature just like any other market commodity; there had not yet come into being the modern royalty system whereby, jointly though no doubt unequally, author and publisher combine to do as well as possible out of the public.

Not that all transactions in the eighteenth century consisted of the outright sale of the copy by the author to the publisher for a lump sum: booksellers occasionally made further payments if a second edition was called for, either *ex gratia*, as Millar gave Fielding another hundred pounds for *Tom Jones*, or by contract—such was Tonson's agreement to "pay Mr. Congreve . . . the sum of twenty guineas whenever his volume of poems—which I am now printing—shall come to be reprinted." There were various other approximations to the royalty system: an author might receive a stated proportion of the profits, as Gibbon got two-thirds on those of the third edition of *The Decline and Fall*, and Johnson a similar share of the proceeds from the publication of *The Idler* in book form; and there were also many kinds of subscription arrangements, very characteristic of the early decades of the century. The author might, in exchange for the copyright, receive so many volumes to sell for his own benefit, or else he might have the whole edition printed at his own expense, get his friends to sell as many as possible, and turn the rest over to the booksellers: in either case the cost of producing the book was defrayed, at least in part, by the subscribers before it was printed.

But the commonest arrangement for authors was still that of the outright sale of their copy, and so the writer who had neither capital nor reputation might earn only a pittance, which was spent long before the book was published; while for the successful writer the system meant that, in the absence of any continuing regular income from royalties, a Johnson or a Goldsmith would spend most of his literary energies on various kinds of casual labor—proposals, dedications, introductions, epilogues, compilations, translations, and so forth.

The negotiating position of the writer with the bookseller was somewhat strengthened by the 1710 "Act for the Encouragement of Learning" which for the first time, apparently, stated that literary compositions in manuscript were the property of their author. Personally I find it difficult to follow some writers who have seen this as the Magna Carta of authorship; but I suppose that some modest jubilation is in order whenever the law is discovered to agree with the expectations of uninstructed reason. Another provision of the Act, limiting copyright to fourteen years and making it renewable only to the author, was probably an indirect step toward the establishment of a royalty system: Pope, for example, sued Henry Lintot on the grounds of this clause, and having thus resumed his rights in *The Dunciad*, he was able to issue the new and enlarged version in 1743—fourteen years after the old.

The 1710 Act, however, was not primarily concerned with the rights of authors; it was, as Pope said, "a bookseller's bill" to make it easier for the trade to take action against piratical printers and publishers; and the need arose partly because of the lapse of the old Licensing Act, and partly because of the intensified competition for copy which came with the increase in the number of booksellers. It is this competition, of course, which is symbolized in the second book of *The Dunciad* where, parodying the traditional games of epic, the Goddess Dulness makes the booksellers run races and perform other, should one say—feats of skill?—with authors—imaginary or real—as prizes. Pope makes Curll run away with all the trophies—"Still happy impudence obtains the prize"—because he was the most famous of the pirates, and had indeed boldly laid both Swift and Pope under contribution: he wrung from Swift the tribute that "one thorough bookselling rogue is better qualified to vex an author, than all his contemporary scribblers in critic or satire."

Curll was only the most prominent of a minority of booksellers who, lacking the capital to attract established authors or to purchase valuable copyrights, employed hacks to turn out various kinds of ephemeral writing which are obvious examples of the literary debasement which ensued from unrestricted competition between publishers for the attention of the public. One of the most conspicuous of these new genres, the one most favored by Curll, and the one most objectionable to Pope, was the scandalous contemporary memoir, biography, or secret history, especially that which took the form of the unauthorized publication of private letters. The tremendous vogue of these piracies, and the extent to which they penetrated public awareness, is suggested by a letter from one J.W. (probably Dr. John Woodward) to John Dunton in 1718, which ends: "You'll hear no more from me. . . . There's no writing to a man that prints everything."[4]

Dunton, incidentally, well illustrates the influence of the more directly commercial context of literature which was coming to the fore. One day, when walking through St. George's Fields with some bookseller friends, he stopped and exclaimed: "Well, Sirs, I have a thought I will not exchange for fifty guineas." The thought materialized as a weekly question and answer paper called *The Athenian Mercury*; and the inanity of some of its contents is representative of the kind of thing Pope was attacking in *The Dunciad*. One question indeed—"Why a horse with a round fundament emits a square excrement?"—typifies the deluge of scatological and pornographic writing called forth by the itching palms of the less reputable booksellers; Pope's revolting depiction of Curll's fall in Corinna's pool, and of his later submingent prowesses, are a fair satiric comment on this aspect of the literary gutter. (The whole subject, incidentally, of the cloacal image in Augustan polemic cries aloud for the attentions of some curious and intrepid scholar.)

A less gamey dullness, however, was much more typical of the commercial kind of writing described by Pope as "daily books and daily bread"; things like Samuel Wesley's "Pindarick Ode on Three Skipps of a Louse," or the endless pamphlet wars on religious, political, and literary controversies. To keep these going, it was often alleged, booksellers forced their hacks to write against their own convictions: Fielding, in *The Author's Farce*, makes his Curll-like—and significantly named—publisher, Bookweight, explain to one of his garret writers that to argue on "the wrong side" of a question is "the properest way to show [his] genius"; and Archibald Campbell develops the theme in his *The Sale of Authors*.

This particular kind of institutionalized subornation and hypocrisy is, of course, the basis of modern journalism, where it goes under the name of conformity to editorial policy: and it is but one of the many examples of how most of the features in the commercial exploitation of the writer today were already beginning to appear in the eighteenth century.

---

[4] Bodleian Library, *Rawl. mss.* D 72, f.66.

It is true that it was the marginal writers and publishers who were then mainly involved; and one could perhaps dismiss Pope's alarm by saying that *The Dunciad* deals with extreme and trivial cases which only represent, in Chesterfield's phrase, "the licentiousness which is the alloy of liberty." But Pope also introduces some of the big booksellers—Tonson, Lintot, Osborne—into *The Dunciad*, and thus implies that the booksellers in general bore some responsibility for the spreading empire of Dulness. At the beginning, for example, he couples the booksellers with the theatrical managers as progenitors of the works of Dulness from:

> . . . the chaos dark and deep
> Where nameless somethings in their causes sleep,
> 'Till genial Jacob, or a warm third-day
> Call forth each mass, a poem or a play.

Actually, it could be argued, genial Jacob Tonson had, in Pope's own case, called forth into print the young poet's first works, and this because, as he flatteringly wrote to Pope, he had seen "a pastoral of yours in Mr. Walsh's and Mr. Congreve's hands, which is extremely fine, and is generally approved of by the best judges in poetry." Here, as in most of his publishing, Tonson was certainly reflecting the best educated taste of his time, and much the same can be claimed, somewhat less convincingly, for most of the other well-established booksellers of the time. In any case, the main income of the big booksellers like Tonson, Lintot, Longman, Millar, Dodsley, and of the wealthy printer-publishers like Buckley, Tooke, Barber, Richardson, and Strahan, came either from copyrights in works of authors now dead (Tonson, for example, claimed an exclusive right to publish Shakespeare and Milton), or from various other monopolies—government printing contracts, or patents giving exclusive rights to publish special kinds of material, educational, legal, or religious, for which there was a continual demand. Their primary interest, therefore, was to defend the prices and the copyrights of these valuable properties, and they were not mainly dependent on current writing. To Horace Walpole's charge in 1764 that "our booksellers here at London disgrace literature by the trash they bespeak to be written, and at the same time prevent everything else from being sold," they could fairly answer that he naturally tended to reflect the hostility of their envious rivals, the printers, and further that the main things which they in fact bespoke were large and valuable projects like Johnson's *Dictionary* or Hume's *History*, works which could not have been produced otherwise. James Ralph—another Dunce, incidentally—pictured in his *The Case of*

*Authors by Profession or Trade Stated* (1758) how "the sagacious bookseller feels the pulse of the times, and according to the stroke, prescribes not to cure, but flatter the disease"; he gave as his example the novel, and it is no doubt true that fiction, from the time of the seventeenth-century publisher "Novel Bentley" until the days of the mass production of fiction in the late eighteenth century by the Noble brothers and the Minerva Press, was much stimulated by booksellers without noticeable regard for literary value. But here again the main booksellers could claim that though of course they catered to all comers, the dominant tendency of their editorial policy was nevertheless to reflect the solid and traditional tastes of the educated reading public, if only because they were the main purchasers of the substantial volumes on which they made their largest profits.

Even so I believe that Pope and the other alarmists were in a sense right: something like Sainte-Beuve's "Littérature industrielle" (1839) was coming into being. In Pope's day it was mainly confined to Grub Street, but as the century wore on the implications of the new context of literature became more evident. The mere fact that even the greatest authors increasingly had their eye on the reading public as a whole, rather than on their patrons or on their peers in taste and knowledge, must have had incalculable effects on the style and content of what they wrote: not all of these effects, one imagines, were bad, and yet they were almost certainly bad for the kind of matter and manner we find in Pope, for example: much of his perfection of form and compressed intransigence of statement must have been lost on what Shenstone called "the mob in reading." Certainly, any commercial pressure towards haste in composition is particularly disastrous for poetry; as Oldham put it in his imitation of Horace's *Art of Poetry*, though not, perhaps, without inviting an invidious reflection:

> But verse alone does of no mean admit;
> Who'er will please, must please us to the height;
> He must a Cowley or a Flecknoe be,
> For there's no second-rate in poetry.

On the other hand, the new situation was uniquely favorable to the very antithesis of poetry, journalism, which provides the readiest means for printers, publishers, and writers alike to engage the attention of the largest number of readers. Goldsmith made the logic of this tendency explicit when he wrote in 1761 that "the effort ... to please the multitude, since they may be properly considered as the dispensers of rewards,"

made writers concentrate on bringing "science down to their capaci-
ties." "This," he continued, "may account for the number of letters, reviews, magazines, and criticising newspapers, that periodically come
from the press." As time went on journalism, by Gresham's law, started
to drive out much of the older literary currency; this at least was what
Crabbe suggested in his "The Newspaper" (1785), a poem which he
considered to be "the only one written on the subject":

> For these [newspapers] unread the noblest volumes lie,
> For these in sheets unsoiled the Muses die;
> Unbought, unblessed . . .

## III

If the more directly commercial context of literature, unintentionally
perhaps, but inexorably, favored the most ephemeral literary forms over
poetry, traditionally and actually the most perennial, it had equally disastrous results, as the Augustans saw it, on those responsible for the
maintenance of the literary tradition. The "Grubean race," as Swift
called them, were the result of the same specialization as had led to the
rise of the bookseller: and like them they responded to the dictates of
economic individualism. People of every class were now flocking to
London as never before, in an attempt to find fame and fortune in the
profession; but, as many economists, from Petty to Adam Smith, pointed
out, all the established professions were vastly overstocked—even
teaching. Once in London, the possibility of living by one's pen beck-
oned, and it had the unique advantage that no special training was required. So Grub Street pullulated with hackney authors: its miseries
were real enough, but they were the result, not so much of the malice or
parsimony of the booksellers as of the economic law that a labor surplus
brings down wages; the social historian, indeed, may see the legend of
Grub Street primarily as an early and revealingly hostile social definition
of a new professional class. Certainly there is evidence that the writers
themselves were feeling the need to establish a less unflattering public
identity, for the expression "author by profession" began to gain currency in the fifties, when it was used by Ralph, Murphy, and others. It is
interesting, incidentally, to note that there was an analogous and almost
contemporary movement in France, by which the term "homme de lettres" came to apply only to writers and not to the *literati*, the men of

taste in general; and in 1764 Jean-Jacques Garnier wrote his monograph on *L'Homme de lettres*.

The emergence of the new social group is an important part of the subject of the *Dunciad*: fitly, for the epic traditionally deals with the birth of a new nation. And if at first its two successive heroes seem incongruous, and we feel like objecting that after all Theobald was not foolish and Cibber was not dull, the context of the new literary professionalism may help us to discover a real kinship between them: both were unauthorized professional intruders into the republic of letters—Theobald, not only an attorney by trade but, like Bentley before him, a pedantic scholar who wouldn't stay where he belonged, and who had the impudence to know better than a man of wit, and even to receive 652 pounds, 10 shillings for his edition of Shakespeare; and Cibber, a vagabond player, now presuming from his success on the stage and from the growing social recognition given to the actor's trade that he was entitled to write a book telling the world about his life and opinions.

The dates of the *Dunciad*, from 1728 to 1743, mark an important transitional era in the history of the profession of writing. Under Queen Anne enlightened political patronage had bestowed wealth and power on the greatest writers of the time, on Prior and Addison and Swift; while the most successful of the booksellers, Jacob Tonson, by maintaining close ties with the literary and political leaders of the time, and by publishing only what was consistent with the educated tastes of his circle, had achieved a unique combination of the tradition of literary patronage and the new power of the bookseller. With the advent of the Hanoverians, Tonson's retirement in 1719, and the dissolution of the Kit-Cat Club soon after, there came a decisive change. Bernard Lintot's list[5] had none of the discrimination that is evident in the elder Tonson's; while the outstanding feature of the thirties in respect to patronage was Sir Robert Walpole's massive purchase of journalistic support without any regard to literary merit. William Arnall, for example, is said to have received more for his polemical writings in four years than did Pope for his Homer; he is, of course, remembered in the *Dunciad*, which belongs to this last era of patronage, which took a flagrantly political form, and which was succeeded by the era which saw the final triumph of the booksellers and the professional authors.

---

[5] See the M.A. thesis "The Firm of Lintot" by Marjorie W. Barnes (London 1942).

It was not easy for Pope to define his position in the new situation which the development of bookselling was creating. He could hardly identify himself with the emergent class of professional writers, and yet the same new social and economic conditions as had produced them were fast making literary patronage obsolete. In any case his religion, his politics, his temperament, and above all, perhaps, the pattern of the new individualism, would have made it very difficult for him to adapt himself to the accommodating role that would be expected of him by a patron, if one had been available. In the event, however, he managed, somewhat like Tonson, to make the best of both worlds. Adopting intact from the old literary order Boileau's role of the poet as the legislator of Parnassus, he removed himself far enough above the common throng to be able to voice "la haine d'un sot livre" with the full sacerdotal commitment. At the same time, however, he was able to assert his independence from patronage through the new resources which the booksellers had made available. Boileau, of course, had loftily refused payment for his works from his bookseller, as did Blackmore, and as Gray and Cowper were to do; but Pope set out to beat venal booksellers and hacks alike at their own game. By an extraordinary example of the interpenetration of opposites, which Professor Sherburn's edition of the letters now enables us to trace in fuller detail, Pope turned his aristocratic friends, not into patrons, but into publishers—he set Lady Burlington, the Earls of Orrery, Islay, and Granville, and the Viscount Simon Harcourt to soliciting subscriptions, dispatching and storing books, keeping accounts and collecting money, and he also made the Earl of Oxford, the Earl of Burlington and Lord Bathurst proprietors of the copyright of *The Dunciad*. Not content with this, Pope set himself up as a kind of unofficial literary agent, for Swift and others; he inspired the starting of a newspaper, the *Grub-Street Journal*, to voice his point of view in opposition to that of the booksellers and their Dunces; and he secured support and influence within the trade by setting up one of his protégés, Robert Dodsley, as a bookseller; thus, incidentally, providing the true apostolic succession in Augustan letters for, of course, it was Dr. Johnson who remarked ironically, "Doddy is my patron."

Pope's phenomenal success was in one sense prophetic: it showed that potentially the new individualist and capitalist order could, under favorable conditions, make possible a much greater freedom for the writer than ever before, and this without any pandering to the taste of the masses. But Pope's personal and unrepeated triumph did not blind him to the likelihood that the main pressure of events was in a quite opposite direction, and so he declared war on the Dunces. The nineteenth-century critics were inclined to write off the war as motivated by personal spite, and this may be in part because the implications of what Goldsmith called "that fatal revolution whereby . . . booksellers, instead of the great, become the patrons and paymasters of men of genius"—were not yet so clear. Now that we have so much more reason than Dr. Johnson to insist on the distinction between a book as a "subject of commerce" and a book as an "increase of human knowledge," and so much more opportunity to observe what happens when the publishing system turns literature into a marketable commodity, we can better admit the truth of Pope's attribution of the rising flood of bad writing "not so much to malice or servility as to dulness; and not so much to dulness as to necessity." Pope had the economic necessities of underpaid hacks in mind, but there is another kind of historical necessity, perhaps, behind the Dunces: Dr. George Cheyne, author of *The English Malady*, diagnosed an even more universal syndrome when he wrote to Richardson that "all booksellers I fear are Curlls by profession": publishers are sinners, we may say, not by choice but by necessity.

Today, Pope's own gallant stance in the face of these intricate necessities must be allowed to excuse his malice and to authorize his pride; we know, now, that he was right to warn us against underestimating the power of the Dunces: "Do not gentle reader rest too secure in thy contempt of the Instruments for such a revolution in learning." The instruments and the revolution have now assumed giant proportions; if there was ever any hyperbole in the famous lines about the coming triumph of Dulness time has rendered it almost imperceptible:

> She comes! she comes! the sable throne behold
> Of Night primeval, and of Chaos old . . .
> Lo! thy dread empire, Chaos! is restored,
> Light dies before thy uncreating word.

If the writer's laws the writer's patrons give, and if today the well-patronized publishers of *Time*, *Confidential*, and the comic books laugh all the way to the bank, can we in the academy, who have inherited the tradition which Pope defended, find any other comfort than the reflection which Lord Chesterfield made, with the professional authors of the time in mind, as he addressed his peers: "Thank God! We, my Lords, have a dependence of another kind"?

# 5

## FLAT-FOOTED AND FLY-BLOWN:
## THE REALITIES OF REALISM

I am, of course, immensely flattered to be invited here, and for many reasons.* As Horace Walpole said about the unexpected success of *The Castle of Otranto*, "It is charming to totter into vogue" (to George Augustus Selwyn, 2 December 1765).[1] It is particularly charming because it lends credibility to the hypothesis of my continuing survival, which is not universally accepted: not long ago I fell into conversation with a student at Berkeley, and when, on parting, I told him my name, he answered with genuine astonishment: "Oh, I thought you were dead." A third reason, no doubt, is that I cannot claim to be wholly a stranger to what Johnson said about Richardson: that he "could not be content to sail quietly down the stream of reputation without longing to taste the froth from every stroke of the oar."[2] My original difficulty in deciding whether to come and, if so, what to talk about arose partly from a sense of decorum which told me that I should not be observed visibly to agitate the stream of reputation myself; and yet this is what

---

* This talk was given as the plenary address to the fourth annual meeting of the Southeastern American Society for Eighteenth-Century Studies, University of Alabama, Tuscaloosa, 12 March 1978. It was first published jointly by the *Stanford Humanities Review* and *Eighteenth-Century Fiction* in 2000, with the permission of the Department of Special Collections, Stanford University Libraries. Bibliographical information supplied by the editors of those publications is signed "Ed."

[1] *Letters of Horace Walpole*, ed. Mrs. Paget Toynbee, 15 vols. (Oxford: Clarendon Press, 1904), 6:367.

[2] Ian Watt, *The Rise of the Novel: Studies in Defoe, Richardson, and Fielding* (Berkeley: University of California Press, 1957), p. 260. References are to this edition.

Paul Hunter in effect has asked me to do. The difficulty is compounded by the fact that I don't want to repeat an earlier solicited transgression in the self-congratulation line, an essay called "Serious Reflections on *The Rise of the Novel*."[3]

Titles beginning with "towards" always make me wonder "Why doesn't he wait till he arrives? Then he'll know if there is anything there worth reporting." In any case, you will not expect any report from me on that vast abstraction, the "Poetics of Fiction." For the "flat-footed" pedestrian of my title is, of course, myself; and I continue to totter along the "fly-blown" paths of "realism." I thought that one reasonably decorous way of fulfilling my assignment would be to avoid tracks I've made already, or that have been much noted by others, and give a biographical account of how some of the less obviously pedestrian elements in *The Rise of the Novel* came into being, mainly through the influence of that least earthbound of all modes of thought, the German intellectual tradition. I will then, still remaining abroad, look briefly at how the various foreign translations and the subsequent receptions of what I normally think of as the *R of N*, drew attention to some of its larger and less-noticed ideological implications. Finally there may be a stopover in Paris, before coming home to speak my mind about the representational status of fiction and, more emphatically, about the need for realism in literary criticism.

### The Three Periods of Composition: Thesis

Looking back on the process of composition of the *R of N*, I have been delighted to discover a truly Hegelian pattern of thesis, antithesis, and synthesis.

The registered topic of my PhD dissertation in 1938 was "The Novel and Its Reader: 1719–1754." The title reflects something of the intellectual atmosphere of Cambridge in the late thirties. There was logical positivism. Some of my friends spent a good deal of time waiting for someone to use the word "why" so that they could jump in with "But

---

[3] Ian Watt, "Serious Reflections on *The Rise of the Novel*," *The Novel: A Forum on Fiction* 1 (1968), 205-18; reprinted, *Towards a Poetics of Fiction: Essays from "Novel: A Forum on Fiction 1967–1976*," ed. Mark Spilka (Bloomington: Indiana University Press, 1977), pp. 90-103. [Reprinted as Chapter 1 in this volume.]

you mustn't say that. The only *real* questions are *how* questions." My
research topic wholly disregarded the "why," assumed the more or less
publicly attested phenomenon of the "rise of the novel," and attempted
to study merely the "how." Behind my approach there lay the deep-
rooted empiricism and moralism of the English—and especially the
Cambridge—tradition. In particular, there was the reader criticism of
I. A. Richards's *Practical Criticism* (1929), certainly the most influential
text as far as the Cambridge English school was concerned: and, no less
important, there was also the combination of the historical and moral
outlook of the Leavises: F. R. Leavis had done a historical thesis on the
cultural milieu of Addison; and Q. D. Leavis had published her thesis
*Fiction and the Reading Public* in 1932. Its dominating assumption was
that in the past there had been a long golden age in which the relation of
author and audience was harmonious and fruitful; but then industrial-
ism, the mass media, philistine commercialism, and metropolitan deca-
dence had produced the situation of "mass civilisation and minority
civilisation," which only Cambridge and *Scrutiny* were attempting to
stand against. The other main influence on my thinking in 1938 was the
Marxist; and its influence was in many ways surprisingly complementary to the others. The materialist outlook of Marxism made it consonant with a great deal of the empirical and positivist tradition in
scholarship; and because it related literature to society, and viewed the
current cultural situation as one of catastrophic decline, there was substantial agreement between the Communist critical position and that of
the Leavises. This is very clear in the work of my friend and contemporary, Arnold Kettle. His valuable *Introduction to the English Novel*
(1951), for instance, reveals a mixture of Leavisite and Marxist orienta-
tions which now seems strikingly anomalous.

### Antithesis: 1946–1948

My own subject was an awkward exception as far as both the
Leavises and the Marxists were concerned, since the novel was fairly
obviously a literary form that had not got worse as we approached the
present. But at the time—1939—I was little troubled by such difficulties;
there were obviously much more serious troubles ahead. The war came
in September. When it terminated, and I was demobilized seven years
later in the spring of 1946, I found myself with no very definite ideas
about what to do next. As a prisoner for three and a half years, I had

accrued most of that pay and over half a year's leave and, in so far as I thought seriously of what I would do when that was finished, the most definite idea I can now recall was that of going into the wine business. But I was destined to be saved for a worse fate than wealth and cirrhosis of the liver. I remember going one day to the British Museum, without any clear purpose, and looking through the catalogues to see what had happened during my long absence; and the dating on my notes makes it clear that, by some piece of luck I cannot now explain I apparently made my painful way in the next couple of months through Georg Lukács's *Die Theorie des Romans* (1920) and Erich Auerbach's *Mimesis* (1946). I say painful mainly because it meant learning German for the third time. Both Lukács and Auerbach actually contributed much more to *The Rise of the Novel* than the few references in the text suggest.

In the spring of 1946 I applied for a Commonwealth Fund Fellowship—now called a Harkness—for two years' research in the United States: and in September I found myself at UCLA. That winter, in a furious burst of energy, I wrote a draft of over 500 pages, got them typed, and won a Research Fellowship at St John's College, Cambridge. But before taking it up, I still had—if I wished—a year and a half left to study whatever I wanted in the United States. In 1947 I did some work at UCLA in anthropology and sociology in what was then an excellently open and lively group of faculty and students; but the most significant single result of this detour into the social sciences was to bring me into touch with someone who was certainly to be more responsible than any other single person for the intellectual shaping of *The Rise of the Novel*, and for the long delay in its completion, the late Theodor Adorno, now well known as a leader of the Frankfurt School, which was then located in the area round the Pacific Palisades. We had hardly met when he said with genuine interest that he would be glad to read my manuscript. When I returned to his house a few days later, he kept me on the doorstep explaining his view of the difficulties involved in using the term "genius"; he then modulated into how he never used the word lightly; and finally, well, modesty forbids that I go on, but the word of praise he used convinced me that he had connected me with the wrong manuscript. Later I got to know Adorno fairly well, and this caused me three kinds of delay. First, I didn't want to be found out, so that for some time it became virtually impossible for me to write anything at all; second, I became aware that, given his intimidatingly large view of what any educated man had at his fingertips, I still had an awfully long way to go; and third, I came to understand what he most liked in my dissertation were in fact independent parallels or extensions of some of the general ideas of the Frankfurt School, notably of some of the ideas expressed in a work which appeared in that year, *The Dialectic of Enlightenment* (1947). The discussion there of the "cunning of technocratic reason" has some parallels with parts of *The Rise of the Novel*: what I had said about *Robinson Crusoe*; what I suggested about the potentialities of mass exploitation contained in the closer identification between the literary work and the reader, which was made possible by the printing press and by what I already called "formal realism"; and more widely, what I said about the larger connections between the city and bourgeois privatisation in the chapter on "Print and Private Experience."

Adorno was an immensely generous and fertile person; there was a purity, almost a childlike innocence, in his enthusiasm for the life of the mind; he put me in touch with the whole tradition of German thought in history, literature, sociology, and psychology; and he did it in the only way it could have been done for me, because I would never have believed that people actually thought like that until I saw Adorno continually doing it.

His most immediate effect on the *R of N* was to make me put aside the manuscript until such time as I should feel new wings sprouting; and meanwhile I began quite another book, which dealt, broadly speaking, with literacy, reading, memory, and technology in the widest possible theoretical context. Had I finished that book—then called "Printed Man"—I might have become a St. John the Baptist to Marshall McLuhan. All that has appeared of it is a long article written in collaboration with an anthropologist friend, Jack Goody, entitled "The Consequences of Literacy."[4]

In my second Commonwealth Fellowship year, 1947–48, I went to Harvard; and there among other things, my exposure to German thought continued. I took Talcott Parsons's seminar on social theory, and learned something about Max Weber. This is reflected, I think, not only in the treatment of economic and institutional forces in *The Rise of the Novel*, but in some of its more abstract guiding ideas—the notion,

---

[4] Jack Goody and Ian Watt, "The Consequences of Literacy," *Comparative Studies in Society and History* 5 (1963), 304-45. Reprinted in *Literacy in Traditional Societies*, ed. Jack Goody (Cambridge: Cambridge University Press, 1968), pp. 27-68.

for instance, of the disenchantment of the world under the impulse of the scientific and economic rationality (*Entzauberung der Welt*) which came with the Enlightenment. I also learned from Parsons—though resisting all the way—to see society in structural-functional terms; that is, to see society not as something which fails to be what I would like, or what it was in the past, or what it should be in the future, but as something which exists, and which manifests its own living, though stress-ridden and ever-changing, equilibrium of institutional and cultural forces. This mode of thought made me very aware of the dubiousness of many of the unchallenged assumptions I had more or less unconsciously picked up from all kinds of sources—Plato, Matthew Arnold, Leavis, Marxism, and the Frankfurt School, for instance. I did not, of course stifle all my personal impulses of social criticism or disgust, but I became much more aware of them; one result, I think, was to give a greater degree of objectivity to the sociological and historical aspects of *The Rise of the Novel*.

A related impulse—towards a more immediate and direct sympathetic penetration of the authors I was studying, and a greater awareness of the activities of my own consciousness in the process—was strengthened by another lucky meeting. Aron Gurwitsch, then teaching mathematics at a small local college, though already editing the *Journal of Philosophy and Phenomenological Research*, introduced me to the thought of Brentano, Husserl, and Merleau-Ponty. What remains most vividly is the tonic vitality of his sardonic contempt for most of the subjects which came up in conversation; but I think I also picked up some ways of going beyond positivism in my treatment of intention, quotidian expectation, and imaginative projection.

### Synthesis: 1950–1956

Back in Cambridge, England, in 1948, the difficulties in finishing the book on literacy, and the not obscurely related one of earning some kind of living, finally impelled me back to the tattered manuscript on the eighteenth-century novel. It was used first as a quarry for isolated articles. The first was "The Naming of Characters in Defoe, Richardson and Fielding" (1949); its traces of phenomenology may explain why it has found its only reprint in Germany. The second article, on "*Robinson Crusoe* as a Myth" (1951), was so influenced by Adorno, and more directly by Weber and Stamm, that one American reviewer, perhaps disturbed by my departure from the then established tendency to see the eighteenth century wholly in eighteenth-century terms, seems to have assumed I must be German. (The next two, one on a mistaken Defoe attribution, and the other on the views of Defoe and Richardson about Homer, reveal fairly directly the diverse influences of positivism and of Georg Lukács.)

When I started working on the manuscript as a whole, I became aware that my present understanding of the subject, and even more my now initiated sense of what a full understanding might be, was leading me towards a much more ambitious enterprise than I had originally conceived, and one which would be even more impossibly long.

How could I combine all the data I had amassed with the ideas I now thought informed them with larger meaning? My resolution of the problem was draconian, both as regards substance and form. As regards substance, I expressed my larger philosophical or historical ideas only where they seemed directly relevant to the matter at hand, and usually only where there was sufficient evidence to illustrate them from the primary sources. On the other hand, I drastically reduced the empirical data, and left little that did not illuminate the larger intellectual perspectives. As to my rhetorical strategy, it was primarily literary, in the sense that I wished to avoid anything that might be indigestible, whether in the way of too much flat empirical documentation, or in the way of sesquipedalian philosophical abstraction.

In a sense, my general method reversed that of Adorno. In the foreword to the English edition of *Prisms*, Adorno pays homage to what "the author has learned from Anglo-Saxon norms of thought and presentation." But it turns out this is purely "as a control, lest he reject common sense without first having mastered it"; and then Adorno paradoxically concludes that "it is only by the use of its own categories, that common sense can be transcended."[5] In a way, Adorno helped me go beyond common sense; but my main aim can be stated in terms of the opposite paradox: to transcend what I had learned from the idealist modes of German thought by translating it into empirical categories and commonsense language.

That final synthesis was largely intuitive; insofar as I can recall any particular influence on my compositional strategy, it must be the echo-

---

[5] Theodor Adorno, *Prisms*, trans. Samuel and Shierry Weber (London: Spearman, 1967), p. 7.

ing memory of what I. A. Richards had told me with characteristically kind indirection after reading the manuscript: "If I were you, Ian, I would keep away from the big transportation companies."

Looking back, then, I can see beneath what I hope is the unassuming surface of *The Rise of the Novel* the troubled undercurrents of a fairly representative set of the main intellectual tendencies of its period of gestation—1938 to 1956. It is essentially a partial, and in many respects amateur, synthesis of two great but very different traditions of thought: first, of the empirical, historical, and moral elements of my Cambridge training; second, of many other theoretical elements in the European tradition—formalism and phenomenology in a minor way, and Marxism, Freud, and the Frankfurt School in somewhat larger part.

It would take me much too long to illustrate this synthesis; and it would also involve my rereading the book. But looking at the first paragraph I notice a certain prefigurative indication of this union of the empirical and the nonempirical; the paragraph proceeds from a how question to a why question: from "how does [eighteenth-century prose fiction] differ from [that] of the past?" to "is there any reason why these differences appeared when and where they did?" (p. 9).

That *The Rise of the Novel* benefited from these various philosophical presences, even though they were at most briefly mentioned in footnotes or the preface, seems to me quite certain; it probably accounts, among other things, for the increasing interest in the book in the last few years; I surmise the basis for its virtually posthumous topicality must in part be that its substance and its emphases were much more in touch with a wide spectrum of the modern ideology than appeared on the surface. This, I think, can be verified by the pattern of its reception.

### European Translations and Reactions

The first two translations appeared in 1974: into German, as *Der bürgerliche Roman*, and into Polish as *Narodziny Powiesci* (the birth of the romance/novel). These two titles were not, I think, mistranslations. The mere absence—not only in German and Polish but in many other languages—of the distinction which is established in English between romance and novel made a literal translation of *The Rise of the Novel* impossible. To call it, instead, "The Bourgeois Romance" was to draw primary attention to the historico-social aspect of the book in a Marxist way; and the same emphasis occurs in the Italian translation—*Le origini del romanzo borghese* (1976). It contains a long essay by the translator, Luigi del Grosso Destreri, "Bourgeois Culture and Popular Culture." Destreri laments that the "so-called sociologists of literature" have not "seriously meditated" on "il Watt," partly because of the book's "logical positivist positions"; he then proposes a "second birth" for the book by making it an occasion for a "larger discussion of the conditions of production of cultural models."

The essay is an interesting one, but I have time to discuss only one issue, which is minor in itself but illustrates both the advantages and disadvantages of my empirical method of composition. Destreri reproves me for "having described but failed to name" the phenomena of alienation and *anomie*, but he praises me for "having placed himself unknowingly in the critical tradition of Lukács and Lucien Goldmann." In fact, I had not, in the 1950s, heard of Goldmann, although he in turn reflected the ideas of some of the Frankfurt figures whose work I knew, such as Franz Borkenau, Walter Benjamin, and Bernard Groethuysen; as to Lukács, I had read, and to some extent accepted, some of his ideas, both Hegelian and Marxist. But I could hardly have made either my debts or my disagreement with Lukács or the Frankfurt School explicit in *The Rise of the Novel* without intruding large conceptual issues which would have diverted my attention, and that of my readers, from the concrete immediacies of my subject. It was for similar reasons that I had even avoided using the word "bourgeois" (except when quoting). Just as the word "alienation," whether used by Hegel, Marx, or later thinkers, implies an anterior state of spiritual, economic, and cultural harmony whose actual historical existence I question, so Marx's sense of "bourgeoisie" implies a whole historical and political theory. I used various concrete aspects of that theory, but avoided the term itself because it invoked metaphysical ideas which I rejected. On the other hand, I did not mention my disagreement, if only because I had no reason to believe that my arguments for it would be particularly interesting to other people, since they had long ceased to be interesting to me.

This abstention from ideological topicality had the sufficient advantage for me of sharpening my focus on the subject at hand; but I have reason to believe that it did not in the event decrease the topicality of what I did say. I know, from articles, conversations, and letters, that readers of *The Rise of the Novel* in Poland, Hungary, and Romania, for instance, have found in it a topical relevance, even a minor controversial interest, which was certainly quite unintended; and this topicality is directly concerned with the very issues that had led me to avoid using the terms "bourgeois," "alienation," and "anomie." The issue, very simply put, is whether bourgeois values, and the whole range of disaffections from society denoted by the terms "alienation" and "anomie," are, as Marx and Durkheim assumed, the temporary result of a particular phase in the development of capitalist production. For the writers in socialist countries, the question—which is diametrically opposed to the assumptions of their prevalent "socialist realism"—is whether the social, spiritual, and literary manifestations of alienated individualism may not in fact have very little to do with who owns the means of production. May it not, rather, be part of the evolutionary process of change from small tribal societies to those of the modern large-scale industrial and urban way of life? May not the whole cycle of what used to be dubbed "bourgeois individualism"—and the kind of novel associated with it—be a necessary historical stage in the literary and intellectual development of all developed industrial societies?

## Some Aspects of the Term "Realism"

I come at last somewhat closer to the topic suggested by my title. If I have to wear a critical label, I have no particular objection to that of "sociological realist" recently pinned on me by Mark Spilka,[6] although my basic reaction is a yawn followed by a plea of *nolo contendere*. My impatience is not so much with the general assumption that "realism" is a pedestrian and flat-footed metaphysical posture, as that in critical usage the term denotes controversies, which, after a century or so, have become distinctly fly-blown. But I think it may be worth while attempting to take up two general aspects of the problem in which the issues of realism are involved. First, a few words on the underlying meaning of the two terms I used, "realism of presentation" and "realism of assessment," in relation to the philosophical ideas which provided the second, or antithesis, stage of the gestation of *The Rise of the Novel*.

## Realism of Presentation

In *The Rise of the Novel*, "realism of presentation" or "formal realism" was a way of differentiating the purely technical aspect of the nar-

---

[6] Spilka, p. viii.

rative representation of the real world from that of the truth or otherwise of the substance of the literary work. I notice that three recent
works on realism make a similar distinction. Thus Ernst Fischer, in *The
Necessity of Art* (1967), speaks of one aspect of realism as "a particular
*method*" of the novels and plays of the nineteenth century. Damian
Grant uses the category "conscious realism"; and in his acute study, *On
Realism* (1973), J. Peter Stern describes realism in literature as "a way
of depicting, describing a situation in a faithful, accurate, 'life-like' manner," and sees the special quality of "fiction in the nineteenth century"
as containing "*more* realistic elements than earlier literature had done."[7]
In *The Rise of the Novel*, I had been dealing with the prehistory of that
process; and what advance, if any, I made over previous treatments was
to connect formal or presentational realism with two different kinds of
causes, kinds which of their nature exposed them very unequally to the
vicissitudes of history.

There were, first of all, the causes which I attributed to philosophical,
social, economic, and educational changes affecting both authors and
audience, changes which led to an emphasis on the individual, on the
particular in time and space, on the material universe, and on quotidian
life: all these and other historical factors had created a substantially new
version of literature's ancient concern with verisimilitude; but since
some of these changes were essentially social, I assumed that not only
the particular content of eighteenth-century fiction, but also some aspects of its distinguishing expressive idiom, were not likely to outlive
their period. But there were other kinds of cause which were much less
subject to historical contingency: first, the authority of the pseudo-realism
of print, which I attributed to the technological medium; and second,
the associated establishment of silent and private reading as the novel's
characteristic mode of performance. These factors, I assumed, derived
from the mode of literary production itself, and had therefore contributed permanent qualitative changes in the expressive idiom of fiction;
the objective and yet private effect of the printed page made possible a
kind of realistic presentation which was likely to endure much longer.

---

[7] Ernst Fischer, *The Necessity of Art: A Marxist Approach*, trans. Anna Bostock
(Harmondsworth: Penguin, c. 1963), p. 106; Damian Grant, *Realism* (London:
Methuen, 1970); J. Peter Stern, *On Realism* (London and Boston: Routledge
and Kegan Paul, 1973), pp. 40-41.

My treatment of formal realism, then, was intended to be quite independent of the kind of consideration involved in using the term realism as the term for a specific literary school of novelists; even less was I concerned with realism as a conscious critical doctrine which allegedly professes that fiction is or should be a photographic verbal reproduction of reality, or a direct, unmediated imitation of life.

The semantic difficulty with realism here seems to be insuperable, largely because we are all—and equally—experts on "reality," and therefore feel authorized to handle its terminology in whatever way we like. As a result the present debate, or rather non-debate, about realism is essentially a form of shadowboxing in which no blows are ever landed because the ring of reality is so large: in fact there are no ropes. The overwhelming de facto victory of the antirealists in the current critical arena depends upon two simple assumptions: that since there was a French literary school in the middle of the nineteenth century which used the term "réalisme," and since this label has also been extended to the whole course of fiction since Balzac and Stendhal to Zola and the good Dean Howells, realism in all guises must therefore be non-modern, and is therefore finished. When the antirealist critic goes beyond this implicitly historical use of the term, the analytic model of realism remains the naïve photographic reproduction of reality. Albert Guerard, for instance, in his fine recent book *The Triumph of the Novel* (1977), categorizes Dickens, Dostoevsky, and Faulkner as "non-realists" because they are patently not pretending to be mirrors or cameras of the ordinary world. But whatever Stendhal or indeed Hamlet or others may occasionally have said, no writer has ever seriously thought that he was just a mirror; but the assumption that realism can only mean the photographic imitation of the outside world affords critics too easy a target to be let die. In any case, my concept of formal or presentational realism was not intended to imply any restriction on its use; the detailed particularity of its representation of the inner or the outer world can be just as easily applied to melodrama, play, fantasy, involution, or what Guerard calls "illuminating distortion." The technical possibilities of presentational realism are in themselves quite neutral; they can serve any number of purposes: and I notice that the three novelists with whom Guerard deals are in fact notable examples of many fictional techniques whose prehistory and analytic basis I was concerned with in *The Rise of the Novel*. All three of them, for instance, to take one obvious example, combine an almost obsessive concern with the physical objects and aspects of the environment with an equal concern to show that the individual's inner life is largely separate and autonomous—a point which is made in different ways by what I say about Robinson Crusoe and Pamela, but which could hardly be made without the way the illusion of print can make the inner and the outer world seem equally "real."

### Realism of Assessment

In *The Rise of the Novel* I attempted to establish another category of a very different kind, realism of assessment, which would take account of all the various ways in which the novel, like all literary forms, contains structuring elements other than those of representational intent. Later writers on realism have used similar terms. Ernst Fischer speaks of "realism of attitude" (*Realimus der Haltung*), Damian Grant of "conscious" or "conscientious" realism, and Peter Stern differentiates "descriptive" from "evaluative" realism.[8] All three of these distinctions take account of the fact that the author's intellectual, emotional, and aesthetic predispositions are inevitably present, at various levels of consciousness, in all prose fiction as well as in any other genre of writing; and these predispositions can go from the simplest preferences in the writer's hierarchy of attention (Ann Radcliffe uses larches rather than magnolias, say) to much larger sets of organizing principles and values. Thus Lukács's admiration for the realists—from Scott and Balzac to Tolstoy—and his rejection of the naturalists, are based upon his own philosophical, political, and aesthetic values, which lead him to reject any mechanical, conformist, or passive attitude to the material and social world.

The conception of realism of assessment was intended, at the higher levels of abstraction, to include not only such distinctions, but others, from the phenomenological insistence on the structuring activity of the consciousness (Jean Starobinski, "conscience structurante") to the ultimate questions of the wisdom and truth of a literary work.

I am properly ashamed to thus affront your sophistication with such fly-blown terms as wisdom and truth; but they are—and not very obscurely—part of my overt concern in *The Rise of the Novel*; and I would like to end by considering what I take to be a much more serious problem than the current critical objections to realism in fiction: the problem

---

[8] Fischer, pp. 116-17; Grant, chaps. 2, 3; Stern, pp. 130-31.

of how and why the dominant contemporary trends in literary criticism have tended to deny or neglect the truth status of literature, and to regard realism of critical assessment as an appropriate concern only for pedagogues with fallen arches.

*Philosophy, Realism, and Literary Criticism:*
*Realism and Structuralism*

It is, I think, very easy to see why the term "realism" arouses no excitement in philosophical circles. Apart from many specialized historical usages which need not concern us here, it denotes, very simply, the acceptance of three general notions: that the world and the people outside us are real; that language enables us to communicate about them to others; and that truth about them is verified through the assent of other observers. In what, as far as our practical dealings are concerned, we all know to be the real world, these notions raise no particular difficulty. I do not imagine that the most reckless semiotician has not been forced to the conclusion that he must eat to live: I do not believe that he approaches his bank in fear and trembling lest the meaning of the words on his cheque be challenged as inherently unreal by the cashier; nor even that the number of dollars concerned has ever been known to provoke paroxysms of interfacing hermeneutic hesitation. I also think it reasonable to believe that philosophy as a specialized social institution could not have begun if it had merely asserted the common assumptions about the reality of the outside world or the possibility of talking about it sensibly to our fellows; the first cheque to a philosopher must surely have gone to the sophist who proved that our material wants were unreal, or that the language we use had in fact no meaning, or at least one that was unsuspectedly problematic.

The whole enterprise of Western philosophy since the pre-Socratics, then, has largely depended on the paradoxical denial of what we all know to be in some simple sense true: and this essentially antirealist view of things was given its decisive modern aesthetic formulation by Kant in *The Critique of Judgment* (1790) when he decisively established the opposition of idealism and realism which is now evident in critical thought.

At the end of the nineteenth century the antirealist position also became dominant in literature when symbolism and impressionism superseded realism and naturalism. The general critical outlook changed ac-

cordingly, and eventually spread to the academy at a time when philosophy was being replaced by literature as the queen of the sciences.
Now, by a familiar dialectical reversal, what passes for philosophy has
largely taken over the field of literary studies. In the last few decades this
process has been materially assisted by the much greater self-confidence,
prestige, and financial rewards of the natural, and to some extent of the
social sciences. This rivalry has led to an enormous compulsion to find
an autonomous and quasi-scientific methodology for the study of literature; and it is now widely assumed that some quasi-philosophical technique is an indispensable prerequisite for approaching or discussing any
literary works.

The most extreme and influential form of this analytic technique is no
doubt structuralism. It is concerned with timeless verities at a much
deeper level than the particularities of individual literary works, and rejects as an exploded—or at any rate rather dull—relic of the past the notion that the referential functions of language, and therefore the representational status of literature, any longer merit the attentions of a sophisticated mind. As Roland Barthes put it in *Le Degré zéro de l'écriture*
(1953), with engaging finality:

*Le réalisme, ici, ce ne peut donc être la copie des choses, mais la connais-*
*sance du langage; l'œuvre la plus 'réaliste' ne sera pas celle qui 'peint' la ré-*
*alité, mais qui, se servant du monde comme contenu (ce contenu lui-même*
*est d'ailleurs étranger à sa structure, c'est-à-dire à son être), explorera le*
*plus profondément possible la réalité irréelle du langage.*[9]

Barthes is dealing with the change from traditional fiction to the
quasi-philosophical verbal engineering of the *nouveau roman*; but he
does make the usual assumption that realism is to be identified with the
mere copying of things. He thus provides me with an excuse for the
brief excursion to Paris I promised you: a sociohistorical explanation of
what some impatient historian might have written had he begun to col-
lect notes for a book on "The Rise of Structuralism."

---

[9] Quoted in Stern, p. 165. In his address Ian Watt translated this passage as follows: "Realism can only be, not the copy of things, but the knowledge of language; the most realist work will not be the one which 'paints' reality, but
which, using the world as a content (a content which is, incidentally, a stranger
to its [the work's] content, that is to say, to its being), makes the deepest possible explanation of the unreal reality of the language" [Ed.].

After the First and Second World Wars there occurred large and continuing migrations of intellectuals from the defeated countries—Russia, Hungary, Romania, Bulgaria, Austria, Czechoslovakia, and Germany. These intellectuals brought with them habits of thought which were based on their experience of academic institutions which had accorded them a considerable social prestige, but no importance whatever in the national and political life as a whole. The circumstances of exile intensified the need for the same habits of thought. The first prerequisite was an intellectual system which provided them an unchallengeable status as a sage; and at the same time that system had to be based on an approach to truth which either disregarded or transcended all national, historical, and psychological differences, and took no notice of the fate which had befallen their own countries, or the various idiosyncrasies and hostilities which they encountered in their countries of adoption.

After 1945, Paris offered them by far the most favorable institutional and intellectual environment; as to some extent it was for French intellectuals also. The humiliation of 1940 Vichy had made a reassertion of national greatness imperative; at the same time the very privileged status of the French higher bourgeoisie had survived almost intact. Indeed, it was soon expanded as far as the academic elites were concerned. For one thing, the needs of reconstruction led the government to set up a strong national research policy (Centre Nationale de Recherche Scientifique); and some humanists incidentally benefited from this, for example, Todorov. At the same time the strong centralizing policy of the French tradition continued, so that the top positions went to a relatively small group of those who came out well in the competitive examinations for the Grandes Ecoles. Even the new emphasis on business and technology was not wholly unfavorable in its effects because, although it ended the former alliance between the Ecole Normale and political power, the system enabled its beneficiaries to combine government positions with impeccable left-wing credentials: Althusser in the Ministry of Education, for instance.

The main structuralists operate at the very top of the Parisian academic hierarchy—Barthes and Foucault at the Collège de France, Todorov and Genette at the Ecole des Etudes Pratiques. They are almost entirely free from any obligatory educational ties or responsibilities. There is no teaching, or almost none—a dozen lectures on a chosen topic per year would be the norm; there is no responsibility for preparing students for examinations or administering a syllabus—that is done by the university proper, in so far as it is done; for the lectures there is no particular presumption that the students will have read any of the texts discussed—it would in fact be quite difficult for anyone to find out what they will be in advance. The essence of the system is to promote brilliantly idiosyncratic verbalization without any fixed or controlling relation to anything outside the Cartesian ego as it thinks: it is all *cogito* and no *cogitamus*. The only real external constraints are those which they share with the Parisian high fashion industry. New structural designs are expected every winter as regularly as hemlines rise or fall in the dress salons, or new automobile models are produced in Detroit. This explains the annual books we have come to expect from the main structuralist writers, books that are more or less bound to express quite different opinions from the author's last because obsolescence is built into the game, and you only get on to the evening talk shows on French national television when you have done something new.

## Philosophical Criticism and Literature

My satiric oversimplification is not, of course, intended to be whole truth, even of my own opinions; I have learned from some structuralists, am on friendly terms with some, and have even been translated for *Poétique*. But I am persuaded that structuralism exacerbates what I regard as a mistaken view of the nature of literary criticism, and am sure that it has disastrous effects as far as most teaching of literature is concerned. The most obvious error is the monstrous assumption that literary criticism, or the philosophy of the literary work, is inherently superior to literature itself, or if not that, at least an indispensable prerequisite for understanding it. The basic notion of the superior role of the critic, is, I suppose, essentially an attempt to retain in a new form the ancient claims of philosophy. But we don't need Blake or Kant or Matthew Arnold to tell us that what literature most characteristically offers is the concreteness of the imagined particular case, so that there is an essential difference between literary and philosophical discourse. The more the critic approaches the generality of philosophical statements the further he inevitably goes from the literature he is talking about. The view that we require a theoretical ontology of the literary work, or of the language, to understand literature seems to me equally mistaken. It assumes that literature, like the Platonic forms, is not visible to the naked eye, and that we need special equipment to be able to see it. But unlike the mysteries of metaphysics, or indeed of faith or science, the literary work is really there, and needs only our own experience of life and language for us to be able to decipher its meaning. For reading literature, as Auerbach puts it, we need no more than our "empirical confidence in our spontaneous faculty for understanding others on the basis of our experience."[10]

Philosophical criticism has the practical effect of impeding the approach to literature in at least three ways. First, if the ordinary reader is persuaded that special analytic equipment is required, he may discover that he cannot master it, or if he does, that it does not in fact help him to understand *King Lear* or *Alice in Wonderland*. Second, if the reader accepts the critic's claim to a transcendental role, he may be humiliated by the discovery that his own explorations are much less exciting: a seer is by definition someone who sees what nobody else can see; the critic-seer makes the ordinary sublunary mortal feel he must be blind to literature; and so he desists from further effort in despair of ever catching even a glimpse of the backside of the moon as the seers seem to do all the time. They belong, essentially, to the greatest lobby in America—the Anxiety Lobby—which ranges from armament manufacturers and Madison Avenue to Ralph Nader and some conservationists.

Last, philosophical criticism tends to view literature in exclusively cognitive terms. The result is that we are made to forget that it is a condition of literature's wider truth to life that it is not exclusively cognitive; that it covers the whole range of human actions and feelings, memories and imaginings; and to treat it as cognitive both in subject and meaning is not only to misrepresent it, but to prevent it from fulfilling literature's capacity to enlarge our imaginative sympathies.

That enlargement is surely one of the primary reasons for the place of literature in the educational curriculum: as Coleridge put it, "the imagination is the distinguishing characteristic of man as a progressive being."[11]

The opposition between theory and the direct imaginative experience of literature is particularly obvious in the case of structuralism. The *en-*

---

[10] Erich Auerbach, *Literary Language and Its Public in Late Latin Antiquity and in the Middle Ages* (London: Routledge and Kegan Paul, 1965), p. 7.

[11] See Lecture 11, *Lectures 1808–1819 On Literature*, ed. R. A. Foakes, 2 vols. (Princeton: Princeton University Press; London: Routledge and Kegan Paul, 1987), 2:193, in *The Collected Works of Samuel Taylor Coleridge* [Ed.].

*fants terribles* of Paris, like those of other places, are in one respect inhuman: they are neither infants nor adults; and their brilliant command of an adult verbal apparatus either masks an absence of other kinds of understanding, or prevents it from appearing in their writing. Their talk is of deep universal structures; but these structures are produced by extravagant exclusions which defy human experience. In any case it is surely unhelpful, in an age when reading occurs less and less, and less and less naturally, to send out the message, not "Come on in, the water's fine," but "Beware the Baleful Binaries, The Dragons of the Deep"; and it doesn't help to map the whole world of literature with markers which turn out to announce the same binary monsters, especially when their names change every year.

One final objection. The actual educational effect of the currency of philosophical criticism is ultimately to hinder rather than to help the promotion of philosophical ways of thought. For, quite apart from the appalling logical inadequacy of such writers as Lacan, the works of the structuralists are usually read second or third hand; a mass of textbooks offer do-it-yourself kits which promise the user a magic transformation into being what he most wants—to be a philosopher without doing philosophy.

This macabre contemporary academic phenomenon was nicely taken off by the short-story writer Leonard Michaels, in a zany version of Swift:

While doing inventory, the manager of a new bookstore in Berkeley discovered that thousands of dollars worth of books had been stolen. They were mainly in philosophy. He decided that people who study philosophy can always think of reasons that allow them to steal. . . . But even if the manager is correct in thinking philosophers can rationalize their criminal peculiarities, what about the other stolen books? These other books were mostly in literary criticism, and, as the manager observes with great bitterness, literary criticism is the philosophy of literature.

As it happens, the most frequently stolen book in literary criticism was Jonathan Culler's *Structuralist Poetics* (thirteen dollars). This book surveys all the new theories in structuralism and semiotics that come largely from France. The theories are excitingly fashionable, though they are only about establishing a systematic relationship between literary texts and the ways critics read them. None of these theories, according to Culler, is too logical.

You might suppose not many people care to read about illogical theories, but Culler writes very intelligently and the theories are interesting. Thus, interesting theories attacked by an intelligent critic make a book irresistible to thieves. The really significant thing, however, is that Culler's book is what you might call the philosophy of the philosophy of literature. Culler's book is, then, the most philosophical book in the store! It excites the sneakiest instincts of acquisition.

God only knows how many copies of *Structuralist Poetics* have been stolen. (The manager of this new store lost seventeen out of twenty, and now keeps Culler under the counter.) But how many copies have been stolen in university towns everywhere! How many philosophers curl up every night with a hot Culler! How many are ravished page after page by delicious analyses of critical theories which talk about nothing but other critical theories! (Would it be too much to say that theories which talk about theories are something like an extraordinary tumescence of the head?)

There is a story about a book thief in Cambridge who was caught stealing a Culler. The police got a warrant, searched his apartment, and found sixty-three Cullers in his hope chest. All of them had been passionately underlined.[12]


## Conclusion: The Rise of the Novel *as Realist Criticism*

You are no doubt wondering not only when I am going to finish, but whether I am going to do so by using *The Rise of the Novel* as an example of how philosophy should serve the purposes of literary study. The answer, I fear, is "yes"; but only in the spirit of a valedictory homily which is primarily intended to express my unchanged general views of the role of literary criticism.

My earlier account of youthful fraternising with German thought will, I hope, acquit me of any boot-faced rejection of philosophy as such. I assume, of course, that as teachers and scholars we have an obligation to try to understand as much as we can of the world we live in, even if this sometimes turns out to mean an attempt to understand misunderstandings. But I cannot believe that we need put down all our assumptions in our writings, and I see no point in attempting a philosophical defense of the common uninstructed judgment that we all know sufficiently well what is real and what words mean and how they enable us to talk about matters of common interest. On some such grounds I see *The Rise of the Novel* as being a realist work of criticism;

---

[12] Leonard Michaels, "Book Thieves and Philosophy," *San Francisco Review of Books* (May 1976).

and this, I suppose, is connected with four aspects of the book which may be worth commenting on: the attitude to philosophy; the attitude to language; the attitude to the reader; and the attitude to the subject.

Philosophically, realism is generally assumed to regard deductive reasoning as a less reliable guide to truth than common experience. This no doubt informs my avoidance of most methodological issues. I assume that philosophy can help the critic in at least three ways: by giving him a sense of how different kinds of problems can be approached; by giving him a sense of conceptual consistency and of the appropriate degree of logic in exposition; and finally, by giving him a notion of the interrelatedness of different bodies of knowledge, the attempt, in Robert Louis Stevenson's phrase, to "circumnavigate the metaphysics," can inform our whole way of seeing a subject. In the course of looking at some early reviews I was interested to see that Irving Howe had written of my method in *The Rise of the Novel*: "the various critical schools of the past few decades. . . come into play. . . as elements that have been assimilated by the critic's sensibility . . . for example . . . the insights borrowed from Marx become his own possession, inseparable from his awareness as a whole."[13]

One is always immensely grateful to critics who help one to make sense of what one has been trying to do. Irving Howe's notion of the *Gestalt* of awareness perfectly expresses what I intuitively felt then, and see more clearly now, as to the primary value of philosophy in enriching literary criticism; and that value, I am convinced, directly depends upon the capacity of the ideas concerned to promote our understanding of literary, aesthetic, and historical experience.

The question of the appropriate linguistic decorum of literary criticism is closely tied to this. It should not assume that philosophical terminology has any superiority of status. Of course, all more or less specialized pursuits have their own vocabularies; plumbers make a nice distinction between a coupling and a union; but the vocabulary of criticism should be as commonsense as possible in its attempt to achieve clarity and accessibility of statement. It should also avoid unnecessary abstraction as a courtesy to the reader, and to the subject. I remember one conversation with Theodor Adorno when, after I'd said what I'd done that morning (checking out some books from the library, going to the laundromat, etc.), and asked "What about you," I was slightly

---

[13] Irving Howe, "Criticism at Its Best," *Partisan Review* 25 (1958), 145 [Ed.].

chilled when he answered: "I have been meditating on erotic and musicological problems."

The effect of long words is a little like that which Fowler attributes to the exact pronunciation of French words in English conversation: "the greater its success as a *tour de force*, the greater its failure as a step in the conversational progress; for your collocutor, aware that he could not have done it himself, has his attention distracted whether he admires or is humiliated."[14]

Any literary criticism whose effect is to humiliate the reader (and I've seen some cases where that seemed its only intention), seems to me to defeat its primary purpose, which is, I take it, to be part of a conversation among lovers of literature. In that sense, the critic's concern for a common orientation with his reader towards literature should produce a style of discourse which is fraternal; that is, discourse whose rhetoric implies the common and equal possession of shared interests and feelings. I treasure a few letters and chance encounters, incidentally, which have indicated that my intentions in this respect did not go unregarded by some readers of *The Rise of the Novel*.

Wittgenstein once said that he didn't dine at high table because "the conversation was neither from the heart nor from the head." How the heart can be represented in critical writing is a very delicate matter; but there should surely be some evidence that the writer's experience of literature has rubbed off on the words he uses and how he uses them. And the "realist" attitude to literature should also, I think, reflect the fact that many generations of human beings have accorded literature, and the arts generally, a special place in their hearts, and one which led them to look up with reverence, admiration, or a sense of personal obligation to those who contributed so much to their lives and their understanding. It is no accident, I suppose I am entitled to say, that *The Rise of the Novel* ends, if I am not mistaken, with the words "Defoe, Richardson, and Fielding . . . [expressed] their own sense of life with a completeness and conviction which is very rare, and for which one is grateful."

As I am, to you, for your presence and your patience.

---

[14] *Modern English Usage, v.* French words [Ed.].

# 6

# DEFOE AS NOVELIST

Defoe was nearly sixty when his first novel, *Robinson Crusoe*, appeared in 1719.* He had been well known to his contemporaries as a journalist and pamphleteer, however, long before he took overtly to fiction. The first work which brought him fame was *The True-Born Englishman* (1701), probably the most influential political verse satire in English after Dryden's *Absalom and Achitophel*. The poem defended William III against those who hated the idea that a Dutch king should govern "true-born Englishmen." Defoe retorted that there was no such thing:

> We have been Europe's sink, the jakes where she
> Voids all her offal outcast progeny.

Defoe, then, was no poet, although his rough vigor of expression cannot be denied. Elsewhere in the poem he handled the couplet better, as in:

> But English gratitude is always such
> To hate the hand which doth oblige too much,

and in the famous opening:

> Wherever God erects a house of prayer,
> The devil always builds a chapel there:

---

* The original version of "Defoe as Novelist," which appeared in Boris Ford's *Pelican Guide to English Literature* in 1957, was contemporaneous with *The Rise of the Novel*. This revised version of the essay appeared in *From Dryden to Johnson, The New Pelican Guide to English Literature*, vol. 4, ed. Boris Ford (Harmondsworth: Penguin Books, 1982), and is reprinted here by permission of David Higham Associates.

> And 'twill be found upon examination,
> The latter has the largest congregation.

Defoe used verse because that, since Dryden, was the favored mode for public polemic; but earning literary glory was not his concern. Thus, in the Preface to *The True-Born Englishman*, Defoe anticipated critical objections with engaging jocularity:

Without being taken for a conjuror, I may venture to foretell, that I shall be cavilled at about my mean style, rough verse, and incorrect language, things I indeed might have taken more care in. But the book is printed; and though I see some faults, it is too late to mend them. And this is all I think needful to say. . . .

Defoe could be cavalier because his main audience cared little for such niceties; they were not the cultivated patrons to whom so much of previous literature had been primarily addressed, but plain middle-class folk who constituted an important new force in the reading public, and were strongly asserting their independence, cultural as well as political. They felt, and Defoe agreed, that

> Fate has but small distinction set
> Betwixt the counter and the coronet,

and that the tastes of shopkeepers who worked behind the counter must also be served.

So if the great Augustans, Swift and Pope, sneered at Defoe as an outsider, he took little notice. With more than his share of the truculent self-reliance of the trading classes, Defoe was less an artist than a literary tradesman; and in a career that was as much devoted to business and politics as to literature, he produced over five hundred separate works, as well as a vast amount of journalism, including the whole of his thrice-weekly newspaper, *The Review*, which ran for nine years, from 1704 to 1713.

Defoe's novels—which are certainly the works that interest us most today—were among the greatest concessions he made to the tastes of the reading public. His own preference seems to have been for more factual and expository forms—for the political, economic, social, and moral improvement of his countrymen. As editor of *The Review*, however, he had learned that his readers often needed to be "wheedled . . . in to the knowledge of the world"; and, to "carry out this honest cheat and bring people to read with delight," he had added to the usual fare of a newspaper a lighter section called "Advice from the Scandalous Club" which dealt humorously with controversial aspects of the social life of the day. This feature was very popular and paved the way to *The Tatler*'s more polished presentation of similar matter; it also taught Defoe much about this side of the public's interests and gave him practice in catering to them.

In any case, Defoe was a professional writer, and always ready to supply whatever the printing press could use. Pope might attack what he called Grub Street and the Dunces that wrote for it; but Defoe saw Grub Street as merely an application of commercial principles to the manufacture of literary goods. As he wrote in a letter signed "Anti-Pope," published in the popular *Applebee's Journal* in 1725:

Writing, you know, Mr Applebee, is become a very considerable Branch of the English Commerce. . . . The Booksellers are the Master Manufacturers or Employers. The several Writers, Authors, Copyers, Sub-writers, and all other Operators with pen and Ink are the workmen employed by the said Master Manufacturers.

It was in the spirit of an "operator with pen and ink" that Defoe turned to supplying the needs of the booksellers (or publishers as we should say now) for fiction. But, as in everything else he wrote, Defoe informed his fiction with so much of his own personality and outlook that it became something quite different from anything that the world had seen before: a form of prose narrative which, if not quite the novel in our sense, was in many respects much closer to it than what had been written before in English. It is, of course, highly appropriate that the rise of the novel—then regarded as a subliterary form—should begin with a subliterary figure like Defoe, a writer responsive to a wider reading public and largely independent of patronage and the critical standards of the literati.

Defoe's most important innovation in fiction was his unprecedentedly complete narrative realism. There is little doubt that it springs directly out of his long practice of journalism. Leslie Stephen long ago described[1] how his early pamphlet, the famous *A True Relation of the Apparition of one Mrs Veal, the next day after her death, to one Mrs Bargrave at Canterbury, the 8ᵗʰ of September, 1705*, contains all the hallmarks of Defoe's later narrative style, including "the manufacturing of corrobora-

---

[1] In his excellent essay, "De Foe's Novels" in *Hours in a Library*, I (London: Smith, Elder & Co, 1874).

tive evidence" and the deflection of attention from weak links in the chain of evidence. Stephen thought that *The Apparition of Mrs Veal* was a work of fiction, but it has since been discovered that Defoe was merely reporting a popular news item of the day in his own characteristic manner. He was to use exactly the same technique when he came to write fiction, and even there we are never quite sure how much is pure invention. *Robinson Crusoe* itself was widely regarded as authentic at the time of publication, and it is still not certain to what extent some of Defoe's works, such as the *Memoirs of a Cavalier*, are fictitious or genuine.

It was certainly Defoe's overriding intention that readers should be gulled into thinking his fictions true. If he did not already know that the illusion of authenticity was his forte, he could have learned it from one of his journalist rivals who wrote in 1718 of "the little art [Defoe] is truly master of, of forging a story, and imposing it on the world for truth." Defoe never admitted that he wrote fiction; and it is typical of him that his greatest success, *Robinson Crusoe*, is prefaced with a statement by the "Editor" that he "believes the thing to be a just history of fact; neither is there any appearance of fiction in it."

This claim to historical truth is false. For, although Defoe took a good deal from the accounts of Alexander Selkirk and other castaways, the story and the character of Robinson Crusoe are very largely of Defoe's invention. But the narrative is presented with so much circumstantial detail that the reader does not think of the book as fiction; and later generations have accorded it a semi-historical status.

Consider, for example, the way in which the famous finding of the green barley sprouts is told:

In the middle of all my labours it happened, that rummaging my things, I found a little bag, which, as I hinted before, had been filled with corn for the feeding of poultry, not for this voyage, but before, as I suppose, when the ship came from Lisbon. What little remainder of the corn had been in the bag was all devoured with the rats, and I saw nothing in the bag but husks and dust; and being willing to have the bag for some other use, I think it was to put powder in, when I divided it for fear of the lightning, or some such use, I shook the husks of corn out of it on one side of my fortification, under the rock. It was a little before the great rains, just now mentioned, that I threw this stuff away, taking no notice of anything, and not so much as remembering that I had thrown anything there; when, about a month after, or thereabout, I saw some few stalks of something green shooting out of the ground, which I fancied might be some plant I had not seen; but I was surprised, and perfectly astonished, when, after a little longer time, I saw about ten or twelve ears come out, which were perfect green barley of the same kind as our European, nay, our English barley.

The main aim of the writing is clearly to keep as close as possible to the mind of the narrator as he struggles to make exactly what actually happened clear to himself and to us. Nothing but the exclusive pursuit of this aim, we feel, would have brought about such abrupt dislocations of rhythm and syntax as are found in the first sentence; no other reason could excuse the repetitions, the parentheses, the stumblings. The final result is that the little bag takes its place with all the other objects of Crusoe's life which have fastened themselves on our imaginations—the first clay pot, the climatically inept fur garments, the umbrella, the boat, the grindstone.

Defoe's style obeys more fully than ever before the purpose of language as his great contemporary John Locke redefined it: "to convey knowledge of things." Defoe concentrates his attention on the primary qualities of objects as Locke had defined them: especially solidity, extension, and number; and he presents them in the simplest language—Defoe's prose contains a higher percentage of words of Anglo-Saxon origin than that of any other well-known English writer except Bunyan. His sentences, it is true, are often long and rambling, but Defoe somehow makes this a part of his air of authenticity. The lack of strong pauses within the sentence gives his style an urgent, immediate, breathless quality; at the same time, his units of meaning are so small, and their relatedness is made so clear by frequent repetition and recapitulation, that he nevertheless gives the impression of perfect lucidity.

Defoe had been exposed to all the influences which were making prose more prosaic in the seventeenth century: to Locke's philosophy; to the Royal Society's wish for a language which would help its scientific and technological aims by keeping close to the speech of "artisans, countrymen, and merchants"; and to the plain unadorned style of later seventeenth-century preaching, which obtained its effects by repetition rather than by imagery or structural elaboration. Most important of all, Defoe's twenty years of journalism had taught him that it was impossible to be too explicit for the audience of "honest meaning ignorant persons" which he kept continually in mind. As a result, Defoe's natural prose style is not only an admirable narrative vehicle in itself: it is also much closer to the vernacular of the ordinary person than any previous writer's, and thus admirably adapted to the tongues of Robinson Crusoe, Moll Flanders, and his other characters.

But the effect of the passage quoted is not just a question of clear description; there is also the effect of Defoe's emphatic pressure forcing us to accept the truth of his narrative. For instance, Crusoe seems to demonstrate his scrupulous care with the truth by admitting that he cannot be absolutely certain about some trivial details—when and where the bag had originally been filled with corn, or what he had actually wanted the bag for later. As readers we reflect that our memory has its little lapses too, and we think the better of Crusoe for frankly confessing his weakness. In this case Defoe is "manufacturing" not so much the "corroborative evidence" that Leslie Stephen spoke of, but the character of a corroborating witness whose fastidious concern for complete veracity authenticates every word he writes. And this particular reminder of the narrator's reliability, we notice, is strategically placed; for it deflects our attention from the weakest link in the chain of evidence—the fact that, as Crusoe admits, "the climate . . . was not proper for corn."

We have been programmed by the way of writing to accept a miracle. The miracle itself reflects Defoe's religious background and his didactic intention. The Puritan tradition saw the whole world, and every incident of individual experience, as alive with secret indications of divine intervention or intention. Crusoe instinctively interprets his experience in this way; he looks for signs of Grace or Reprobation not only in the ears of corn, but in everything else that happens to him. *Robinson Crusoe* is not just—or even primarily—a travel story; it is also, in intention at least, one of what Defoe called his "honest cheats," a sincere attempt to use fiction, a godless form of literature, to the purposes of religion and morality. Crusoe's story is supposed to demonstrate how God's Providence saves an outcast who by leaving his family and forgetting his religious training has sinned against the divine will out of a "secret burning lust of ambition for great things."

The book we know was called *The Life and Strange Surprising Adventures of Robinson Crusoe*. It was a phenomenal success, and to cash in on it Defoe wrote two continuations: *The Farther Adventures*, and *The Serious Reflections of Robinson Crusoe*. In the latter Defoe repeats the moral and religious aim he had avowed earlier; his book "is calculated for, and dedicated to, the improvement and instruction of mankind in the ways of virtue and piety, by representing the various circumstances to which mankind is exposed, and encouraging such as fall into

ordinary or extraordinary casualties of life, how to work through difficulties with unwearied diligence and application, and look up to Providence for success."

We tend to interpret *Robinson Crusoe* rather differently today; we are
able to do so because Defoe's was a much secularized puritanism, and it
relied more on "unwearied diligence and application" than on faith. Defoe's heroes habitually seem to act on the assumption that it is prudent
to keep your powder dry so that you won't have to put the imponder-
able effects of your trust in God to the test. Crusoe's religious rumina-
tions are like bouts of benign malaria, easily shaken off; they indicate no
organic spiritual change. Thus, as soon as Crusoe remembers that previously he had "shook a bag of chicken's meat out in that place . . . " his
wonder ceases; and, as a result, he confesses that "my religious thankfulness to God's Providence began to abate too, upon the discovering
that all this was nothing but what was common." The same operative
primacy of nonreligious considerations is evident in the book as a
whole. For, of course, Crusoe is well rewarded for his sins: without
them he would hardly have risen above the "middle station of low life"
to which he had been born, and become a wealthy merchant, plantation
owner, slave trader, and colonizer.

If today we are skeptical about the book's religious significance, we
see much else in it which was no part of Defoe's intention. We see
Robinson Crusoe as the symbol of economic man,[2] who, by recapitu-
lating on his island all the basic productive processes, provides the
economists with their favorite example. We see him too as the very pro-
totype of the empire builder, leaving a crowded homeland for the wide-
open places where he establishes a little city in a tropical forest and converts the heathen. We may notice too that, just as economic individualism in general stands in the way of harmonious personal and social relations, so Crusoe's radical egocentricity leads him to sell the Moorish boy
Xury, who has saved his life, to the Portuguese trader for sixty pieces of
silver, and later to treat Friday in the manner of a benevolent slave
owner rather than that of a friend. Defoe, it seems certain, was not conscious of the prophetic nature of his tale; but he had experienced the
crucial social and economic processes of his time more fully and deeply
than anyone, and, as an experienced reporter, without illusions, he re-

---

[2] See my "*Robinson Crusoe* as a Myth," in *Essays in Criticism* 1 (1951), 95-119,
for a treatment of this aspect of the book.

vealed their effects on human behavior and mental habits with unthinking fidelity.

Not that Defoe was unaware of the symbolic quality of Crusoe's experience. In the preface to the *Serious Reflections* he hints that the story
is an allegory of his own life: and though this assertion is mainly an af-
terthought to defend himself against the critics who had charged that
*Robinson Crusoe* was fiction, his plea has a certain essential truth. Defoe tends to identify himself with all his protagonists and most fully
perhaps with Crusoe; his own life, too, had been one of solitary and heroic achievement against great odds. In an eloquent chapter, "Of Solitude," which begins the *Serious Reflections*, Defoe converts Crusoe's
island existence into an image of man's perpetual aloneness. This
springs from his basic egocentricity:

. . . it seems to me that life in general is, or ought to be, but one universal
act of solitude. Everything revolves in our minds by innumerable circular
motions, all centering in ourselves . . . we love, we hate, we covet, we enjoy,
all in privacy and solitude.

*Robinson Crusoe* is one of the great myths of modern civilization; the
story celebrates Western civilization's material triumphs and the strength
of its rational will to conquer the environment: and it also prefigures the
spiritual loneliness and social alienation which have accompanied its
progress.

Some of this loneliness is itself a reflection of a force which did much
to build modern civilization—Puritan individualism. The Puritans saw
the activities of the world as a diversion from man's proper spiritual
purpose, which was the scrutiny of his conscience for signs of his probable destiny in the divine plot of redemption and damnation. So Defoe
makes Crusoe write in his *Serious Reflections*: "It is the soul's being en-
tangled by outward objects that interrupts its contemplation of divine
objects"; and he concludes that "the business is to get a retired soul."
This can be done anywhere, and so Crusoe affirms

that I enjoy much more solitude in the middle of the greatest collection of
mankind in the world, I mean, at London, while I am writing this, than ever
I could say I enjoyed in eight and twenty years' confinement to a desolate
island.

We must not underestimate Defoe's dissenting background. If he is
not as serious as Bunyan, he has many of his qualities; if he does not
convince us that considerations of piety are really the controlling factors

in his stories, at least they are there, and their presence gives Defoe's novels a real, though problematic, moral dimension.

Indirectly, Puritanism also helped to develop Defoe's literary realism. Defoe shares its hatred of fiction, as he tells us in the *Serious Reflections*: "This supplying a story by invention is certainly a most scandalous crime, and yet very little regarded in that part. It is a sort of lying that makes a great hole in the heart, at which by degrees a habit of lying enters in." Pressure of circumstances led him to write novels: but one feels that, with a curious obliquity, Defoe resolved to make his lies as like truth as possible so that his scandalous crime would escape detection.

If Defoe's Puritan forebears need not have turned too often in their graves at *Robinson Crusoe*, their slumbers must have been more seriously incommoded by the major works of fiction which succeeded it. Their protagonists were not merely successful sinners, like Crusoe, but successful criminals, whores, and pirates. The best of these later works are probably *Moll Flanders* (1722), *Colonel Jack* (1722), and *The Fortunate Mistress* (1724), usually called *Roxana*; all three are closer to being novels than *Robinson Crusoe*, which is too little concerned with personal relationships and too restricted in emotional scope. But all Defoe's other narratives are worth reading, especially *Captain Singleton* (1720) and *A Journal of the Plague Year* (1722), which are closer to the quasi-historical mode of *Robinson Crusoe*.

The earlier pages of *Colonel Jack* are perhaps Defoe's finest piece of writing; they have all his characteristically vivid reporting, his penetrating sociological understanding of the conditions which make children into criminals; and they also have an insight into the whole moral world of a young waif which he hardly equaled elsewhere. The final scenes of *Roxana* have a powerful dramatic interest unique in Defoe: the desperate expedients of the heroine to avoid discovery by the daughter she has abandoned have great psychological and narrative tension; they also— and this is rare in Defoe—embody the story's moral theme in the action; we see how Roxana's life of prostitution is exacting a terrible punishment on both mother and daughter.

But it is *Moll Flanders* which, at least since the praise of E. M. Forster and Virginia Woolf,[3] has been generally accepted as the best of Defoe's

---

[3] Their judgments, and much else, are conveniently available in the Norton Critical Edition, *Moll Flanders: An Authoritative Text, Backgrounds and Sources*, ed. Edward Kelly (New York: W. W. Norton, 1973).

novels. It is richer in range of feeling than *Robinson Crusoe*; it is full of
Defoe's best-written episodes; the heroine is perhaps Defoe's most successful piece of portraiture; the theme is concerned, not with a fight
against Nature, but with something more typical of the novel, the individual's struggle against society; and the plot, though rambling and
confused, is based on a pattern of personal relationships which is finally
rounded out with a degree of unity by the restoration of Moll to her
husband and her son, and a final curtain closing on a peaceful old age of
penitence and prosperity.

Much of *Moll Flanders* is concerned with plain reporting of the heroine's loves and larcenies, often brilliantly done in a narrative manner
very similar to that in *Robinson Crusoe*. No novelist can succeed unless
he is a good reporter, and there is a long and honorable tradition in the
novel which makes the depiction of social reality its main aim. But there
is more than this in *Moll Flanders*—much humor and drama, and some
genuinely novelistic presentation of personal relations.

The humor is often of a blunt cockney variety, as when Robin quiets
his sister who opposes his marriage with the penniless orphan Moll:
"Prithee, child, beauty's a portion, and good humour with it is a double
portion; I wish thou hadst half her stock of both for thy portion." And
Moll adds: "So there was her mouth stopped." We also get more complex effects, sometimes ironical in their psychological point: as when
Moll, having robbed a child, reflects that she had "given the parents a
just reproof for their negligence, in leaving the poor lamb to come home
by itself, and it would teach them to take more care another time"; or
when, giving her son a gold watch, "I desired he would now and then
kiss it for my sake. I did not, indeed, tell him that I stole it from a gen-
tlewoman's side at a meeting house in London. That's by the way."
There are also examples of a more polished wit that recalls Addison or
Swift: Moll comments of her first lover, the elder brother, that "though
he had levity enough to do an ill-natured thing, yet had too much
judgement of things to pay too dear for his pleasures."

*Moll Flanders* has more conscious craftsmanship than *Robinson
Crusoe*, and its orientation to the social and emotional world brings it
much closer to the novel. The account of the first seduction and many of
the episodes with the Lancashire husband combine vivid reporting with
a command of character and emotion that foreshadow the later triumphs of the novel form. Such a scene occurs when, after a long absence, Moll Flanders is reunited with her Lancashire husband:

He turned pale, and stood speechless, like one thunder-struck, and, not able to conquer the surprise, said no more but this, "Let me sit down"; and sitting down by a table, he laid his elbow on the table, and leaning his head on his hand, fixed his eyes on the ground as one stupid. I cried so vehemently, on the other hand, that it was a good while ere I could speak any more; but after I had given some vent to my passion by tears, I repeated the same words, "My dear, do you not know me?" At which he answered, "Yes," and said no more a good while.

This passage, and a few others, have a supremely evocative quality; they show how powerful Defoe's narrative manner could be when focused on human feeling. But such passages are rare. Selected quotations normally give us a much more favorable opinion of Defoe than reading the whole work would; and *Moll Flanders* is no exception. Its pages contain a great deal of uninspired filling-in; and this is one reason for believing that Defoe's stature as a novelist has tended to be overestimated of late.

His central defect is a lack of serious order or design, a lack which is manifested, not only in the development of the story, but in the psychological and moral aspects of his work. What little narrative unity there is comes from the fact that it is Moll Flanders who is the chief character throughout; but this unity is largely submerged in an undiscriminating attempt to tell all that happened in a busy and eventful life.

The moral disunity of the work is even more striking. The purported moral does not tally with the plot. Defoe says in his preface that "there is not a wicked action in any part of it, but is first or last rendered unhappy"; yet actually the heroine does not have to disgorge her ill-gotten gains, and they are the basis of her final prosperity. Even if Defoe had avoided this contradiction, the quality of his moral would have little to recommend it, since it amounts to little more than telling the reader to look to his silver and be on his guard against pickpockets. The actual moral which emerges is even worse: the story suggests that honesty may not be the best policy, and that if you want to live in a genteel style, prudent and enterprising crime may prove more effective than plying your needle; you can always settle your spiritual account when the one at the bank has been taken care of.

This crassly material perspective is revealed in the moral reformation scene which occurs when Moll brings home to her husband all the wealth from her mother's plantation,

. . . the horses, hogs and cows, and other stores for our plantation; all which added to his surprise, and filled his heart with thankfulness; and from this time forward I believe he was as sincere a penitent and as thoroughly a reformed man as ever God's goodness bought back from being a profligate, a highwayman, and a robber.

Reformation by cows and hogs. The book is indeed an example of "mercantile morality that Defoe has apparently neglected to measure."[4] So much so that many modern readers have assumed that the whole moral aspect of the book must be consciously ironical.

The psychological defects of the book are less obvious and could not be demonstrated without lengthy analysis. It can only be suggested, therefore, that Moll Flanders is not seen objectively by Defoe as a character in the round; like many of his characters, she is at times indistinguishable from her author, despite the various "feminine" traits she is given, particularly in her first love affair with the elder brother, and in her regular concern for genteel lodgings, clean linens, and the creature comforts of her males. But the autobiographical form, which Defoe always uses in his fiction, makes it particularly difficult for him not to identify himself with the heroine; it certainly makes it difficult for his picture of her to have much depth, since we do not know what the other characters think of Moll Flanders, and see her only as she sees herself. It is certainly suspicious that nearly all the other characters are shown treating her with adoring and selfless devotion, whereas she is never completely honest with anyone. If we try to get deeper, and ask whether she or her author are aware of her duplicity, we find that Defoe has not told us enough of the relevant facts for an opinion to be possible. It seems that Defoe did not ask such questions himself, or conceive that his readers would. Defoe keeps us informed, as no other novelist does, of his heroine's holdings in cash and personal effects: he does not bother to make clear her emotional development, or to take stock of her real character.

Nor, apparently, does Defoe consider the nature of her personal relationships any more seriously. We are told nothing about most of her lovers or her children: it appears she had a dozen or so of each, but it is impossible to be sure, because most of them are treated very cursorily. She is properly maternal on being reunited with one son, Humphry, in

---

[4] See Mark Schorer's Introduction to *Moll Flanders* in the Modern Library College Edition (New York: Random House, 1950).

Virginia; but what of the remaining seven children whose deaths have not been indicated? The answer is surely that all these are mentioned merely as items of realistic detail, and that after they have served that purpose Defoe does not give them another thought, and does not intend the reader to; we are certainly not meant to draw the conclusion that she is a heartless mother, nor, indeed, any conclusion, but only to forget as easily as she does. Everything in the narrative seems real, but most of it has no existence once it is offstage: for Defoe, convincing the reader of the reality of the story is not only the means, but the end. There is no developing personality in Moll to be observed, no moral or psychological pattern to the loosely-strung-out network of personal relations. Defoe is too intent on getting away with the reality of his characters to try to get into them.

Defoe's forte as a writer is the brilliant episode. His imagination creates events and characters, and sets them solidly in their background; in that respect his narrative is much in advance of anything that fiction had seen before; but the novel as a literary from could be considered established only when realistic narrative was organized into a plot which, while retaining Defoe's lifelikeness, also had some intrinsic unity of development; when the novelist's eye was focused on character and personal relationships as essential elements of the continuity of the novel and not as incidental matter to be used in furthering the verisimilitude of the actions described; and when all these things were related to a unifying theme, a controlling intention. It was left to Richardson and Fielding to take these further steps.[5]

---

[5] See my *The Rise of the Novel: Studies in Defoe, Richardson and Fielding* (London: Chatto & Windus, 1957). Its interpretation of *Robinson Crusoe* and *Moll Flanders* has been challenged by many, perhaps most, subsequent critics. On the economic interpretation of *Robinson Crusoe*, see especially Maximilian E. Novak, *Economics and the Fiction of Daniel Defoe* (Berkeley and Los Angeles: University of California Press, 1962). Sixty or so contributions to the debate about *Moll Flanders* are discussed in C. J. H. O'Brien, *Moll Among the Critics* (Armidale, N.S.W., Australia: University of New England Publishing Unit, 1979). George A. Starr, *Defoe and Spiritual Autobiography* (Princeton: Princeton University Press, 1965), and J. Paul Hunter, *The Reluctant Pilgrim* (Baltimore: Johns Hopkins University Press, 1966), have made important contributions to our understanding of the religious aspect of Defoe's fiction. The coherence and subtlety of Defoe's art have found many defenders; one notable recent study is John J. Richetti, *Defoe's Narratives, Situations and Structures* (Oxford:

They did so, and very consciously. But now that later novelists have gone so much further than they did, and in so many ways, we tend to read Richardson and Fielding in the perspective of the novel tradition as a whole, and they may suffer in the comparison. Defoe, on the other hand, does not really compete, and thus history has lent his artless veracity an adventitious charm: we rejoice to see a writer so innocently unaware of how novels are supposed to be written, and we are tempted to find irony and moral sophistication because we cannot credit that so remarkable a writer and so amazing a man could have produced so many contradictions in a spirit of genuine naïveté. That, at least, is the main problem his novels pose for readers today.

It was not a problem for his contemporaries; and after his death, on 24 April 1731, the few belated obituaries concerned themselves with quite other aspects of his life: *Read's Weekly Journal*, for instance, wrote of "Mr Defoe, Sen.[ior]" that "He had a great natural Genius, and understood very well the Trade and Interest of this Kingdom . . . "; no obituary mentioned the novels which were to make his name live.

---

Clarendon Press, 1975). A recent, comprehensive, and balanced critical assessment, as well as a very attractive and reliable account of the life, is provided in James Sutherland, *Daniel Defoe: A Critical Study* (Cambridge: Harvard University Press, 1971). Pat Rogers, *Robinson Crusoe* (London: George Allen & Unwin, 1979), gives—among much else in the way of reliable historical and literary introduction—an up-to-date and acute analysis of the economic and religious interpretations of *Robinson Crusoe*.

7

# THE NOVELIST AS INNOVATOR:
## SAMUEL RICHARDSON

I suppose the usual assumption about the birth of the English novel is that although Samuel Richardson was undoubtedly the father, his first-born child, *Pamela*, was probably an unplanned accident.* The literary histories leave us with the image of a plump, prosperous printer, odiously complacent and nauseatingly moralistic, who accidentally produced a work which was undeniably the literary sensation of its day, which still has some faint historical importance, but which no modern reader can possibly take seriously. Much of the evidence certainly supports this view. Richardson did turn to writing more or less by accident, and a long time after he had completed the traditional career of the virtuous apprentice, married the master's daughter and set up on his own. As a London printer, one way he got publishers to put business in his way, he wrote, was "because of the Readiness I showed to oblige them, with writing Indexes, Prefaces, and sometimes, for their minor Authors, *honest* Dedications; abstracting, abridging, compiling, and giving my Opinion of Pieces offered them."

This was just hack work and it was not until he was nearly fifty that Richardson had anything to do with writing fiction. Then, one day, he tells us:

Two Booksellers . . . entreated me to write for them a little Volume of Letters, in a common Style, on such Subjects as might be of Use to those Country Readers who were unable to indite for themselves. Will it be any Harm,

---

* This essay, which began as a talk for the BBC's Third Programme, was published in *The Listener* (February 4, 1965), 177-80, and in *The Novelist as Innovator*, ed. Walter Allen (London: BBC, 1965).

said I, in a Piece you want to be written so low, if we should instruct them how they should think and act in common cases, as well as indite? They were the more urgent with me to begin the little volume for this Hint. I set about it, and in the Progress of it, writing two or three Letters to instruct handsome Girls, who were obliged to go out to service . . . how to avoid the snares that might be laid against their Virtue.

There came into his mind a true life story he had once heard about a servant girl who had finally made it clear to her upper-class master that he would never be able to consummate his designs except on matrimonial terms. So for the time being Richardson set aside writing the commissioned collection of *Familiar Letters* and wrote *Pamela*.

Still, it was not just a fluke. For one thing, the idea had long been on his mind. As he later wrote:

For twenty years, I had proposed to different Persons (who thought the Subject too humble for them) [the story] of *Pamela*, and it was owing to an Accident (the writing of the little Piece of *Familiar Letters*) that I entered upon it myself. And its strange Success at Publication is still my Surprize.

This is not the only place where Richardson speaks as though *Pamela* had been largely a question of luck, not cunning; and that, of course, would fit in with one picture of the evolutionary process: the first novel would be an accidental mutation that just happened to suit the literary environment, and therefore became the dominant form of the ensuing two centuries. But Darwinian evolution hardly seems to apply to human affairs, and to look at *Pamela* in this way involves an affront to our most basic critical assumptions about literature—that it is an art, and that though literary intention and achievement are by no means the same thing, they are at least related. I think that the reputation of *Pamela* has suffered because of the assumption that it was an accident. The novel and literature itself seem somehow to stand to lose if Richardson really did not know what he was doing.

I

But I think he did, and so I would like to look at the whole question again, partly because it is still of considerable interest and partly because I think that one possible answer raises larger critical problems that are important for the tradition of the novel as a whole. First, let us look at the opening paragraph of *Pamela*:

LETTER I. Dear Father and Mother, I have great trouble, and some comfort, to acquaint you with. The trouble is that my good lady died of the illness I mentioned to you and left us all much grieved for the loss of her: she was a dear, good lady and kind to all us her servants. Much I feared, that as I was taken by her ladyship to wait upon her person, I should be quite destitute again and forced to return to you and my poor mother, who have enough to do to maintain yourselves, and as my lady's goodness had put me to write and cast accounts, and made me a little expert at my needle, and otherwise qualified above my degree, it was not every family that could have found a place that your poor Pamela was fit for: but God, whose graciousness to us we have so often experienced, put it into my good lady's heart, just an hour before she expired, to recommend to my young master all her servants, one by one, and when it came to my turn to be recommended (for I was sobbing and crying at her pillow) she could only say: "My dear son!" and so broke off a little; and then recovering, "remember my poor Pamela"—And these were some of her last words. O, how my eyes run, don't wonder to see the paper so blotted.

Of course, it all sounds completely artless, just one sentence following another in Pamela's mind as she writes her letter home. One could argue that just achieving this convincingly casual effect is part of Richardson's art. But at best, that would be only the lowest kind of art, mere mimicry, Richardson as parrot. The real case for Richardson must be made on other and better grounds; on the grounds, I suggest, that behind the aimless prattle there is also an author's mind in control—and in control, not only of a convincing narrative voice, but of the shape of the fiction as a whole. A second look at the passage reveals, for example, that all the themes of the story are sounded, and sounded in a way that expresses the nature of their eventual conflict. There is the economic motive: Pamela's dependence, and her fear of being forced to return and be a clog on her parents. There is the class issue: Pamela's awed respect for her social betters, and her feeling of being herself "qualified above her degree"—she is already on the way up and scrubbing floors is out. Then there is Pamela's obtrusive religious piety, coupled with her complacent assurance that God's graciousness is specially extended to her and her family. And finally there is the ironic climax that what God should most specifically have done for her is to "put it into my good lady's heart . . . [to] say 'My dear son! . . . remember my poor Pamela.'"

Mr. B. does indeed remember Pamela, and not at all as his mother intended—the complexities of that situation are clearly foreshadowed in the rest of Pamela's first letter. There, both Mr. B. and Pamela are shown as already aware of the need for concealment, not to say deceit: when Pamela sends home the guineas she has been given by the footman John, she tells us that she wraps "them up close in paper, that they mayn't chink." And at the end of the letter, when Mr. B. catches Pamela in the act of writing the letter—she is in her "late lady's dressing-room"—he says: "You are a good girl, Pamela, to be kind to your aged father and mother. I am not angry with you for writing such innocent matters as these, though you ought to be wary what tales you send out of a family." It is a prophetic remark, but no more prophetic than when we see Pamela's reactions to Mr. B. On the one hand, she is "scared out of her senses" by her master's approach, and is "all in confusion" at being in his mere presence; but on the other hand, she is also very proud when Mr. B. "took me by the hand, yes, he took my hand before them all." This conflict between sexual hope and fear is beautifully summed up when Pamela concludes her first letter: "Indeed, he is the best of gentlemen, I think . . . "

He may not be quite the best of gentlemen, but he is the best for her. And when, after finishing *Pamela*, we look back, we can see that all its main themes have been completely prefigured in that opening letter. Which means that, at least at the level of ordinary literary craftsmanship, Richardson had considerable and conscious narrative skill, and this means that in *Pamela* we are in the presence of an ordering of human life, not merely a formless and haphazard imitation of it.

Unfortunately, several further objections arise. First, that though Richardson had a plan, he carried it out at excessive length, that the book is too long for its subject and that, at times, the writing is just life-likeness, or preaching, for its own sake and without reference to the fiction as a whole. I am afraid that this is often my own impression, and it is not easy to find a satisfactory defense. Historically, though, it does seem clear that the prevailing attitude in 1740 was that one cannot have too much of a good thing. Certainly many other authors proceeded to act on that assumption. There were many continuations of *Pamela*, and in the end, Richardson himself was driven to add two more volumes, called *Pamela in her Exalted Condition*.

There is another partial defense or at least explanation which is probably more important. It concerns the whole question of the scale on which the novel makes its representation of life. The novel in general has a characteristic impulse to bring the reader very close to the day-to-day texture of experience, and this means that it always tends towards

diffuseness and prolixity: in Richardson's case, the closeness of the perspective, the total, uncensored, unabbreviated reporting of the heroine's
experience, was something quite new in literature and so it is hardly
surprising that, at times, it got out of hand.

Yet the main objection to *Pamela* has always been not so much that it
was too long, but that Richardson did not see that his heroine was
really, to use the traditional terms, a scheming little minx whose pre-
tended virtue was only a means for pursuing her aim of marrying Mr. B.
The charge was made almost as soon as the book came out in 1740, and
the most famous protagonist of this interpretation is Fielding. His
heroine, *Shamela*, as the change in name shows, is revealed as a hypocritical but experienced young slut who relates the hilarious sexual in-
eptitudes of Mr. Booby, as Squire B. has been dubbed, and the compensating expertness of the local parson, Williams, to her incredulous
mother, a London bawd.

II

Here we come to the central critical issue. Can Richardson have been
an artist in any sense worth the name if he produced a work where the
chief character could be open to such diversity of psychological interpretation, where the Pamela whom he had naively presented as an instruc-
tive example of Virtue Rewarded was more plausibly to be seen as a
complete sham? I myself would hardly like to base the defence on the
literary proposition that ambiguity is good in itself. It all depends,
surely, on whether the conflicting meanings involved are self-defeating
or mutually enriching. But in the case of *Pamela*, I certainly believe that
the ambiguity of interpretation to which the text is susceptible does, in
fact, add to the total meaning; that it is an ambiguity of which Richardson was at least in part aware; and—more important—that the greatness of Richardson's literary achievement should be seen as an example
of how his narrative technique enabled, and indeed encouraged, him to
reveal much more about his heroine and her story than was consistent
with his conscious didactic purpose.

The discrepancy between Richardson's avowed purposes and the tenor
of the text as a whole is certainly remarkable. The opening paragraph, for
example, is hardly what one would expect from the preceding title page:

Pamela: or Virtue Rewarded: In a Series of Familiar Letters from A Beautiful Young Damsel To Her Parents. Now first Published in order to cultivate

the Principles of Virtue and Religion in the Minds of the Youth of Both Sexes. A Narrative which has its Foundation in Truth and Nature; and at the same time that it agreeably entertains, by a Variety of curious and affecting Incidents, is intirely divested of all those Images, which, in too many Pieces calculated for Amusement only, tend to inflame the Minds they should instruct.

The emphasis is flatly moralistic; it does not prepare us at all for the mixture of motives one actually finds in the heroine, for all the fluctuations in class attitudes, the attraction-repulsion towards Mr. B., the pride and self-satisfaction, the assumption that Providence is especially interested in one's material benefits. What the title page of *Pamela*, and the preface that Richardson later added, tell us is merely how Richardson wants the story to be seen, or, what amounts to the same thing, what face value his heroine would like to be taken at. It is a question of the public posture only, as befits a title page, or a lady who now has a position to maintain in society. But, surely, one can reasonably doubt whether the public posture is the whole story of Pamela's psychology, and this without going over to the opposite extreme with Fielding.

Private experience, the day-to-day contacts, and our inner thoughts and feelings about them, are never simple, as we all know: motives and emotions and reactions are usually mixed, and never more so than in the relations between the sexes. Our speech and our public attitudes in general normally conform to the systems of moral and religious value current in society. This is not usually out of hypocrisy but because these values have been internalized in the conscience, roughly what Freud called the superego, which is usually the most articulate part of the mind, because it has largely been formed by the talk of others, by what people in society profess, expect, and applaud. But even the most strictly moralistic person is normally aware that this public moral posture is not the only part of the mind, that there are many other unconscious or preconscious or merely unstated interests and wishes, which are not much talked about by ourselves, or by other people, but are very important. As we grow up, we gradually learn to understand that the discourse of others represents an accommodation between public attitudes and private pressures, and the most persistent of these pressures of course originate in the libido, or the id, to use Freud's terms for the source of our impulses towards financial, aggressive, and sexual satisfaction. And, as we noticed, it is precisely these impulses which are prefigured in Pamela's first letter, but not in the title page.

So one way out of the dilemma which Fielding's *Shamela* seems to pose is to accept the view that Pamela is neither all superego, as Richardson sometimes suggests, nor all libido, which would be one way of putting Fielding's views. Instead, she is merely, like everybody else, a mixture. And so, before we assume that her contradictory attitudes must be evidence of hypocrisy, one must be very sure that they are not merely the usual human muddle—a muddle in the person, not the book, I should add. For Pamela's motivations and actions throughout seem to me to be wholly credible and consistent with any adequately complex notion of human behavior. And we have considerable evidence that Richardson himself was fully conscious of the ambiguities of the human mind. "I was not more than thirteen," he later wrote in a letter about the writing of *Pamela*,

when three . . . young Women, unknown to each other, having a high Opinion of my Taciturnity, revealed to me their Love Secrets, in order to induce me to give them Copies to write after, or correct, for Answers to their Lovers' Letters: Nor did anyone of them ever know, that I was the Secretary to the others. I have been directed to chide, and even repulse, when an Offence was either taken or given, at the very time that the Heart of the Chider or Repulser was open before me, overflowing with Esteem and Affection; and the fair Repulser dreading to be taken at her Word; directing *this* Word, or that Expression, to be softened or changed.

From very early days, then, Richardson, "not fond of Play, as other Boys," and called "Serious and Gravity" by his schoolmates, had been a quietly fascinated observer of the obliquities of human behavior. He had also been devoted to letter-writing and to storytelling, and he had had unique opportunities for knowing the inner mind of people like Pamela. So on the question of Richardson's degree of awareness about his creation, it seems reasonable to say that, in general, although a writer does not always know what he has written, he cannot write what he does not know. In Richardson's case it was the stimulus of an accidental request for a letter-writing manual which elicited *Pamela*. But it was no accident that it was Richardson who was asked, Richardson who complied, and Richardson who then embodied in epistolary form a particular story, and an area of human understanding, which had long been his.

That Richardson actually intended the discrepancy between his didactic intention and the actual psychological tenor of the narrative is quite

another matter, and seems highly unlikely. On the other hand it would
be quite normal for explicit good intentions to turn out rather more
mixed in practice. We notice that Richardson at once asked the booksellers if he could expand his original brief and make the letters useful as
models not only of letter-writing but of feminine virtue. But when
Richardson put himself into the mind of Pamela, and wrote what he
knew she would say in the circumstances, other parts of his mind came
into play. The pedestrian moralizing of the superego had obtruded itself at first, but the cover afforded by his mask of being the mere editor of pretendedly real letters written by a servant girl allowed Richardson, perhaps for the first time in his life, to express a much wider spectrum of human complexity. And when he had finished, he realized very
well what he had done, as can be seen in his letters. Thus, to one friend,
Dr. George Cheyne, he wrote: "In my Scheme I have generally taken
Human Nature *as it is*; for it is to no purpose to suppose it Angelic, or
to endeavour to make it so."

So Richardson can be taken as embodying an early case of what the
American writer Mark Schorer, applying the formalist concerns of mod-
ern criticism to the novel in a now celebrated essay, calls "Technique as
Discovery."[1] His theory, briefly, is as follows:

Modern criticism has shown us that to speak of content as such is not to
speak of art at all, but of experience; and that it is only when we speak of
the *achieved* content, the form of the work of art as a work of art, that we
speak as critics. The difference between content, or experience, and achieved
content, or art, is technique. When we speak of technique then, we speak of
nearly everything. For technique is the means by which the writer's experience, which is his subject matter, compels him to attend to it; technique is
the only means he has of discovering, exploring, developing his subject, of
conveying its meaning, and, finally, of evaluating it.

The epistolary form, it would seem, which has often been regarded as at
best a cumbrous eccentricity, was for Richardson the literary mode which
"compelled him to attend to his subject," his experience. I would not
argue that he also evaluated it, at least in *Pamela*, because one of the
disadvantages of the letter form is that it makes it very easy for the
author to identify himself completely with the letter-writer and forget
everything else. But it is probably out of this completeness of identifica-

---

[1] Mark Schorer, "Technique as Discovery," *Hudson Review* 1:1 (1947), 67-87.

tion that there arises the main importance of *Pamela* in the tradition of the novel.

## III

I have suggested that Pamela is hardly, if at all, aware of the discrepancies between her ethical and religious ideals on the one hand, and the direction of her other impulses and actions on the other. This is as much as to say that, in a strict sense, she has no ego, that her personality has not matured to the point that there is a reasonably stable and controlling center which understands and adjusts the contradictory claims of the conscience and the emotions. This unformed fluidity of character is what makes her so revealing a recorder of the messages of her own inner life; she floats freely in the sea of circumstance, reacting to each random impulse of superego or libido. Even when she has every reason to fear rape, she continues to work on Mr. B.'s waistcoat: it is her job, she is good at it, she would still like to please Mr. B.; it is the only way, given her circumstances, that she can express her love. Critics, of course, have mocked the professed purity of her motives in staying so long in his house, but this is surely because they expect a higher degree of self-awareness and a more complete control of the total personality over its divergent impulses than can really be expected in a fifteen-year-old girl, especially given the rigid kind of ethical and religious formation that puritanism has given Pamela. With so rigid a superego, how can we be surprised that, like so many other people, she seems to live on the unstated premise: "How could I say what I ought if I let myself know what part of me thinks?"

In this subjection to the world of impulse, *Pamela* seems to me to be a precursor both of much that is best and much that is worst in the tradition of the novel. At its best, the novel can show human beings in the process of development in a way that other literary forms cannot. In a sense, Emma Woodhouse and David Copperfield, Stephen Dedalus and Paul Morel also portray the egos of young protagonists gradually learning to relate dissonant impulses to each other, to circumstance, and to the people they meet. And this is probably why it is that in the novel there has been so much emphasis on the distinction between round and flat characters. Compared to drama or epic, the novel has tended to choose young protagonists whose developing reactions to ordinary human life are interesting precisely because they embody the psychological drama whereby the ego is formed. Once formed, surely, such characters, like Pamela in the second two volumes, will become flat. Only if they are involved in great events—such as befall Ulysses, say, or Macbeth—are fully formed characters likely to interest us as much. To adapt Freud, the greatest single subject of the novel is to show how where superego and libido were, there ego shall be.

But will it? For *Pamela* also inaugurates a new version of the age-old fantasy of wish fulfillment, and one of the reasons for *Pamela*'s influence in the tradition of popular romantic fiction is that its epistolary technique made possible a more complete identification between heroine and reader than in previous literary forms. One of the conditions for this identification probably is the very absence of the defined and stable personality in the heroine. As readers we are surely more alike in our wishes than in ourselves; so it is the very absence of defining characteristics that would exclude us from full participation in Pamela's psyche which makes it possible to achieve the supreme objective of mass art, that total (and sickening) collusion of two "I's," the hero's and the audience's, as they jointly throw down the gauntlet to reality—and triumph.

I have pursued these speculations about *Pamela* at some length because it does not seem to me that the problems involved have yet been satisfactorily resolved, either with regard to *Pamela* or with regard to the more theoretical implications. One of the issues raised, though, whether Richardson was aware of what he was creating and of the literary problems entailed by his chosen narrative form, is very easy to answer. For after the anticlimax of the second part of *Pamela*, Richardson went on to write *Clarissa*, which many critics both in his day and ours have placed among the few great masterpieces of the novel.

As early as *Pamela*, Richardson had owned that although he was surprised to discover that he had "so much invention," he was also convinced that he had founded "a new species of writing." It so happens that we have much more copious evidence, mainly in letters, about the rest of Richardson's writing life, so that we know exactly what he thought about all the problems that are raised by *Clarissa* and *Sir Charles Grandison*. Thus to charges that *Clarissa* was going to be too long, as a result of the epistolary method, Richardson replied:

Length will be naturally expected, not only from what has been said, but from the following considerations: That the Letters on both sides are written while the Hearts of the Writers must be supposed to be wholly engaged in their Subjects: The Events at the Time generally dubious: So that they abound, not only with critical Situations; but with what may be called instantaneous Descriptions and Reflections; which may be brought Home to the Breast of the youthful Reader—As also, with affecting Conversations; many of them written in a Dialogue or Dramatic way.

Richardson was equally emphatic on the question of unity and, more significantly for our theme, he also showed that though in *Clarissa*, as in *Pamela*, he normally spoke of his heroine as a model of piety and virtue, he fully realized that perfection would actually be both unreal and uninteresting. One way out of this danger in *Clarissa* was to make his heroine unaware of her love for the licentious Lovelace; and on one occasion, he explained this in terms that can also be applied to *Pamela*:

As to Clarissa's being in downright Love, I must acknowledge that I rather choose to have it imputed to her (his too well-known bad character consider'd) by her penetrating Friend (and then a reader will be ready enough to believe it, the *more* ready, for [Clarissa] not owning it or being blind to it herself), than to think *herself* that she is.

In *Clarissa*, we also have a triumphant demonstration of how to avoid the formal drawbacks of the letter form. There are two sets of correspondences, with the reader looking at the story both through the letters of Clarissa to her friends, and through those of Lovelace to his. More important, the correspondents of the protagonists enable us to have a more stereoscopic vision both of their motives and of their actions, and this stereoscopic vision is applied to the kind of basic problem implicit in *Pamela*: Clarissa unwittingly reveals our tendency to love those we know we should not, and not to act as we know we should to those we do love. In *Clarissa* these basic conflicts, and much else, are expressed in a fictional design of great psychological complexity and uncompromising moral rigor; as was brought home to me in my teaching last spring when I became aware that, for a class of students at the University of East Anglia, *Clarissa* had the most immediate significance and impact. It was not just a question of its historical importance. I had never thought that the identity crisis was new or that it had not always been the unavoidable problem of what used to be called the formative years, but I understand better why there is still a direct appeal in *Pamela* and *Clarissa* for those who can see in Richardson, beyond the narrowness and the prolixity, a profound commitment both to his technique and to what it enabled him to discover about the ambiguities and complexities of how we come to be as we are.

8

## ON READING *JOSEPH ANDREWS*

Most novels pretend to be life and not art; their characters and actions normally claim our attention in much the same way that actual people and real events do; the novelist typically rests his case, like the newspaper or ordinary conversation, on being real rather than true, or at best true only in the sense that witnesses uses the term, rather than philosophers.* As readers of novels, the prevalent assumption goes, all we have to do is to follow, to be immersed, to fall for the fiction; and the only equipment we need bring to the task is sufficient experience of life to be hooked by its imitation.

Of course, good novelists have always expected much more from their readers than an enthusiastic docility of sympathy; in different ways they make an implicit plea that we give their novels a more thoughtful kind of attention, and pause over the work as a whole long enough to take the measure of its offered truth. Since the days of Jane Austen and Stendhal, however, novelists have not made their demand explicitly, told us directly that reading their fiction as art is part of the price of admission. But this is exactly the demand that Fielding makes in *Joseph Andrews*, as we can see from his title page, his preface, and his first chapter. For us today to begin to understand the terms of Fielding's demand, we must imagine ourselves in the situation of his original audience, faced by what he calls a "kind of writing . . . not . . . hitherto attempted in our language"; we must remember that *Joseph Andrews* appeared in

---

* Ian Watt's "On Reading Joseph Andrews" originally appeared as the Afterword to Henry Fielding's *The History of the Adventures of Joseph Andrews* (New York: Harper & Row, 1966), and is reprinted by permission of HarperCollins Publishers.

1742, before there were any novels; or at least only one, Richardson's *Pamela*.

*Pamela* was published in 1740. As everybody has heard, it is about a poor young servant girl called Pamela Andrews who steadfastly resists her master's various attempts to seduce her—the understatement becomes increasingly glaring as the novel progresses. Eventually, however, Pamela's virtue is rewarded, and she marries her master, Squire B—. How far this summary, or even the usual treatment of *Pamela* in the literary histories, is unjust to Richardson, need not detain us here; what matters is that Fielding was outraged both by the book and by its phenomenal success. He first wrote an outrageously funny, acute, and bawdy burlesque of it, in which Richardson's virtuous female innocent was turned into a designing trollop called Shamela, while her incredibly inept would-be rapist was dubbed Squire Booby, and treated accordingly. *Shamela* was no more than a pamphlet; but less than a year later Fielding returned to the subject in a much longer work whose title alone, *Joseph Andrews*, would certainly have reminded his readers of Richardson's *Pamela*. In two ways. First, of course, the surname prepares us to meet the famous Pamela's brother—and indeed, Pamela herself later on; and second, the Christian name Joseph, given, as Fielding tells us, "for good reason," recalls Joseph's namesake in Genesis, whose resistance to the adulterous enticements of Potiphar's wife (chapter 39) makes him the most conspicuous, and, unless memory fails, the only, exemplar of male chastity among the Old Testament heroes.

After *The History of the Adventures of Joseph Andrews* Fielding's full title goes on *And of his Friend Mr. Abraham Adams, Written in Imitation of the Manner of Cervantes, Author of Don Quixote*. Here we have two further literary cross-references. To begin with, Mr. Abraham Adams bears the names first of the Old Testament patriarch, and then of his and our ultimate ancestor, the father of all mankind. It is the parallel with Cervantes, however, that is stated explicitly. The parallel has many aspects. Most obviously, Parson Adams, as Fielding's presumable equivalent of Don Quixote, is to become the dominant character in the novel, despite the priority allotted to Joseph Andrews in the title. More generally, the multifarious chance contacts of the two travelers on the roads and in the taverns become, in Fielding as in Cervantes, a way of mirroring the full range of the world's selfishness, brutality, and stupidity. Cervantes also provides Fielding with a literary model for counterpointing the narrative episodes with a miscellany of droll conversations, interpolated stories, and direct authorial comments, so that the activities of the fictional characters are placed against a much wider background, which includes the history, the literature, and the philosophy of the past. There are many other parallels between Fielding and Cervantes, and there are importance differences; but they are perhaps of less importance to the modern reader, who is, for instance, not likely to find any significant resemblance between Joseph Andrews and Sancho Panza except that they are servants; nor, more important, can the reader fail to notice that unlike Don Quixote, Parson Adams is not mad, and that his goodness, learning, and Christian devotion, however impercipiently and imprudently applied, receive Fielding's emphatic endorsement, as we are told at the end of the "Author's Preface."

This Preface is the first, and perhaps the most famous, critical statement in the history of the English novel. Its main concern is to relate past literary traditions to Fielding's particular intentions in *Joseph Andrews*. It was natural that Fielding should wish to clear his novel from any parallel with two established literary genres—romance and burlesque. The chivalric romances which Cervantes had mocked, and even more the heroic romances of seventeenth-century France, were so sprawling, unreal, and extravagant that they had brought the whole notion of prose fiction into ill-repute; if the new species of fiction was to receive a fair hearing it had first to disassociate itself completely from its earlier forms.

Burlesque raised a quite different issue. Travesty, mock-heroic, and burlesque, from Butler's *Hudibras* to Pope's *Rape of the Lock*, had been favorite literary forms among the Augustans, and Fielding himself had triumphed in them, notably in his play *Tom Thumb the Great*, and in *Shamela*. But burlesque made the development of any serious extended narrative very difficult, because if the reader was always feeling he should focus on the literary parallel being mocked, he could hardly give consistent attention to the primary narration; and the novel, after all, required that the author establish for his reader a reliable and responsible relationship between his fictional world and the real one. Fielding therefore abjured burlesque at least as regards "sentiments and characters," and confined himself to "the just imitation of nature."

To a classically educated writer in the eighteenth century, however, the notion of imitating nature in the sense of directly reporting human life without regard for established literary forms and techniques, would, if conceivable, have seemed crassly wrongheaded. Fielding thus needed to find what established literary modes would provide him with appropriate literary precedents and perspectives for his new enterprise; and from this imperative there came the celebrated theory of the comic epic in prose.

The formula was not wholly new, and it is not in itself very complicated; but its application to *Joseph Andrews* raises several problems. We can recognize the operation of the epic analogy easily enough; it applies very largely to the burlesque imitations of epic diction, as in Fielding's descriptions of the dawn or the inflated heroic rhetoric of Lady Booby; and there is also some guying of traditional epic motifs, such as the description in the second chapter of Joseph's genealogy and of his miraculous boyhood feats. Since the parallel is used mainly to burlesque the more superficial aspects of the epic, however, and since the use of prose is fairly obvious, the operative emphasis in Fielding's formula lies on the word "comic."

The general implications of the term would have been both familiar and unquestioned for an eighteenth-century reader. Everyone assumed, to use Fielding's phrase, that the plot and incidents of comedy should be "light and ridiculous"; that its characters should be "of inferior rank . . . and manners"; and that its aim was to correct human weaknesses through ridicule. The main difficulty lay in what application to give to the term "ridiculous"; and Fielding's two assertions, that "the only source of the true Ridiculous . . . is affectation," and that "affectation proceeds from any one of these two causes, vanity or hypocrisy," are neither wholly satisfactory in themselves, nor unambiguously applicable to all the elements in *Joseph Andrews*. One difficulty is that the word "ridiculous," while logically denoting everything that we laugh at, usually has the more restricted and contemptuous connotation of "that which excites *derisive* laughter." Fielding, accepting the implications of this narrower meaning, decides that the proper comic target can only be those aspects of human behavior which are "affected" or "put on," and are therefore, according to classical theory at least, capable of amendment when mocked by the satirist.

In the eighteenth century the word "affectation" had a somewhat wider sense than the normal modern meaning of "some obtrusive and intentional artificiality of speech or manner"; to "affect something" had originally meant to want or aim at it; and so in Fielding "affectation" covers the whole range of roles and attitudes where people consciously or unconsciously set out to be something other than their real, honest, proper, or natural selves. This wider sense makes possible Fielding's subdivision of affectation into vanity—overestimating one's actual merits—and hypocrisy—pretending to a virtue one doesn't have. Even so, the attempt to be schematic does seem to lead Fielding to impose unnecessarily narrow limits on his subject matter. One can see why the comic writer should not portray serious vices, since they oughtn't to be laughed at, and can hardly be reformed by satiric ridicule; but it is obvious that the traditional comic or satiric theory must interfere with Fielding's larger aim—to present a "just imitation of nature"; and though Fielding confesses this, admitting that "it is very difficult to pursue a series of human actions, and keep clear from" worse evils than affectation, his Preface does not wholly resolve the contradiction.

There is also another kind of restriction involved in Fielding's theory of the comic novel: if its subject is the ridiculous, it does not cover the many cases where we laugh *with*, rather than *at* the characters. For instance, we smile with melancholy sympathy at Parson Adams's perpetual innocence in assuming that people are more unselfish and truthful than they really are, but we would call his behavior humorous rather than ridiculous; Fielding's theory seems to have no place for the kind of laughter which is one of his supreme gifts, or for the creation of characters who are humorous rather ridiculous, notably Parson Adams. One could take Adams's pride in his classical or medical learning as being an example of affectation, of vanity; but it would probably be wrong to make too much of this and place Parson Adams among the characters who are being satirized; after all, Adams has real learning, and his enthusiasm for it is not an affectation; while his exceptional virtues and our admiring sympathy surely place him outside the range of Fielding's corrective theory of satiric comedy.

There are, of course, other and larger senses in which *Joseph Andrews* is a comic novel. Fielding had spent the earliest years of his literary career in writing comedies and farces for the theater, and in *Joseph Andrews* he develops his narrative largely through a succession of scenes which we can easily imagine on the stage. The attempted seduction of Joseph by Lady Booby (I, v), with its classic dramatic pattern of a piquant and artfully prolonged misunderstanding, is only the first of countless scenes which remind us of stage comedy, largely because their conflicts and misunderstandings and duplicities are usually broader and more pointed than those we normally encounter outside the theater. If we compare these scenes in *Joseph Andrews* with the kind of narrative the novel has since accustomed us to, we find that Fielding, unlike most novelists, is much more interested in exploiting the comic possibilities of the repetition and elaboration of a few stock themes than in the progressive development of character, and of actions which are the outcome of character.

Fielding's preference, of course, controls the way in which he portrays character. Comedy normally presents its actors from the outside rather than from the inside, and for two reasons. The very rapidity on which comic effect depends means that there is no space available to tell us just what the protagonists thought and felt at the time; and secondly, both our sympathy with the characters, and our sense of the reality of what happens to them, must be kept within definite limits because we wouldn't enjoy the comedian's falling flat on his face if we thought it hurt him as much as a real fall would hurt us. Thus Fielding's comic distancing in *Joseph Andrews* keeps us, for example, from taking the pains and dangers of Parson Adams too seriously; not so much because we notice that he is strong, brave, and irrepressible, but because we know that he is clad in the ultimate invulnerability to punishment that protects all the sympathetic inhabitants of the magic world of comedy.

Fielding's mainly external way of presenting character and action is, then, typical of comedy but diametrically opposed to the usual kind of psychological presentation to which the novel has accustomed us. This, of course, does not mean that Fielding lacks psychological understanding, but only that he conceives of it in quite different terms from ours. As a psychologist he begins, not with the individual case, but with a notion, based on past observation, of the main tendencies in human motivation; and as a novelist he thinks his task is not so much to create fully individualized characters as to provide illustrative character-types and exemplifying episodes for his previously established generalizations about individual, social, and occupational psychology. Thus he hopes that the reader will pause and see, for instance, that although we meet many innkeepers and their wives in *Joseph Andrews*, even the last one to be introduced, the landlady of the New Inn (III, iv), though quite different from all others, is equally characteristic of her profession and her sex. Similarly Fielding draws the attention of the "judicious reader" (I, vii) to how he has "greatly laboured to describe, the different operations of this passion of love in the gentle and cultivated mind of Lady Booby, from those which it effected in the less polished and coarser disposition of Mrs. Slipslop."

When, finally, we pass from Fielding's Preface to the main body of the novel, our attention is caught by the division into books and chapters. The divisions themselves are a token that in *Joseph Andrews* the reader is to be given, not an amorphous slice of life, but a narrative that, following the precedent of epic and of most classical works (and contrary to that set by Defoe and Richardson), has been arranged and framed into a regular pattern, a formal order. That this formal order is not exclusively narrative we can see from the way that each book begins with a chapter of general literary and critical commentary, an obtrusive intermission of the story which shows that Fielding, unlike most later novelists, is making no effort to hide himself; that he is offering, not the pleasures of make-believe, but the satisfactions involved in the recognition of the operations of intelligence and art. The critical chapters are our guides to this satisfaction; and so, hardly less explicitly, are the chapter headings themselves. Their ironic attitude to the narrative that they categorize is yet another device for distancing the events of the novel, for insisting that its fictional content is not something that, like life, proceeds autonomously under its own momentum; the novel is, rather, under the control of the author, who asks not so much that we believe in what he is telling us, but that we notice what he is doing with it. Here, of course, the critical chapters and the chapter headings are only the most conspicuous manifestations of the intrusive commenting narrator who pervades *Joseph Andrews* as a whole; a narrator who is facetious and philosophic by turns, never committing himself completely to any position, always obstinately independent and predictable only in the omnipresence of his voice.

So much, very summarily, for some of the main literary assumptions on which *Joseph Andrews* is based. They combine to produce a work which yields greatest rewards if it is read in a special way; not so much as one reads most novels, but rather as one listens to music, and listens in the sense, not that our ears are carried along by the sound, but that our mind attends to the total pattern that is being evolved. In music we must consciously recall an earlier theme if we are to observe the current variation on it, and if the recapitulation of one melody has heightened our expectation that its companion will shortly appear, our satisfaction will be increased when it does.

In *Joseph Andrews*, as in music, repetition and variation are the key to the narrative development. For instance, the first scenes in the book show the parallel efforts of Lady Booby and her waiting woman, Mrs.

Slipslop, to overcome Joseph's virtue; then both of these ineffectual efforts at seduction are repeated almost immediately in somewhat different keys; and finally Joseph is dismissed. Later, the first book is brought to a close with another double-seduction sequence, when the chambermaid Betty, having been repulsed in her amorous assault upon Joseph, yields in turn to the importunities of Mr. Tow-wouse. Here we have repetition of the opening theme with significant variation. Betty is honest, generous, and accommodating; she thus offers a pointed contrast to the hypocrisy and selfishness of Lady Booby and Mrs. Slipslop, while her being unfairly turned out of the house establishes a parallel with Joseph: feminine hypocrisy metes out similar punishments to chastity and unchastity alike. The double-seduction theme with which Book I opens and closes is recapitulated in the last book. During the "curious night-adventures" of chapter 14 Beau Didapper makes the last of his attempts on Fanny's virtue, but mistakes the room and instead barely escapes from the lustful embrace of Mrs. Slipslop. Here the repetition has two significant differences: first, it ends the various unsuccessful attempts on Fanny's virtue which have occupied the later part of the novel, as those on Joseph's do in the earlier part, and thus shows us that the lovers have finally completed their parallel probations; and second, the scene ends with the crowning irony that, in the confusion succeeding his rescue of Didapper from Slipslop's grip, Parson Adams symbolically succeeds where others have failed and—in innocent obliviousness—spends the rest of the night in Fanny's bed.

The counterpoint of character, action, and meaning in *Joseph Andrews*, then, demands a somewhat different sort of attention from that which most novels exact; and once we are attuned to Fielding's characteristic methods we will no longer be outraged even by his most blatant divergences from the conventions of modern realistic fiction. We will, for instance, recognize that even the long interpolated stories of Leonora and of Mr. Wilson can be defended not only as sanctioned by epic and Cervantic precedent, but also as consistent developments of Fielding's major themes—chastity and unwary youth, education and the corruptions of the fashionable world, the virtues of the country and the vices of the city. In any case, since Fielding as commentator has priority of status in *Joseph Andrews*, he is not really changing his basic narrative approach when he introduces a new set of players in the middle of his comedy. Even Fielding's often-criticized means of removing the final impediment to the marriage of Joseph and Fanny through the disclosure that Joseph's left breast is ornamented by "as fine a strawberry as ever grew in a garden," is peculiarly appropriate to the circumstances. Fielding could not honestly pretend that in real life difficulties are normally resolved so easily—footmen don't often turn out to be gentlemen merely to make the course of true love run smooth; an ostentatiously unrealistic resolution is therefore, as Fielding says, "a perfect solution," and one wholly consistent with the conventions of artificial comedy, which often uses a striking but implausible recognition scene to bring about the denouement. Further, Joseph's birthmark, which is itself appropriately bucolic and festive in nature, also brings Mr. and Mrs. Wilson out of the limbo of their interpolated story on to the main stage where, as opposite numbers to Gaffar and Gammar Andrews, they can play their part in the jollities of the wedding finale.

Yet, when all is said about what is idiosyncratic in the form of *Joseph Andrews*, it is also a novel; it is mimetic in a way that music is not; and from Fielding's time to ours all kinds of readers, whatever their degree of awareness as regards Fielding's special literary intentions, have found in *Joseph Andrews* a vital and congenial representation of the realities of many kinds of experience. Although, among other things, *Joseph Andrews* is probably the most attractive introduction to the world of eighteenth-century England, it is not just a period piece; for it continues to demonstrate the most tattered of literary truisms, that what has life, lives.

# 9

# THE COMIC SYNTAX OF *TRISTRAM SHANDY*

Laurence Sterne received no notice in the annual bibliography of the *Philological Quarterly* for 1953.* Since then there has been a rapid increase in published studies, but there are, as yet, few signs of converging perspectives in our view of *Tristram Shandy*. There are, of course, many things that recent studies have enabled us to see more clearly—its philosophical and literary traditions, the details of sources or of characterization; but these approaches hardly resolve the elementary problems which the reader faces as he tries to come to grips with the text. One of these problems, which persists even after many readings, concerns the unity of *Tristram Shandy*. A good deal has been done to demonstrate unity of plot and character, using the criteria that are traditional in dealing with the novel; what follows explores a very different, though not necessarily contradictory, approach to the problem.[1]

---

* "The Comic Syntax of *Tristram Shandy*" appeared originally in *Studies in Criticism and Aesthetics, 1600-1800: Essays in Honor of Samuel Holt Monk*, ed. Howard Anderson and John S. Shea (Minneapolis: University of Minnesota Press, 1967), and is reprinted by permission of the University of Minnesota Press. Parts of this essay are from Ian Watt's introduction to the Riverside Edition of *Tristram Shandy* (Boston: Houghton Mifflin, 1965). [Ed.]

[1] See, for example and in addition to works cited later, Robert Curtis Brown, "Laurence Sterne and Virginia Woolf: A Study in Literary Continuity," *University of Kansas Review*, 26 (1959), 153-59; Sigurd Burckhart, "*Tristram Shandy*'s Law of Gravity," *English Literary History*, 28 (1961), 70-88; Henri Fluchère, *Laurence Sterne, de L'Homme à l'Oeuvre* (Paris: Gallimard, 1961); Charles Parrish, "The Nature of Mr. Tristram Shandy, Author," *Boston University Studies in English* 5 (1961), 74-90; W. B. Piper, "*Tristram Shandy*'s Digressive Artistry," *Studies in English Literature* 1 (1961), 65-76; J. M. Stedmond,

We can probably recognize a passage taken at random from *Tristram Shandy* more quickly than one from any other book. The tone, the style, the attitude toward the reader, and the events, all are quite special; and they don't vary substantially from page to page or from beginning to end. One thing that is consistent in *Tristram Shandy* is its narrative voice.

Consider, for example, the opening paragraph:

I wish either my father or my mother, or indeed both of them, as they were in duty both equally bound to it, had minded what they were about when they begot me; had they duly considered how much depended upon what they were then doing;—that not only the production of a rational Being was concerned in it, but that possibly the happy formation and temperature of his body, perhaps his genius and the very cast of his mind;—and, for aught they knew to the contrary, even the fortunes of his whole house might take their turn from the humours and dispositions which were then upper-most;—Had they duly weighed and considered all this, and proceeded ac-cordingly,—I am verily persuaded I should have made quite a different fig-ure in the world, from that in which the reader is likely to see me. (I, i)

Taking notice of the promise of the title, we see that in a sense we are getting what we expect in this first chapter—the hero's begetting. It is whimsically done, to be sure, if only because we are unaccustomed to thinking about this particular action from the point of view of the end product; but after all, we may reflect, the author is only taking the con-ventions of autobiographical fiction with unprecedented literalness, and, with a vengeance, beginning at the beginning. Such a view of the text, which would still see it primarily as a novel, would continue to find some support from the ostensive narrative subject of the next six books; they proceed from Tristram's conception to his parturition, bap-

---

"Genre and *Tristram Shandy*," Philological Quarterly 38 (1959), 37-51; "Style and *Tristram Shandy*," *Modern Language Quarterly* 20 (1959), 243-51; and "Satire and *Tristram Shandy*," *Studies in English Literature* 1 (1961), 53-63; Gerald Weales, "*Tristram Shandy*'s Anti-Book" in *Twelve Original Essays on Great English Novels,* ed. Charles Shapiro (Detroit: Wayne State University Press, 1960). The James A. Work edition of *Tristram Shandy* (New York: Odys-sey Press, 1940) has been used throughout. [For a recent treatment of *Tristram Shandy* with references to Ian Watt's work on Sterne, see Carlo Ginzburg, "A Search for Origins: Rereading *Tristram Shandy*," in his *No Island Is an Island: Four Glances at English Literature in a World Perspective* (New York: Colum-bia University Press, 2000), pp. 43-67—Ed.]

tism, and breeching. But, of course, Sterne's main interest doesn't really lie with the traumatic consequences of these no doubt important events in his hero's life, as we can see from the way that none of them plays any part later except as a topic of jest, and, more important, that virtually nothing else about Tristram's life emerges.

At this point, if not before, we must take account of Sterne's epigraph, from Epictetus: "It is not things themselves that disturb men, but their judgments about these things." What matters, Sterne is telling us, is not particular actions, but the reflective consideration of them in the judging mind. In the passage quoted, for instance, even the grammar makes the action subordinate to reflection about it: we have to get through the first two lines—"I wish either my father or my mother, or indeed both of them, as they were in duty both equally bound to it, had minded what they were about"—before we know the cause of the speaker's impatience; and when it is specified it comes in a subordinate clause: "when they begot me."

There is a further departure from the usual fictional emphasis on narrative event when Tristram proceeds:

—Believe me, good folks, this is not so inconsiderable a thing as many of you may think it;—you have all, I dare say, heard of the animal spirits, as how they are transfused from father to son, etc. etc.—and a great deal to that purpose:—Well, you may take my word, that nine parts in ten of a man's sense or his nonsense, his successes and miscarriages in this world depend upon their motions and activity, and the different tracts and trains you put them into, so that when they are once set a-going, whether right or wrong, 'tis not a halfpenny matter,—away they go cluttering like hey-go mad; and by treading the same steps over and over again, they presently make a road of it, as plain and as smooth as a garden-walk, which, when they are once used to, the Devil himself sometimes shall not be able to drive them off it. (I, i)

Here Tristram seems to be thinking less of the event than of his auditors as he anticipates their derisive incredulity that, even after some forty years, he should still be so disgruntled at the thought of parental irresponsibility. "Believe me, good folks, this is not so inconsiderable a thing as many of you may think it;—you have all, I dare say, heard of the animal spirits." "And if you haven't, you peasants, cringe," implies Tristram's lofty "I dare say"; and the paragraph continues to focus our attention so completely on Tristram's present claim on our commisera-

tion and on the dangers of not granting it that we have almost forgotten
Mr. and Mrs. Shandy.

They reappear for the final brief paragraph of the first chapter, but in
a way that continues their subordination to Tristram's directing mind in
at least three respects:

*Pray, my Dear, quoth my mother, have you not forgot to wind up the
clock?* Good G__! cried my father, making an exclamation, but taking care
to moderate his voice at the same time,—*Did ever a woman, since the creation of the world, interrupt a man with such a silly question?* Pray, what
was your father saying?—Nothing. (I, i)

Again, the narrative event is merely an occasion for talking. This
time, however, the talk isn't soliloquy but conversation: first, conversation between the characters; and second, between the narrator and his
audience. It's out of the combination of these two elements that the
humor and suspense of the chapter arise; and these in turn ultimately
depend upon Tristram's presence, more specifically on his withholding
from his audience the narrative information required to understand the
scene until it is needed for his comic climax: obviously all the connubial
converse about the clock, and Tristram's reflections about it, remain
fairly obscure until the reader's oscillation between bewilderment and
understanding is finally resolved through Tristram's answer to the question interposed by his imaginary reader. "'Pray, what was your father
saying?'"—"'Nothing.'"

The design of the first chapter as a whole, then, reveals that Tristram's primary emphasis is rhetorical rather than narrative; we have to
wait another three chapters before we fully understand Mrs. Shandy's
question about winding the clock, but the chapter has perfect formal
completeness in its own rhetorical terms, since the reader's questions in
the first paragraph begin to be answered in the second, and are fully
disposed of by the final clinching implication of the word "Nothing."
Narrative as such is not autonomous or primary; it is merely the initial
fictional pretext for a complex pattern of conversations: conversation
between characters, in the first place; and, more important, conversation
between Tristram and his readers. It is essentially the completion of this
interplay, rather than that of a narrative episode, which determines
Sterne's organization of his basic compositional unit, the chapter.

As we go on, indeed, it becomes apparent that the same rhetorical
imperatives govern the interrelationship between chapters. Thus if we

turn to the climax of the other main plot of *Tristram Shandy*, the court-ship of Uncle Toby and the Widow Wadman in the last two books, we find exactly the same subordination of narrative development to the autonomous demands of rhetorical effect. In Book VIII, for example, when, at long last, the Widow Wadman trains upon Uncle Toby the full firepower of her amorous eye, under the pretense that there's a speck of dirt in it which he must remove: "—I am half distracted, Captain *Shandy*, said Mrs. *Wadman*, holding up her cambric handkerchief to her left eye, as she approached the door of my Uncle *Toby's* sentry-box—a mote—or sand—or something—I know not what, has got into this eye of mine—do look into it—it is not in the white—" (VIII, xxiv)

Up to now this is straightforward comic narrative, but there follows a long commentary by Tristram, who concludes Chapter 24 with the ad-juration: "If thou lookest, uncle *Toby*, in search of this mote one mo-ment longer—thou art undone."

In Chapter 25, after Tristram's long military simile, "An eye is for all the world exactly like a cannon," has reminded us of the parallel between the wars of love and those of Uncle Toby, we are finally taken back to the fictional scene:

I protest, Madam, said my uncle *Toby*, I can see nothing whatever in your eye.

It is not in the white; said Mrs. *Wadman*: my uncle *Toby* looked with might and main into the pupil—

Once again the comedy of misunderstanding is interrupted by the narrator's bravura description of the eye's message, and the chapter ends when he finally interrupts himself with the reflection: "But I shall be in love with it myself, if I say another word about it.—It did my un-cle *Toby's* business."

That the interlocking of chapters is conceived primarily in rhetorical rather than fictional terms is clear enough: here a single narrative inci-dent is related in two separate chapters, each with a parallel composi-tional structure, emphasized by the choric repetition of their closing phrase: "thou art un*done*"; and, "It *did* my uncle Toby's business."

The narrative event—Toby's falling in love—is a momentous one that has long been heralded; but Tristram does not use it for a full descrip-tive or psychological presentation of the event in it own right. Of the three main comic climaxes, for instance, only one, Mrs. Wadman's repe-tition of "It is not in the white," belongs within the fictional framework;

the other two depend either on byplay with an imaginary reader—"it was not, Madam, a rolling eye"—or on Tristram's sudden transition from his own imaginary reaction to the widow's left eye to his confidential anticipation of poor Toby's doom: "It did my uncle Toby's business."

The structure of Sterne's larger compositional units, then, is based on the rhetorical patterns arising out of the complex tripartite pattern of conversation between the narrator, his fictional characters, and his auditors. Exactly the same can be said of the smaller compositional units, from the clause to the paragraph; *Tristram Shandy* has at least one kind of unity, unity of style; and behind the style there is, of course, the man and his view of life.

"Writing, when properly managed, (as you may be sure I think mine is) is but a different name for conversation," Tristram himself tells us. His prose reflects the brilliance and ease of a great age of conversation whose most splendid historical record is Boswell's *Life of Johnson*. Sterne's style retains some elements of the careful parallelism and balance of sound, syntax, and meaning that we think of as typical of the Augustans. In the opening sentence, for instance, there is the balanced pattern of consonantal stops, "b," "d," and "t," which gives a certain sense of order to the petulant impression of the sounds themselves: "I wish either *my father* or *my mother*, or indeed *both* of *them*, as *they* were in *duty both* equally *bound* to it, had *minded* what they were *about* when they *begot* me. . . . " The symmetry, however, is largely concealed by the tone of conversational abandon, most evident in the colloquialism ("minded what they were about"); the reader at once feels that he is being directly addressed in an easy and unbuttoned way, and that the units of meaning are being strung together in the most spontaneous way.

The most obvious indication of this conversational style is the punctuation, and especially the use of the dash. In the short chapter about Widow Wadman's eye (VIII, xxv), for example, there are more dashes— eighteen—than any other mark of punctuation; and even though the proportion is rarely as high elsewhere, there must be very few pages of *Tristram Shandy* which do not have many more dashes than is usual in any but the most amateurish writing.

The reasons for this great reliance on the dash go deep into the nature of Sterne's creative strategy. The dash is virtually proscribed in expository prose, presumably because it flouts the standard requirement that the verbal components of a sentence should be articulated into a coherent syntactical structure, a structure in which the subordination and superordination of all the parts should express the unity and direction of the sentence as a whole. Sterne's affront to conventional syntax is essential to establishing the qualities he required for Tristram's voice; Sterne didn't want unity or coherence or defined direction, at least in any conventional sense; he wanted multiplicity, not unity; he wanted free association of ideas, not subordination of them; he wanted to go backwards or forwards or sideways, not in straight linear paths.

We are, of course, quite used to these kinds of discontinuity in ordinary colloquial conversation. In the Widow Wadman's speech, for instance ("A mote—or sand—or something—I know not what, has got into this eye of mine—do look into it—it is not in the white") the dash is used as much to mark pauses as anything else; whatever meaning may be left obscure by the syntax is clarified by the implied situations and gestures; and it is the dashes that force the reader to imagine them. Elsewhere the dash is used merely for aggregating units, as in the dazzling series of descriptive phrases about the Widow Wadman's left eye; and here we observe the usefulness of the dash in Sterne's characteristic exploitation of the rhetorical expectations aroused by any extended verbal series. But the most important strategic function of the dash, both in these passages and in general, is to serve Tristram as a nonlogical junction between different kinds of discourse: between past and present; between narrative event and authorial address to the reader; between one train of thought and another in Tristram's mind.

Sterne needed a much looser and less directed junction between units of meaning than normal syntax allows, for his psychology, for his narrative mode, for his manipulation of the reader, and for expressing his view of life. Dashes were invaluable for enacting the drama of inhibited impulse, of the sudden interruptions and oscillations of thought and feeling, which characterize Tristram both as a person and as a narrator. One obvious example of the latter occurs when there is an abrupt and unheralded shift in the point of view of the narration. Consider, for example, in the chapter cited above, the passage where the narrator comments: "there never was an eye of them all, so fitted to rob my uncle *Toby* of his repose, as the very eye, at which he was looking—it was not, Madam, a rolling eye. . . . " Here the dash enables Tristram to turn suddenly from Toby to reprove an imaginary female interlocutor for her licentious ocular deportment. Similarly the rhetorical finality of the close of the chapter depends upon the dash on which hinges Tristram's sudden temporal transition from his own present attitude toward the eye to its devastating effect, nearly two generations ago, on Captain Shandy: "It did my uncle Toby's business."

Tristram's prose style, then, embodies the multiplicity of his narrative point of view; it is idiosyncratic because it serves a unique, and often puzzling, combination of functions. One of these, at least, demands further attention here, since it is both important in itself, and closely related to some of the main differences of interpretation to which *Tristram Shandy* has given rise.

Tristram's voice, as we have seen, is uniquely adapted to rapid transitions, and they are an essential element in his humor. Kant wrote that "laughter arises from the sudden transformation of a strained expectation into nothing"; Sterne is a master at such transformations, undermining the expectation that has been built up by suddenly making Tristram change his point of view. The end of Le Fever's life, for example, offers a famous example: we are at the deathbed:

The blood and spirits of *Le Fever*, which were waxing cold and slow within him, and were retreating to their last citadel, the heart—rallied back,—the film forsook his eyes for a moment,—he looked up wishfully in my uncle Toby's face,—then cast a look upon his boy,—and that *ligament*, fine as it was,—was never broken.—

Nature instantly ebbed again,—the film returned to its place,—the pulse fluttered—stopped—went on—throbbed—stopped again—moved—stopped— shall I go on?—No. [VI, x]

Here, of course, the humor arises out of the abrupt transition from narration to a direct address to the reader, which suddenly relieves the reader just at the moment when his suffering from the pathos of Le Fever's death has become unendurable; and the relief is easily achieved because only a dash is needed to switch us from the world where fiction seems real (as is typical in the novel) to the world where Tristram can jog the reader's elbow to remind him that fiction is, after all, only fiction.

Tristram's attitude to his audience is in part that of the ventriloquist and in part that of the jester. Where he is recounting the actions and dialogues of the Shandy household, multiple impersonation is called for; and Tristram is as expert in vocal mimicry as in the external description of the dialogues between his characters. It is interesting, in this connection, to note Sterne's admiration of the famous Parisian preacher Père Clement, who, he wrote, converted his pulpit into a stage, so that "the variety of his tones [made] you imagine there were no less than five or six actors on it together."[2]

But the main dialogue which Tristram carries on is with the reader; at least half of *Tristram Shandy* is taken up not with narrative but with direct address to the audience by Tristram, often about matters only tangentially related to the story.

For this dialogue, the first need is for Tristram to ensure that his readers never lose themselves so completely in the story that they forget the monologist behind the footlights. One way of reminding the readers of his presence is for Tristram to break down the cold impersonality of print, whose impassive objectivity encourages us in most novels to forget the literary mirror in which the fictional world is reflected. The typographical tricks, the short or blank or misnumbered chapters, the squiggles, the black or marbled pages, the index fingers, though they may not always amuse us, at least serve to remind us that the image reflected in the mirror is less real than the mirror itself: that the mirror, not the reflections in it, has priority of status.

Many of Sterne's other typographical usages also serve to call us back from the show to the showman. Italics, for example, enact the actor's emphasis—the raised voice, the confidential whisper, or the wink; while capitals and Gothic letters supply heavier emphasis for a moral reflection, a scholarly reference, or a tear. Asterisks and blank spaces similarly provoke our active response, and lead us to ask what they stand for, or to supply something for ourselves, whether correctly or not we often don't quite know; they are the graphic equivalents of the figure of aposiopesis—rhetorically intentional hiatus—which Tristram so often employs. Faint but pursuing, we do our best to puzzle out the asterisks and fill up the gaps; and we are occasionally given the ostentatiously grudging reward which the professional stage performer usually bestows on the unfortunate amateur from the audience who has offered his cooperation. For instance, when Walter and Toby have been left halfway down stairs, and Tristram wants to start the next scene with Walter back in bed, he turns to us with patronizing indulgence: "—So then,

---

[2] *Letters of Laurence Sterne*, ed. L. P. Curtis (Oxford: Clarendon Press, 1935), p. 155.

friend! You have got my father and my uncle *Toby* off the stairs, and seen them to bed?—And how did you manage it?—You dropped a curtain at the stair-foot—I thought you had no other way for it—Here's a crown for your trouble." (IV, xiii)

As to the particular roles Tristram assumes in his address to the reader, they are as varied as his moods. He often seeks to excite pathos, but in different ways: as a Shandy baby he invites commiseration for the early catastrophes of his life; his appeal is more deeply felt and less ironic when he shares with us his mature recollections of his father and his uncle; and there are other times when the Shandy story is forgotten and he implores our pity merely as an author who has just been battered by critics and reviewers. But of course pathos is only one of Tristram's moods, and it usually ends with a smile as he asks us: "Pray reach me my fool's cap" and reassumes his favorite pose—the jester's.[3]

As regards his psychological relationship to his audience, Tristram has many tricks for provoking an active and emotionally charged participation, besides his various ways of keeping us guessing. His main gambit is the traditional one of divide and rule. The audience is imagined to comprise various groups of which the most vocal are a miscellaneous collection of unsympathetic auditors against whom, in mere self-defense, Tristram has to mobilize the rest of his hearers. There are the great Lords who demand submission and dedications; there are solemn critics, pedants, Dutch commentators, church dignitaries, and men of civic substance, who are usually addressed with mock deference as "Your Worships" or "Your Reverences." Equally hostile, and even more threatening, are the censorious prudes; always on the lookout for scandal and obscenity, they are usually addressed as "Madam"; and the appellation nearly always serves as a signal to the reader that there is some dubious imputation in the air. The only morally unobjectionable way of drawing our attention to such bawdy, of course, is to deny it with obtrusive indignation. Thus, for instance, when Tristram has mentioned Jenny as "his friend," he at once has "Madam" challenge his description of the relationship:

Friend!—My friend.—Surely, Madam, a friendship between the two sexes may subsist, and be supported without—Fy! Mr. *Shandy*:—Without any

---

[3] See E. N. Dilworth in *The Unsentimental Journey of Laurence Sterne* (New York: Octagon Books, 1948), and A. E. Dyson's brilliant essay "Sterne: The Novelist as Jester," *Critical Quarterly*, 4 (1962), 309-10.

thing, Madam, but that tender and delicious sentiment, which ever mixes in friendship, where there is a difference of sex. Let me intreat you to study the pure and sentimental parts of the best *French* Romances;—It will really, Madam, astonish you to see with what a variety of chaste expressions this delicious sentiment, which I have the honour to speak of, is dressed out. (I, xviii)

In this passage we also have an example of the exploitation of imaginary differences between different parts of the audience; for if there are insufferably dull and hostile characters around, there are also a few close friends, some of them imaginary, like Jenny, others real, like Eugenius and Garrick; and the reader, alarmed at the possibility that he might be numbered among the priggish and the pretentious, strives his utmost to achieve the perfect sympathetic understanding which will allow him to be enrolled in the charmed circle of Mr. Shandy's friends, a circle where, as a bonus, he will be on nodding terms with the great Mr. Pitt, and even join in Tristram's patronizing rejoinders to St. Thomas Aquinas and "Mr. Horace."

Among this ideal audience benevolence and good humor reign; and compelling the reader to adopt this mood was half Sterne's battle in achieving other literary effects. Aristotle pointed out that people don't normally laugh when they are alone, as readers usually are; so it is an essential prerequisite of Sterne's humor that he should create the sense of an active and friendly relation between himself and his audience, especially the unprudish and benevolent members of it; they must be brought to strain every nerve to achieve that *dies praeclarum* when they will be accepted as close friends by Mr. Shandy. For reasons further clarified by a remark in the pseudo-Aristotelian *Problemata*: "Why are people less able to restrain their laughter in the presence of friends? Is it because, when anything is especially elated, it is easier set into motion? Now benevolence causes elation, so that laughter more easily moves us." (950 a. 18)

For Sterne and his readers, benevolence meant, above all, a readiness to shed a sympathetic tear. The Le Fever passage may be taken as an illustration of how the flow of feeling also helps Tristram's humorous designs; it also, of course, raises the oft-mooted question of whether the climactic comic twists Sterne habitually gives to sentimental episodes means that he is really attacking or ridiculing the pathetic and benevolent feelings he so often arouses and indeed seems to applaud.

In the passage about Le Fever's death, for example, reader and author were deeply united in the fellowship of suffering before they pulled back to smile at the unexpected reality which their joint imaginings had momentarily assumed: "Shall I go on?—No." Community in commiseration is a precondition of community in merriment, Sterne seems to affirm. Our age tends to a circumspect gravity as well about life as about literature, which probably makes it difficult to fully appreciate Sterne's attitude. But we must remember that the eighteenth century's growing approval of humor runs exactly parallel to the growth of its cult of sentiment and benevolence. And not only chronologically: Shaftesbury[4] and Hutcheson[5] were the great precursors of both trends; and we can now see that the growing approval of laughter, and of emotional responsiveness in general, may be regarded as parallel manifestations of the dethronement of reason as the primary human faculty.[6]

Sterne's humor, it may be said, largely depends upon the force of this dual exploitation of man's sympathetic and risible faculties. In Restoration comedy, or in Swift and Pope, we think not so much of humor as of wit; behind the epigrammatic brilliance we sense a mocking rejection of the objects satirized; and if emotions are aroused, they are the negative ones—scorn, distrust, hatred. This was in keeping both with Hobbes's view of the aggressive function of laughter, and with the neoclassical critical theory whereby the aim of satire was to mobilize the reader's feelings against illusion, affectation, and vice.

But in *Tristram Shandy* there is no vice; illusion and affectation are there, of course, but they are fantastic, amusing, and even, in their way, necessary: as with Walter and Toby, for instance, they are merely hobbyhorses. It's relevant here to observe that "hobby," in the sense of a favorite pastime, acquired its modern approbative sense only in the nineteenth century; originally it was a hobbyhorse, or an imitation horse, such as was used in the mummers' dance or as a child's toy; so a concern with hobbyhorses in an adult had, to an earlier generation, seemed a frivolous derogation of man's stature as a rational animal. But Sterne welcomed all such toys; he was willing to approve "an uncle

---

[4] In, especially, *Sensus Communis: An Essay on the Freedom of Wit and Humor* (1709).

[5] Francis Hutcheson, *Thoughts on Laughter* (1725-1727).

[6] See Stuart M. Tave, *The Amiable Humorist* (Chicago: University of Chicago Press, 1960).

Toby's siege—or an *any thing*, which a man makes a shift to get a-stride on, to canter it away from the cares and solicitudes of life."

A special stylistic strategy was required to express the coexistence of humor and sentiment, and indeed of a very large diversity of attitudes, in a context that did not impose or imply a rationally ordered hierarchy of values. This can perhaps be best illustrated by comparison. The typical epigram, like the typical sentence, goes in one direction. When the Lincolnshire lady was ill-advised enough to show Dr. Johnson her underground grotto, and then inquired "if he did not think it would be a pretty convenient habitation?", Dr. Johnson retorted: "I think it would, Madam, for a toad." Either you're for houses or you're for grottoes; Johnson's wit directs our attention to the incompatibility between the categories. Sterne's outlook, on the other hand, is much more pluralist, and so is his style. His ostentatiously permissive syntax allows each category its own independent existence; the dash makes no assertion of relation, but allows the sense to flow forwards and backwards between the phrases which it conjoins, very much at the reader's pleasure; the emphasis is up to us, and if there is exclusion, it is we who make it. Tristram, we feel, would have answered the Lincolnshire lady's query so as to leave open all the diverse possibilities on both sides; perhaps by saying "I *think* it would, Madam—for us—or—for a toad."

This sort of intentional leaving of the final evaluative attitude up to the audience is a very common technique in the stage comic; Mort Sahl is only the most extreme example of a style which depends entirely on the unstructured, parenthetic conjunction of diverse propositions and attitudes. At a much more highly controlled and complex level, we get an equally free choice in *Tristram Shandy*. Shakespeare's Yorick was a jester in a tragedy. Sterne's Yorick affirms a more programmatic kind of coexistence: sentiment and humor—and much else—should be regarded, however illogically, as somehow mutually consistent categories; we reject at our peril the exclusive claims either of the heart or of the head, or, for that matter, of the imagination, even if they seem to be in conflict.

At this point it is perhaps worth insisting that this open-ended mode of writing is very different in aim from such modern manipulations of point of view as "interior monologue" or "stream of consciousness." For "stream of consciousness" is normally supposed to be the expression of the unconscious and inarticulate flow of impressions, whereas Tristram is surely highly self-conscious and obtrusively articulate. Sterne would seem to agree with Locke that an unconscious idea is a contradiction in terms,[7] and deals mainly with conscious, and indeed rationally conceptualized, matters. In addition Tristram's thoughts are quite overtly addressed to an audience, whereas stream of consciousness pretends that the reader does not exist. The steam of consciousness, in fact, takes the inner world of the individual character to the extreme limit of subjective realism; while Tristram's rhetoric is largely devoted to subverting the literal reality of fiction so that the reader's attention shall be focused on the reality not of the narrative but of the narrator.

Some critics, it is true, have seen the total of Tristram's reminiscences—that is, the whole book—as constituting a subjective individual portrait, much as Joyce and Proust portray their characters by presenting their inner thoughts. But although there is nothing exactly out of character in Tristram's thoughts, they surely don't seem aimed at indirect character portrayal. Rather, the apparently random association of thoughts in Tristram's discourse surely reflects a comic exploration of the extremely varied possibilities of Locke's view of pathological mental processes. Faced with the observation that "There is scarce any one that does not observe something that seems odd to him, and is in itself really extravagant, in the opinions, reasonings, and actions of other men,"[8] Locke explained that such failures of the human understanding result from the irrational association of ideas.

In the opening passage, we have a classical example of Mrs. Shandy's association of ideas between the dual monthly routines of Mr. Shandy in his timekeeping and his connubial roles. But there is nothing very unconscious about this in the modern sense; Pavlov's dog, had it the gift of tongues, would, under similar circumstances, have echoed Mrs. Shandy's words. In any case Sterne's emphasis is not on exploring the preconscious or unconscious mind of Mrs. Shandy so much as on using a logically inappropriate conjunction of ideas for comic purposes; and these comic purposes depend upon the reader's being keenly alive to the rational and conscious level of discourse from which Mrs. Shandy deviates.

Tristram's voice is by no means an irrational one, but a rational instrument for the revelation of human irrationality. Belonging to the Age of Reason helped Sterne to see and demonstrate that human behavior is not based on reason; in the end Locke had taught him, not so much that

---

[7] *Essay Concerning Human Understanding*, II, i, 1-4.
[8] *Ibid.*, II, xxxiii, 1.

the human mind is a blank tablet, as that philosophical attempts to transcend ordinary human experience end up in a blind alley.

On the other hand, Sterne is as far from the intellectual satire of Swift as he is from the stream of consciousness, because his account of the non rational aspects of human behavior does not condemn them. Sterne is as committed to the realities of the feelings and of the senses as he is to the life of the mind; he doesn't commit himself to the prior claims of reason and order, as wit and satire usually tend to do.

Here we can find abundant support in recent scholarship, in John Traugott's *Tristram Shandy's World* (Berkeley and Los Angeles, 1954) or instance, or in Ernest Tuveson's *The Imagination as a Means of Grace* (Berkeley and Los Angeles, 1960) for seeing *Tristram Shandy* as the most inclusive literary expression of a movement whose greatest philosophical representative is David Hume. Faced by the apparent failure of man to live up to his alleged nature as a rational animal, and forced to be dubious about the probability of success in Locke's effort to tidy matters up, this movement turned its attention to the complexities of actual human behavior and to the mysteries of psychological identification between individuals. Tristram's personal "Essay Concerning Human Understanding" showed that understanding, if it came at all, came not through the rational faculty, nor through ordinary verbal communication, but through the operation of sympathy and imagination—the two faculties which were beginning to replace the traditional duality of passion and reason as the primary elements in man's understanding of his nature. Tristram's voice, if we attend to it, does not merely direct our attention to the traditional subject of comedy—human folly; it also suggests that we must go beyond the premature exclusions to which the rational mind's awareness of irrationality is always prompting us, and enlarge the area of our imaginative sympathy.

Consider, for example, Trim's great harangue on mortality, in which Tristram's directing presence deftly combines humor and pathos, and defies us to reject any of the human inconsistencies involved. Susannah the chambermaid, Jonathan the coachman, Obadiah the outdoor servant, the unnamed cookmaid, and the foolish fat scullion, are all gathered in the kitchen after hearing the news of the death of Bobby, Tristram's elder brother. Jonathan has just remarked that Bobby "was alive last Whitsuntide":

—O *Jonathan*! 'twould make a good-natured man's heart bleed, to consider, continued the corporal (standing perpendicularly), how low many a brave and upright fellow has been laid since that time!—And trust me, *Susy*, added the corporal, turning to *Susannah*, whose eyes were swimming in water,—before that time comes round again,—many a bright-eye will be dim.—*Susannah* placed it to the right side of the page—she wept—but she court'sied too.—Are we not, continued *Trim*, looking still at *Susannah*—are we not like a flower of the field—a tear of pride stole in betwixt every two tears of humiliation—else no tongue could have described *Susannah's* affliction—is not all flesh grass?—'Tis clay,—'tis dirt.—They all looked directly at the scullion,—the scullion had just been scouring a fish-kettle.—It was not fair.—

—What is the finest face that ever man looked at!—I could hear *Trim* talk so for ever, cried *Susannah*,—what is it! (*Susannah* laid her hand upon *Trim's* shoulder)—but corruption?—*Susannah* took it off.

Now I love you for this—and 'tis this delicious mixture within you which makes you dear creatures what you are—and he who hates you for it—all I can say of the matter is—That he has either a pumpkin for his head—or a pippin for his heart,—and whenever he is dissected 'twill be found so. (V, ix)

We find it difficult to decide what are the appropriate criteria for the indeterminate literary genres, the kinds of writing where the total literary structure is an aggregate rather than an organic whole. Formally, as Northrop Frye has suggested,[9] *Tristram Shandy* may be regarded as a hybrid between the novel and the Menippean satire, or, as he prefers to call the genre, an Anatomy, like the works of two of Sterne's great forebears, Rabelais and Burton.

But if we must decide not so much the fictional category, as the primary principle of unity, of *Tristram Shandy*, it must surely be Tristram's voice. Through it Sterne discovered a principle of order which resides not so much in linear development in time as in a kind of timeless consistency of texture; it is this which has primary autonomy, and which controls every narrative element, from the phrase to the paragraph, the chapter, and the book. So, by "the comic syntax of *Tristram Shandy*," I mean only that the syntax, "the orderly or systematic arrangements of parts or elements" as the *Oxford Dictionary* defines it, of *Tristram Shandy*, is essentially a complex but consistent mode of comic speech which unites all its parts and attitudes, loosely no doubt, but with per-

---

[9] *Anatomy of Criticism* (Princeton: Princeton University Press, 1957), pp. 302, 308-12.

fect appropriateness (this mode of speech is perhaps strictly speaking more humorous than comic, but my title defers to the trochaic rhythm of Sterne's). In any case it is this voice which joins the novelistic to the more miscellaneous elements of the book; which unites the pathetic and the laughable, the intellectual and the emotional; and which, above all, engages the author and the reader in so living a conversation that one no longer asks, as one does of a novel, for an ending.

Yeats called art "the social act of a solitary man." Sterne was a solitary; but toward the end of his life he found a way of talking which created its own society. The members of this society, comprising both the fictional characters in the book, its circle of readers, and its narrator, all have a very special literary quality; their voices are attuned to the endless dialogue within, which is so much more inconsequential, indecent, and above all—shall we face it—trivial, than the public dialogues we can hear going on around us, or that we find recorded in most of literature; Sterne's sad recognition of this enabled him to create a mode of speech which compels what he most desired—our acknowledgment of intimate kinship. And once the Shandean laughter has punctured the authorized hyperboles which make it so difficult for us to recognize our real identity, the remembering mind can sometimes go on beyond this to discover in and through Tristram's comic syntax that real feeling and a kind of logic somehow subsist and trace a shadowy coherence upon the muddled and miscellaneous indignities of our personal lot.

# 10

## TIME AND FAMILY IN THE GOTHIC NOVEL:
## *THE CASTLE OF OTRANTO*

Long ago Matthew Arnold,* confronting what Darwin had recently demonstrated to be our common ancestor—"a hairy quadruped furnished with a tail and pointed ears, probably arboreal in his habits"—was moved to wonder how "this good fellow" could ever have "carried in his nature, also, a necessity for Greek."[1] It was even longer ago that an unpromising stripling named Conrad was dashed to pieces by some archaic military hardware in the courtyard of the Castle of Otranto; and even today we still hardly know how it was that this "enormous helmet, a hundred times more large than any casque ever made for human being, and shaded with a proportionable quantity of black feathers"[2] also carried in its nature an evolutionary necessity for Emily Brontë's Heathcliff and Faulkner's Thomas Sutpen.

Two aspects of that necessity are the subject of the present inquiry. What gave *The Castle of Otranto*—at first sight the most sensationally unpretentious novelette that can well be imagined—its power to bring into being a whole new fictional mode that has been characteristic of the last two centuries? What was the essential imaginative matrix which

---

* "Time and Family in the Gothic Novel: *The Castle of Otranto*" appeared originally in *Eighteenth-Century Life* 10:3 (October 1986), 159-71. Copyright 1986. All rights reserved. Reprinted by permission of Duke University Press.
[1] "Literature and Science," *Philistines in England and America*, ed. R. H. Super (Ann Arbor: University of Michigan, 1974), p. 64. The Darwin citation is from *The Descent of Man*, Part III, ch. 21.
[2] Horace Walpole, *The Castle of Otranto: A Gothic Story*, ed. W. S. Lewis (London: Oxford University Press, 1964), p. 17. Later quotations are from this edition.

struck off, not only the nine hundred–odd works that are listed—however dubiously—in Montague Summers's *A Gothic Bibliography* (1941), but also many later novels that are often placed in the Gothic tradition? I will suggest that two elements in that matrix, the function of time and the treatment of the family, provide a set of particular characteristics in the very miscellaneous literary phenomena to which the label "Gothic" is currently applied.

The very word "Gothic" suggests that the genre has got something to do with time. It is hardly too much to say that etymologically the term "Gothic Novel" is an oxymoron for "Old New." When Horace Walpole subtitled *The Castle of Otranto* "A Gothic Story" in the second edition, to him the term "Gothic," as he had already made clear in the original Preface, meant "the darkest ages of Christianity," or, more generally, merely "very old." "Novel," on the other hand, originally meant the "new"; and such were the contemporary subjects of what, in 1764, were beginning to be called novels. Walpole himself was aware that the essential originality of *The Castle of Otranto* depended on this temporal dichotomy of past and present:

> It was an attempt to blend the two kinds of romance, the ancient and the modern. In the former all was imagination and improbability: in the latter, nature is always intended to be, and sometimes has been, copied with success.[3] (p. 7)

A closer scrutiny reveals that the relation of ancient and present time in Walpole's narrative is somewhat more specific and complex in nature; obviously, all the events take place in Gothic times, but that past itself has considerable depth, and the psychological present in which the characters live is only the immediate surface on which the power of a long anterior past is manifested.

The distant pastness of the whole tale is insisted on in Walpole's title-page and Preface. The original Italian version, he asserts, was printed in black letter—what we now call Gothic type—in 1529; but internal evidence points to a much earlier date of composition; and the actual period of the action, we are told, must go further back still, to some time

---

[3] Walpole said much the same thing in a 16 March 1765 letter to Joseph Warton, where he wrote that he wished to "blend the marvellous of old story with the natural of modern novels" (W. S. Lewis, ed., *The Yale Edition of Horace Walpole's Correspondence* [New Haven: Yale University Press, 1937-83], 40: 377). Subsequently cited as *Corr.*

between 1095 and 1243, the dates of the first and last crusades, "or not long afterwards." This defines what we may call the period both of the narrative present of the story and of its anterior past. The events of the plot, in what the reader experiences as the narrative present, take only three days. The action begins on Conrad's fifteenth birthday, which is supposed to be the day of his wedding to Isabella—a wedding which will strengthen the position of his father, Manfred, Prince of Otranto; but it is in fact the day of Conrad's death. From the opening of the temporal sequence is a progression whose intervals are related to calendar time by signals in the narrative—sunset, moonshine, dawn, etc.

The plot, in five chapters like the acts of a tragedy, is equally linear, logical, and concentrated. In the first chapter, Conrad is crushed by the gigantic helmet. Then a handsome young peasant announces that this helmet is "exactly like that on the figure in black marble of Alfonso the Good . . . in the church of St. Nicholas" (p. 18). Almost immediately that particular helmet is reported missing: an ominous coincidence. Meanwhile, Manfred resolves that he must cast aside his wife, Hippolita, and marry Conrad's intended, Isabella. Horrified, Isabella attempts to escape and in her flight through a subterranean passage sees a ghostlike figure who turns out to be the handsome peasant, called Theodore. He tries to help her but in the process is discovered by Manfred, who is on the point of sentencing Theodore to death when the news comes that an armed giant—or at least an awfully big leg and foot—has been seen lying in the long gallery.

The remaining chapters work out these puzzles. The next day Father Jerome, a priest at the convent near the church of St. Nicholas, announces that Isabella has taken sanctuary there. Theodore is once again on the point of being executed when a birthmark on his neck luckily reveals that he is really Father Jerome's son. Then a great procession arrives, with a gigantic sword that is carried by a hundred knights. (This echo of the "hundred times" larger scale of the helmet illustrates Walpole's rough-and-ready use of numbers to indicate the supernatural dimension of his narrative.) The leader of the knights, who remains masked, eventually proves to be Isabella's father, the Marquis of Vicenza. He found the sword in the Holy Land; and on its blade is written

> Wher'er a casque that suits this sword is found,
> With perils is thy daughter compass'd round:
> Alfonso's blood alone can save the maid,
> And quiet a long-restless prince's shade. (p. 79)

We surmise that the matching accessory which "suits this sword" must be the huge casque that landed on Conrad. As to who "alone can save the maid" (presumably Isabella), it must surely be Theodore, who must therefore be of Alfonso's noble blood. As for "quieting" the "long-restless prince's shade" we are given many clues as to what person may own the "shade." The first and most obvious comes very early: "ancient prophecy which was said to have pronounced, 'That the castle and lordship of Otranto should pass from the present family, whenever the real owner should be grown too large to inhabit it'" (pp. 15-16). Manfred has shown no sign of abnormal growth; and so he cannot be "the real owner," and eventually proves to be the grandson of Richard, Alfonso's false chamberlain, who long ago poisoned his master and made himself the owner of Otranto by a forged will. We must, then, wait until someone's shade gets big enough to wear the helmet; that shade, of course, proves to be Alfonso's own. He is literally a shade—a ghost—and when he throws the castle down according to the prophecy, Manfred is frightened into abdicating, and Alfonso's grandson, Theodore, is restored to the rule of his rightful principality.

The essence of *The Castle of Otranto*, then, is the progressive revelation of the secrets of the two family pasts; but its interest for the reader depends not on this in itself—the disclosure of the rather murky genealogies of the descendants of Alfonso and Richard—but on the excitement generated by how the ghostly survivors of the anterior past operate on the affairs of the fictional present, which wholly preoccupies them. Past and present are, it seems, locked together; the living characters are the captives of the past, while the characters of the past—notably Alfonso—live on as spirits only to be their vigilant captors. The anterior past has all the power. Whenever the present generation attempts to avoid its fate, as when Manfred attempts to marry off his son, its effort is wholly ineffectual. The only imperative causality in the life of the present, apparently, is to complete what was done long ago; only when the helmet, sword, armor, and the giant hands and feet are finally reconstituted can Theodore succeed to Otranto, and the perturbed spirit of his ancestor leave its sublunary caves and rise in apotheosis through the clouds to be received into the arms of his patron St. Nicholas.

The history of the word "Gothic" supplies one basic clue to the meaning of the power and the appeal of the past. *The Oxford English Dictionary* informs us that in the sense of medieval, "Gothic" was early used with the pejorative connotation expressed by Dryden: "all that has something of the Ancient gust is called a barbarous or Gothique manner" (1695).[4] Such reprobation continued well into the eighteenth century, partly because no reasonably precise architectural or chronological meaning was as yet attached to "Gothic."[5]

But long before there was any genuine understanding of what we call Gothic architecture, there arose the fashion for imitations of Gothic buildings and ruins. Walpole's own house, Strawberry Hill (begun 1749), was the most celebrated of many early examples; and literature, in Richard Hurd's *Letters on Chivalry and Romance* (1762), for example, reflected a parallel countermovement to the previous prejudice against the barbarism of the Gothic. "Gothic," in Walpole's day, was exchanging the disgrace of being old-fashioned for the distinction of being antique.

The Augustan nostalgia for its antithesis was itself dependent on the new sense that the present was radically separate from the past. That historical awareness began in the Renaissance, which looked back at the classical world through the darkness of the Gothic period; but both the increasing body of historical knowledge (to which Walpole himself made many contributions), and the conscious Augustan effort to follow Roman models, developed historical consciousness much further. Anachronism in Renaissance painting or drama seems unconscious; in Walpole it is a conscious fashion which also reflects his spiritual and aesthetic needs.

The new need for conscious anachronism brings us to the psychological basis of the tension in Gothic between past and present—the individual's awareness of the quotidian dullness of the present and the con-

---

[4] s.v. Gothic, 4.

[5] Renaissance usage, as in Giorgio Vasari (1551), merely connected the term with the *maniera tedesca* of the Goths who had sacked Rome and destroyed the classical orders of architecture. Our less derogatory and more historical classification awaited François Blondel the Younger, who in 1771 established the distinction between *architecture gothique ancienne*—the 6th to the 11th c. (the word "romanesque" wasn't to appear until 1819)—and the *architecture gothique moderne*, from the 12th c. to 1515, the accession of François Premier. In 18th-c. England, although many of his contemporaries made a vague equation between "Gothic" buildings and the Saxon period, Walpole in general equated "Gothic" with the pointed arch and perpendicular ornamentation (Kenneth Clark, *The Gothic Revival* [New York: Holt, 1962], pp. 46-65), although the issue is not raised in *The Castle of Otranto*.

sequent longing for something totally different. This contrast was to lead the rich, and later their humbler imitators,[6] to cover the land with castles and mansions, suburban villas, and country cottages—all in the Gothic manner—and the same contrast was to become a great theme of the Romantic poets. But the spiritual appeal of the Gothic past is already explicit in Walpole. Thus he writes in a letter to George Montagu (5 January 1766):

Visions, you know, have always been my pasture, and so far from growing old enough to quarrel with their emptiness, I almost think there is no wisdom comparable to that of exchanging what is called the realities of life for dreams. Old castles, old pictures, old histories, and the babble of old people make one live back into centuries that cannot disappoint one. (*Corr.*, 10:192)

In earlier ages there had been nothing picturesque about wearing swords or going into gloomy dungeons;[7] their appeal to the imagination depended on a social order based on life insurance rather than carrying swords; on *habeas corpus*, the rule of law and the beginnings of an organized police force. As Thomas Blackwell put it in his contrast between Homeric times and his own: "The marvellous and wonderful is the nerve of the epic strain: but what marvellous things happen in a well-ordered state? We can hardly be surprised."[8] Or Walpole, speaking of the modern novel: "the great resources of fancy have been dammed up, by a strict adherence to common life" (p. 7).

Escaping the milieu of the common life, Walpole's title proclaimed as the chief protagonist in his novel what was to become the most characteristic symbolic element in Gothic fiction generally, the castle. The "dramatized decay" of the ruin, as Kenneth Clark terms it (*Gothic Revival*, p. 30) inspired fascination and awe, and the later part of the century saw ruins become a major preoccupation of art, architecture, and landscape. And in the Gothic novel, the castle becomes connected with

---

[6] As Ernst Fischer puts it, "The bourgeois wanted to disguise his capital in fancy dress" (*The Necessity of Art* [Harmondsworth, Middlesex: Penguin: 1971], p. 208).

[7] Walpole was delighted with a dungeon at Hurstmonceaux, an elaborate 15th-c. castellated mansion, because it "gives one a delightful idea of living in the days of soccage and under such goodly tenures" (*Corr.*, 37:138, to Bentley, 5 Aug. 1752).

[8] *Enquiry into the Life and Writings of Homer* (London, 1735), p. 26.

the family because it is essentially the material survivor of a powerful lineage, a symbol of the continuing life of its founder. Only, therefore, when Otranto's living heir, Theodore, is safely in the courtyard can "the walls of the castle" be "thrown down by a mighty force," and the form of its founder, Alfonso, "dilated to an immense magnitude," appear "in the center of the ruins" (p. 108). Within the walls the most common material objects are likenesses—either portraits or sculptures—which, like ancient documents, attest the continuing presence of the dead. The portrait of Alfonso, his statue, even the helmet, armor, and sword—all assert his paternal power. So do the ancient prophecy and the riddling quatrain.

From likenesses of the dead to the world of the supernatural is no great leap for Walpole's liberated "resources of the fancy"—as Alfonso presumably discovers when he steps down out of his picture frame. Walpole was at some pains to excuse the element of superstition in his story on the grounds that it was typical of the times depicted, and that he had in any case much restricted its operation, as compared to earlier writers of romance, where "the actors seem to lose their senses the moment the laws of nature lose their tone." So in general his motive for seeking the greater imaginative freedom of the supernatural must be seen as yet another aspect of how Gothic was a reaction to the intellectual temper of the century. Walpole liked *The Castle of Otranto* most among his works, he wrote to Madame du Deffand, because there alone he had given "reign to . . . imagination. . . . I am even persuaded that in the Future, when taste will be restored to the place now occupied by philosophy, my poor Castle will find admirers."[9] His own time, alas, wanted "only cold reason," which had established a rigid distinction between the natural and the supernatural after Newton had cast light on nature's laws, and definitively depersonalized the physical world.

The systematizing of this division between the natural and the supernatural orders inevitably affected general attitudes to the past and to the unseen world. By the time of Pope the supernatural had become to the enlightened a dubious and rather fanciful rival order, like the sylphs in *The Rape of the Lock*; and by the middle of the century such beliefs were becoming a sign of religious archaism, as in John Wesley and Parson Adams. To give the occult power of the past a real existence in fic-

---

[9] Letter dated 13 March 1767 (*Corr.*, 3:260), trans. from the French by the author.

tion it was now necessary to set the narrative back in time into the Gothic past, to the times before the Reformation when Roman Catholic superstition held sway, and to the countries—most notably Italy—where it was still rampant.

To an Enlightenment skeptic like Walpole, of course, religious superstition was equally repulsive to political liberty and scientific reason; but it remained congenial to the aesthetic imagination. Hence Walpole compromised with his times both by setting the events back in times and places where credulity was universal, and by presenting his supernatural interventions in a selective way.

Walpole's supernature is entirely populated with beings who, for all their monstrous size and power, are essentially historical beings with rational human aims. This is typical of the Gothic novel in general; supernature is both secularized and individualized. Alfonso the Good, or whichever of his unseen adjutants is currently on duty to ruffle the helmet's plumes at the appropriate time, seems to be wholly concerned with bringing about a more satisfactory state of affairs in the secular world of his genealogical descendants; and when this rectifying mission has been accomplished, he can be trusted to hand Otranto back to the custody of Newtonian physics.

There are other orders of experience besides the supernatural which exist outside time as it is viewed by natural science: there is the sacred time of myth and ritual and the mystics; and—much more important for the Gothic tradition—there are the special kinds of time in which dreams and the unconscious have their being; and both are peculiarly open to the irruptions of the forces of the past.

In dreams, time is intensely real in the sense that we are immersed in a series of scenes which follow each other with hallucinatory vividness: it is very much a question of now, and now, and now. The connection of these scenes is not causal; the fragments are real, but they have their own kind of temporal order which is unconscious or imaginative, rather than consecutive in any logical way. The specific time-setting of the dream is typically unlocalized or shifting; but when we recall the dream later we often realize that we have revisited various scenes of our long-past life, though not in their chronological order. What initially provokes the dream, though, is normally some present occasion; and this provides a basic structural analogy to the symbiosis of past and present in Gothic.

The closeness of the two kinds of mental representation—dreams and Gothic fiction—is reflected in two well-known facts. First, dreams, particularly nightmares, are common in Gothic novels; many of the best are like nightmares—*Frankenstein* or "The Fall of the House of Usher." Second, many Gothic novels apparently began as actual dreams. In her Preface, Mary Shelley, for instance, says *Frankenstein* did, and so does Walpole in a letter to William Cole (9 March 1765):

Shall I even confess to you what was the origin of this romance? I waked one morning in the beginning of last June from a dream, of which all I could recover was, that I had thought myself in an ancient castle (a very natural dream for a head filled like mine with Gothic story) and that on the uppermost bannister of a great staircase I saw a gigantic hand in armour. In the evening I sat down and began to write, without knowing in the least what I intended to say or relate. The work grew on my hands, and I grew fond of it—add that I was very glad to think of anything rather than politics . . . (*Corr.*, 1:88)

We can be fairly confident, I think, that Walpole's dream was a transposition of sights familiar to him partly from Strawberry Hill and particularly, as he wrote, from the great court of Trinity College, Cambridge.[10] We can also see how the symbolic meanings of these images reflect the unconscious life.

The unconscious shares with Gothic the characteristic that anything (we are credibly informed) can happen there, and that its psychological spectrum reflects the extremes of what we seek and what we fear much more dramatically than is common either in the novel or in real life. There is a further parallel: both dreams and the unconscious share with Gothic fiction the tendency to deal with present problems through a special reliving of the past. As Auden puts it in his elegy for Sigmund Freud, "He wasn't clever at all: he merely told/ the unhappy Present to recite the Past."

This particular aspect of Gothic—the unhappy present reciting the past—is clearest, I suppose, in the later Gothic tradition, in Dickens, with Miss Havisham immobilized in the posture of frustration, or in Ibsen's *Ghosts* and *John Gabriel Borkman*, where the past has irrevocably foreclosed the possibilities of the present. In all these, once again we

---

[10] As Warren H. Smith showed in a letter to the ed., *Times Literary Supplement* (23 May 1936), p. 440.

have a double past; for the crucial events of the past, whether betrayal, theft, murder, rape, or incest, were themselves the residue of an infinitely earlier past which lived on in the archaic violence of the unconscious.

The unconscious, as we have all learned, is very like a Gothic castle: not the clean, well-lighted, and cellarless place of the modern single-family residence, but a many-tiered vertical maze—and a dark and dirty one at that. Its many levels connect only through narrow, turning staircases and concealed trapdoors; and its towers, vaults, caverns, and dungeons are both the natural scene of death and terror and rape, and established symbols for our unconscious drives. Their sexual symbolism is now an open book to a normally contaminated mind; but it may be worth suggesting how the facts that, as Freud put it, "We are not masters in our own house," and that there are rooms in it that we may never really see, both supply an enduring psychological basis for the appeal of the Gothic genre, and help explain its frequent concentration on family relationships.

Melodrama and Gothic are not always clearly distinct genres, and the reader's responses to their characters usually differ. In melodrama, we hiss at the villain. In Gothic our attitude is more complex; the villain nearly always excites some degree of identification, whether he is predominantly evil, like Mrs. Radcliffe's Montoni in *The Mysteries of Udolpho*, or predominantly sympathetic, like Ambrosio in *The Monk*,[11] Melmoth, or Heathcliff. Most typically the reader had a divided sympathy, and this ambivalence seems to follow the division between the id and the superego.

Here, too, Walpole is a precursor. His hero, Manfred, is on one hand a cruel and tyrannical usurper whose mind often turns, in Walpole's phrase, "to exquisite villainy"; yet on the other hand, something in us finds much to admire and to envy in his cunning and self-confident resolution to pursue his aims; Walpole's own unconscious sympathy is made clear very early when he gives Manfred so firm a command of irony at the expense of superstition and sentimental pretense. Like Wal-

---

[11] In *The Monk* the literal haunting of the narrative present by an anterior past mainly occurs in the subplots (the legend of the bleeding nun, e.g.). As far as the protagonist is concerned, it is his own atavistic passions that are gradually revealed, to the astonishment of his admirers (including himself), and that lead to rape, murder, and his own damnation.

pole, we know we ought to condemn Manfred, but we find we cannot; he appeals to a division in us between the conscious and the unconscious, between the public and the private, between the day and night sides of the personality. These tensions provide a complexity which does something to atone for the thin psychological characterization of *The Castle of Otranto*, and is also typical of Gothic fiction. When there is character development in the Gothic, as in *The Monk*, it is a morally emblematic series of accelerating villainies rather than a psychologically cumulative process; more typically, the Gothic character is sustained by a labile balance between the past and the present, between the unrestrained impulses of the id and the controls of reason and normality.

Perhaps it is this unconscious irresolution that explains one puzzle about so many Gothic novels. At times Manfred and Montoni seem so potently and enviably demonic that we see no reason whatever that their victims, or their whole social order, should survive at all. Yet we also find these Gothic supermen having occasional spasms of normality—moral qualms, moments of kindness, ordinary muddled human sympathy. Their destructive power is apparently not limitless, and oddly defeats our expectation. This contradiction becomes more apparent in the nineteenth century, when the Gothic theme becomes psychologically internalized in such characters as Ahab and Heathcliff: they seem much more terrifying persons than their actions turn out to be.

It may be that the essential explanation of why Gothic villains never realized their full destructive potential is in the Freudian view of the relation between parents and children. Perhaps Manfred, for instance, alternates between the demonic and the normal because Walpole was torn between deep admiration for his father, and an equally deep fear of his father's power. Of course Horace Walpole knew that he was no more likely to continue the family's greatness than was Conrad; and so the dread giant hand on the bannister belonged to the paternal authority that was both desired and hated. But it also had its limits—Sir Robert was now dead.[12]

---

[12] The relationship of the Gothic novel to the archetypal and primordial structures of psychological development have been illuminatingly explored in Leslie Fiedler's *Love and Death in the American Novel* (Cleveland: Meridian, 1962), and Frederick Crews's *The Sins of the Fathers* (New York: Oxford University Press, 1966); while more recently, Maurice Lévy, in his *Le Roman gothique anglais 1764-1824* (Toulouse: Faculté des Lettres et Sciences Humaines, 1968),

In any case it is surely within the nucleus of the family that the basic conflicts of the Gothic take place; and for at least three reasons. First, that the most universal of man's social and moral regulations all concern the interplay of power, property, marriage, and sex within the family; second, that these regulations, and the forces which oppose them, are internalized in the unconscious; and last, that these conflicts directly and continuously affect the relationships of the past and the present in the individual's experience. Here again Walpole anticipated later developments; the moral of his work, he wrote in the Preface to the first edition, was "that *the sins of the fathers are visited on their children to the third and fourth generation*" (p. 5).

The psychological contradictions concerning character and the family, it should perhaps be added, work both ways: Freudian theory can itself be seen as a Gothic myth. It presents the individual, much as Gothic does, as essentially imprisoned by the tyranny of an omnipotent but unseen past. The oedipal situation, or more generally, the terrible authority of the parents in the unconscious, is the Freudian equivalent of the supernatural or demonic power of the Gothic protagonist. The parallel is strengthened by the prevalence of paternal incest in Gothic fiction (of which Manfred's passion for Isabella, the girl who was to have been his daughter-in-law, is an example).[13] There is a further parallel in that tradition of Gothic which goes from *The Castle of Otranto* to "The Fall of the House of Usher" and *The House of the Seven Gables*, where the supreme power is the patriarchal authority of the long-dead lineal ancestor, who is still the real, though invisible, master of the house and its occupants.

More generally, we can conclude that although a sense of the mysterious and immobilizing power of the past is one of the characteristic features both of psychoanalysis and Gothic fiction, that power is normally humanized as far as our quotidian experience is concerned. In this respect it seems that characterization in the Gothic novel has a somewhat

---

has investigated those aspects of the Gothic novel which appealed to the French surrealists, notably to André Breton and Paul Eluard. See also *The Female Gothic*, ed. Juliann E. Fleenor (Montreal: Eden, 1983).

[13] Walpole's play, *The Mysterious Mother*, contains a double incest: the mother sleeps with her son, and later kills herself when he marries their joint offspring. The Freudian aspect of *The Castle of Otranto* is treated in Martin Lallich's *Horace Walpole* (New York: Twayne, 1971), pp. 101-4.

similar function to that allotted the individual in psychoanalytic theory: to mediate between the conflicting demands of two sides of the unconscious, the superego and the id.[14]

So much for the psychology of the Gothic. I have obviously not been attempting a complete account either of *The Castle of Otranto* or of its genre. Such an account would have to concede that it is often forced, sometimes dull, and stylistically Walpole's worst piece of prose writing—with hardly a suggestion of the brilliance and understanding of the letters or the memoirs, for instance. *The Castle of Otranto*, in fact, very largely lacks the courage of its Gothic convictions; and yet its basic structure contains enough of the essential features of the later Gothic tradition both to explain its historical importance in establishing the new form, and to help us understand some of its characteristic elements.

Walpole himself shared much of the optimism of the Enlightenment; in his Gothic tale, therefore, the past is fairly benign: Manfred repents, and Theodore is returned to his rightful place. For the most part Mrs. Radcliffe followed this comfortable ideological perspective. After the end of the eighteenth century, however, the Gothic tradition took a darker turn. Gothic was still the world of the ancient romance, in the sense that it was a kind of fiction in which all the most violent and destructive extremes of human possibility could be realized, as opposed to the novel, which habitually confines its characters and events within the more normal quotidian spectrum of action and motive. But whereas Walpole had allowed the more affirmative forces of justice and virtue to vanquish evil, Monk Lewis and Charles Maturin and later Gothic writers operated more and more within the darker shades of the moral spec-

---

[14] The implications of this for characterization have been well demonstrated in Francis Russel Hart's essay "The Experience of Character in the English Gothic Novel." Hart argues that we must not make the common assumption that the Gothic protagonists are merely flat emblematic portrayals of the demonic in the non-representational world of the romance; they are that, and they are also human beings; and so the central mystery in Gothic novels is one where "autonomous natural existences—characters—come to assume demonic roles" and this is the "terrifying truth in an enlightenment context . . . that the demonic is no myth, no superstition, but a reality in human character or relationship, a novelistic reality" (*Experience in the Novel: Selected Papers from the English Institute*, ed. Roy Harvey Pearce [New York: Columbia Press, 1968], p. 99).

trum; the past is evil and tends to triumph; the fate of both the Monk and of Melmoth is eternal damnation.

Whether the balance of power in the world of the Gothic novel is held by good or evil, however, it is typically—though not always—a world where, in a variety of forms, the redoubtable past haunts the impotent present; it is the past which holds the key.

The Gothic tradition in its specialized historical sense is usually agreed to end with *Melmoth the Wanderer* in 1820: more precisely, perhaps, we might say that one branch of it continues in an increasingly subliterary and specialized tradition about vampires and werewolves, while the other branch continues to deepen the main moral perspectives of Gothic in works which in other respects come closer to the main tradition of the novel.

The immediate setting in an historical past, and the use of the supernatural, became rarer in this later and looser version of the Gothic; and at the same time it incorporates many of the interests and techniques of the main fictional tradition. With the Brontës,[15] for instance, it assimilates the fuller psychological characterization and the denser presentations of the environment of the Victorian novel in general.

On this issue the roles of time and the family offer an interesting contrast in two acknowledged classics of the Gothic in its wider sense. In *Wuthering Heights*, for instance, the most memorable part of the narrative—from chapters 3 to 17—deals with events of a generation ago (between 1771, the arrival of Heathcliff at Wuthering Heights, to the deaths of Catherine and Hindley Earnshaw in 1784); Lockwood learns of them after his calls at Wuthering Heights in 1801. To that extent the story enacts a double plunge backwards into time: to the days of Cathy's marriage, and then further back to her childhood with Heathcliff; and this backward movement itself takes us even further back symbolically to an unconscious world of eternal primitive possession. On the other hand, the optimistic conclusion of the novel—Heathcliff's death and the marriage of Catherine and Hareton—occurs in the present tense of the novel, in 1802 and 1803. This contrast suggests an inherent contradiction in the book. One way of looking at it would be as a working out of the dual role of the Gothic hero: the dark powers of the

---

[15] See especially Robert B. Heilman, "Charlotte Brontë's 'New Gothic'," in *From Jane Austen to Joseph Conrad*, ed. Robert C. Rathburn and Martin Steinmann, Jr. (Minneapolis: University of Minnesota, 1958), pp. 118-32.

id have their way for a time, but they succumb to the attrition of moral and social norms in the end. As Thomas Moser has argued,[16] the later parts of the book really amount to a final denial of Emily Brontë's initial psychological premises: the bad, exciting past is not omnipotent; the demonic Heathcliff, of all people, goes soft; Cathy and Wuthering Heights cease to be haunted by him; and the Gothic world fades into the dull domestic Victorian one almost without a protest.

On the other hand Hawthorne's *The House of the Seven Gables* (1851) is much closer to the *Otranto* pattern. There is—first of all—the Gothic present embodied in the colonial house itself which has survived into the eighteen-fifties. The movement back in time reveals the secrets of two anterior pasts: that of one generation back, when Clifford Pyncheon was sentenced to prison, thirty years before, for the alleged murder of his uncle, Jaffrey Pyncheon; and that of about two centuries before, when Colonel Pyncheon had originally seized the land from Matthew Maule, and has him executed for a wizard. In the narrative present, Judge Pyncheon, sitting beneath the portrait of the founder of his lineage, Colonel Pyncheon, dies choked with blood according to Maule's curse, the same fate that had befallen the original Colonel Pyncheon and his descendant, Jaffrey Pyncheon. The past is beginning to be expiated, and the present must now be reconstituted. The old deed to the Indian lands is discovered by the lodger, Mr. Holgrave, who turns out to be a descendant of Matthew Maule, and of his son, Thomas, who had built the house; and time can start going forward again, instead of back, when Holgrave, now called Maule, gives his family name to Phoebe, the only representative of the Pyncheon lineage who has a future.

In the twentieth century, certainly, there has been no inclination to underestimate the extent to which we are haunted by the past and the family; and so the Gothic theme has surfaced in many new, concealed, or unexpected forms. In Faulkner's *Absalom, Absalom!*, for instance, the central pattern is very clear; the two generations which haunt Sutpen's Hundred are traced back to the intractable brutalities and the mysterious inheritance of Thomas Sutpen: the densely layered family history of the Sutpens cannot, any more than the past of the South, be altered; Quentin Compson, and other defeated survivors of history, can

---

[16] "'What is the Matter with Emily Jane?' Conflicting Impulses in *Wuthering Heights*," *Nineteenth-Century Fiction* 17 (1962), 1-19.

only attempt to understand its multifarious power. One could also argue that the tradition continues in the literature of the mindless molecular now, and even that, the present times being what they are, contemporary fiction in general is rapidly becoming more and more indistinguishable from the Gothic novel—in Thomas Pynchon, Joyce Carol Oates, or Kurt Vonnegut, for example.

In general, we can be reasonably certain that, unlike the Gothic language, the Gothic novel is unlikely to disappear. As long as we are ambivalent about our incomparable modernity; as long as our political sky gets blacker daily with chickens coming home to roost; as long as children have parents, and so do parents; as long as we continue to experience boredom, night, sleep, and fear; as long as we fail to experience freedom and happiness; the past, alas, will continue to haunt us, and see to it that we spend much of our lives on Gothic time.

# 11

## JANE AUSTEN AND THE TRADITIONS OF COMIC AGGRESSION

I've long been intending to develop some things that were omitted from *The Rise of the Novel* to make it shorter and clearer in structure.* The sequel is to be called *Gothic and Comic: Two Variations on the Realistic Tradition*. As regards the comic tradition, one of the central arguments is that when Jane Austen began to write there was no established narrative tradition that would serve her turn. More specifically, earlier writers of English comic novels, such as Fielding, Smollett, and Fanny Burney, had in different ways adopted the polar opposition between good and bad characters which is typical of stage comedy from the Greeks on. Through the finer and more detailed psychological calibration of her narrative, Jane Austen made the hero and heroine psychologically complex, and therefore capable of internal and external development. By this means the traditional conflict of "good" and "bad" characters in comedy was internalised as a conflict within and between the "good" characters; and this enabled Jane Austen to discover the answer to Horatio Bottomley's prayer—"I pray that the bad may be made good, and the good nice, and the nice, interesting."

The prayer is very rarely answered—alas!—either in life or in art; but one can surely say about Elizabeth Bennet and Emma Woodhouse that they are not only good and nice, but interesting. They are made inter-

---
* "Jane Austen and the Traditions of Comic Aggression" appeared originally in *Persuasions: Journal of the Jane Austen Society of North America* 3 (December, 1981), 14-15, 25-28. Reprinted with permission. For an earlier treatment of Austen, see Ian Watt's introduction to the Harper's Modern Classics edition of *Sense and Sensibility* (New York: Harper & Row, 1961). [Ed.]

esting because they are idiosyncratic mixtures of character traits, mixtures by no means limited to the good and unexceptionable qualities. For the purposes of comedy there remained a further task—the protagonists had to take over many of the aggressive functions which stage comedy has traditionally allotted to other actors—to the witty helpers, blocking characters, and villains. It is this, I think, that constitutes Jane Austen's greatest originality as an artist; and I would add that this literary originality is based on her psychological and moral realism, which gave the aggressive impulses a role which went far beyond the thought of her time, and, in some ways, of ours.

I will first illustrate the general idea by looking at *Emma* and *Pride and Prejudice*; and then I will consider *Sense and Sensibility* as an early stage in Jane Austen's development of the treatment of aggression.

Jane Austen's novels contain three main types of comic aggression, and all of them involve the "good" characters as well as the others. The first category—which I will call the social—is concerned with how people have different ways of hitting back at the restraints which social life exacts.

Most of the social gatherings described by Jane Austen provide illustrations. In the first social occasion in *Emma*, for instance, the party at the Westons' is dominated by the dialectic of constraint and hostility, and it thus serves as symbolic prelude to the novel's climactic scene on Box Hill. On the one hand, there are the positive, outgoing feelings, however strained, which are directed towards congeniality and sociability, and are expressed through compliments, jesting, and amiability; on the other hand, there are the contrary negative impulses of resentment at whatever threatens or inhibits the individual's status, habits, or convictions.

Every topic of conversation, we notice, evokes some note of hostility. For instance, Isabella Knightley's maternal zeal leads her to an odiously gratuitous pretense of benevolence in connection with Mrs. Churchill: "What a blessing that she never had any children! Poor little creatures, how unhappy she would have made them!" Then Mr. John Knightley comes in to give an alarmist account of the snow, concluding with these words to Mr. Woodhouse: "This will prove a spirited beginning of your winter engagements, sir. Something new for your coachman and horses making their way through a storm of snow."

Others try to comfort poor Mr. Woodhouse, but his tormentor is "pursuing his triumph rather unfeelingly," and continues sardonically:

"I admired your resolution very much, sir . . . in venturing out in such weather, for of course you saw there would be snow very soon. Every body must have seen the snow coming on. I admired your spirit; and I dare say we shall get home very well. Another hour or two's snow can hardly make the road impassable; and we are two carriages; if *one* is blown over in the bleak part of the common field there will be the other at hand."

John Knightley's gleeful malice towards poor Mr. Woodhouse's timidity is authorized by his ideology; he is unkind only in the pursuit of a higher truth. The truth is the pointless folly of social life in general, and it has as its primary axiom that dinner-parties are "in defiance of the law of nature"—an axiom which strikes a death blow at two of the cardinal values of comedy—laughter and feasting.

Here, as in most of the social gatherings in *Emma*, harmony only prevails when the group is happily engaged in the malicious criticism of third parties. The most intransigent and socially destructive manifestation of aggression occurs when some challenge arises to the imperative need of the individual ego to maintain its own image of itself in the face of the outside world. This need produces the cruelest deliberate act in *Emma*, when Mr. Elton refuses to dance with Harriet Smith at the ball in the Crown; his pride has been offended, and seeks revenge. In Jane Austen, however, unconscious cruelty is much commoner, and most often arises from a mere refusal or inability to understand other people. Mr. Woodhouse, for instance, is genuinely kind in his way; but, lacking the controls of intelligence or awareness, his phobias often lead him into the milder forms of cruelty, invective and lying. Thus his tyrannical valetudinarianism leads him to disappoint Mrs. Bates's eager anticipation of a "delicate fricassee of sweetbread and asparagus," on the grounds that the latter were not "quite boiled enough"; the same phobia emerges in a more rancorous verbal form when the arrival of gruel in his family circle becomes the occasion for "pretty severe Philippics upon the many houses where it was never met with tolerable."

It would certainly be wrong, I must observe, to infer that Jane Austen condemns all social forms of aggression. For one thing, it is manifested by every character in *Emma* about whom we can make a judgment, except for two, and they are the exceptions that prove the rule: I mean Mrs. Bates and Harriet Smith—good people no doubt, but intellectually null, with one of them—Harriet—not yet arrived at maturity, and the other—Mrs. Bates—long past it.

I come now to the other two kinds of comic aggression—the interpersonal and the internal—as they are manifested in *Pride and Prejudice*. The personal relations between Elizabeth and Darcy are dominated by the aggressive elements in their characters; these alone replace the roles of the villains, the blocking characters, and the mistaken identities in traditional comedy. This replacement depends on two narrative techniques: first, the aggressive impulses at play in the comic arena are psychologized in the "courtship" of the protagonists; and they are also psychologized as conflicts inside the egos of both lovers.

These conflicts in the personalities of Elizabeth and Darcy provide the mechanism of the main plot. At first the aggressive aspects of their characters block their separation even before they are actually acquaintances. Darcy's pride leads him to reject Bingley's suggestion that he dance with her—"She is tolerable; but not handsome enough to tempt *me*; and I am in no humour at present to give consequence to young ladies who are slighted by other men." Elizabeth overhears him, and her offended pride, exacerbated by Meryton gossip and Wickham's lies, insulates her from Darcy's rapidly changing feelings. The whole of their relationship is thus presented as an adaptation and recombination of one of the most standard modes of comic aggression, invective, to the purposes of psychological and moral realism. Elizabeth and Darcy begin by insulting the other to third parties; later their acquaintance develops almost exclusively through bouts of contemptuous raillery which are as close to the verbal combats of Greek comedy as the manners of Regency England allowed.

The reason for the tradition of invective in comedy is presumably that it offers a symbolic release from the constraints on which civilisation depends; as Freud put it, "The man who first flung a word of abuse at his enemy instead of a spear was the founder of civilisation." But in the kind of novel which Jane Austen wrote the invective and the wit-combats cannot be treated as they usually are in stage comedy, in Aristophanes, for example; they cannot merely stop, and be succeeded by a quick change to feasting, song, dance, and marriage. For in *Pride and Prejudice* the substance of the debate between the two lovers is very real—it expresses the deepest divisions in the way the protagonists see the world and experience the circumstances of their place in it. Jane Austen's moral solution to these divisions is exactly what the solution, if any, would be in real life: the pains of self-education—the realisation of the errors, the delusions, and the prejudices of the self. In narrative terms Jane Austen brings the pattern of invective to a climax by a dual psychological transformation: interpersonal aggression is internalized in both hero and heroine.

In Darcy's case we do not see the process of self-punishment at work; but we can surmise that nothing else would lead him to propose marriage to Elizabeth. Then her insulting rejection apparently causes Darcy to take his self-punishment much further and he writes his abject explanatory letter. Now it is Elizabeth's turn. At first reading she is sure that "it was all pride and insolence," as regards Jane, while as regards Wickham, "she wished to discredit it entirely." Elizabeth then protests "that she would never look in (the letter) again," and we are already expecting the quick change of mind which the comic reversal requires. It soon comes: "in half a minute the letter was unfolded again." Elizabeth faces "the mortifying perusal of all that related to Wickham." From this second perusal there slowly emerges the deep personal humiliation of having to recognize how completely she has been taken in by this handsome scoundrel. From this traditional comic discovery of having been deceived, Elizabeth's negative emotions, which had previously all been directed outwards against Darcy, rapidly now alter their course and are directed inwards in a self-discovery of unflinching psychological rigor:

"How despicably have I acted!" she cried.—"I who have prided myself on my discernment!—I, who have valued myself on my abilities! who have often disdained the generous candour of my sister, and gratified my vanity, in useless or blameable distrust—How humiliating is this discovery!—Yet, how just a humiliation!—Had I been in love, I could not have been more wretchedly blind. But vanity, not love, has been my folly.—Pleased with the preference of one, and offended by the neglect of the other, on the very beginning of our acquaintance, I have courted prepossession and ignorance, and driven reason away, where either were concerned. Till this moment, I never knew myself."

Now Elizabeth must come to terms with the fact that in many matters she shares with Darcy the same moral impulses, of which the most basic is to face the truth, even when it is deeply mortifying to the self. As a result Elizabeth joins Darcy in emerging from her deepest humiliation with a salutary increment of self-knowledge: they both undergo a parallel process of education through mortification.

*Sense and Sensibility* offers many examples of social, interpersonal, and internalized aggression. At the same time *Sense and Sensibility* is also, as one would expect from an earlier work, much closer than *Pride and Prejudice* or *Emma* to the classical tradition of comedy, and to Fanny Burney. The characters in *Sense and Sensibility*, for instance, tend to be more simply good or bad; the plot develops almost entirely through external events rather than inward changes in the protagonists; and although at the end Marianne and Edward Ferrars blame themselves for their past actions, they do so in spoken apologies to Elinor, and so there is no real analogy to the mortification scénes of Elizabeth or Emma.

First, social aggression. In *Sense and Sensibility* the battlefields of civility are littered with casualties. The most openly hostile characters are those who are wholly concerned with improving their financial and social condition; the way that John and Fanny Dashwood treat Mrs. Dashwood, Elinor, and Marianne is as gratuitous and persistently malicious as the behavior of any stage villain. Having forced her husband to betray his promise, and his father's last wishes, Fanny Dashwood persuades herself—and John—that it is they who have been wronged; in the last tortuous extravagances of aggressive projection, John and Fanny even come to the persuasion that Elinor is as falsely designing as they are, and that she is trying to ensnare Fanny's brother, Edward Ferrars, in marriage. So, we observe, Fanny's observations of Edward's affectionate manner to Elinor give rise to her rudest outburst: "it was enough . . . to make her uneasy; and at the same time, (which was still more common), to make her uncivil. She took the first opportunity of affronting her mother-in-law on the occasion, talking to her so expressively of her brother's great expectations, of Mrs. Ferrars's resolution that both her sons should marry well, and of the danger attending any young woman who attempted to *draw him in*; that Mrs. Dashwood could neither pretend to be unconscious, nor endeavor to be calm."

Jane Austen pursues her theme remorselessly; and we see manipulative aggression becoming compulsive in the best stage traditions of the miser's monomania. The parallel hostility of Lucy to Elinor is expressed in false pretenses of friendship which make it merely a polite variation on the same theme of ruthless social competitiveness. For example, when she meets the Dashwood sisters in London, Lucy gushes:

"I should have been quite disappointed if I had not found you here *still*," said she repeatedly with a strong emphasis on the word. "But I always thought I *should*. I was almost sure you would not leave London yet awhile, though you *told* me, you know, at Barton, that you would not stay above a *month*. But I thought, at the time, that you would most likely change your mind when it came to the point. It would have been such a great pity to have went away before your brother and sister came. And now to be sure you will be in no hurry to be gone. I am amazingly glad you did not keep to *your word.*"

Lucy's attempts at poisoned badinage are as unsatisfactory as her grammar; a fatal garrulity betrays her intentions long before she has finished, and thus reveals her unwitting violation of the first law of sarcasm—a rapidity that leaves no time for a riposte, let alone a yawn.

Lucy Steele, like John and Fanny Dashwood and Mrs. Ferrars, is a one-dimensional comic villain; she evokes unremitting dislike from the reader and the narrator alike. The other main group in the cast of *Sense and Sensibility* are also one-trait comic characters whose function is to be the butt of the narrator's running joke. Whenever they appear, we are asked to join in mocking Sir John Middleton's smothering hospitality, his wife's bored egocentricity, Mrs. Jenkins's misguided preoccupation with matchmaking, Mr. Palmer's boorish rudeness, and Mrs. Palmer's silly laugh.

Mr. Palmer cannot be denied the honor of being the ancestor of John Knightley; he never says anything that is not aggressive, and utterly refuses the slightest concessions to social civility. At Barton Park he draws even that most minimal of conversational counters, the weather, into his aggressive symbolic system: "'How horrid all this is!' said he. 'Such weather makes every thing and every body disgusting. Dullness is as much produced within doors as without, by rain. It makes one detest all one's acquaintance. What the devil does Sir John mean by not having a billiard room in his house? How few people know what comfort is! Sir John is as stupid as the weather!'" Elinor, astonished at Mrs. Palmer's forbearance at her husband's rudeness, observes him closely, and decides that he is not "so genuinely and unaffectedly ill-natured or ill-bred as he wished to appear. . . . It was the desire of appearing superior to other people."

The nearest parallel in *Sense and Sensibility* to the wit-combats of Darcy and Elizabeth are—I suppose—the dialogues between Elinor and Marianne. There are, of course, many important differences: for one thing, the fairly strict dichotomy in the novel between good and bad characters means that Elinor and Marianne are often the victims of unprovoked social aggression from the rest of the world, so that the reader usually sympathizes with them against all the unfair, unjust, and hostile circumstances in which they find themselves; secondly, Elinor comes to us as a person having, unlike Marianne, nothing to learn, so that there is a built-in asymmetry in the relations between the two sisters; and thirdly, their dialogue does not lead to change or permanent understanding. *Sense and Sensibility* was originally entitled "Elinor and Marianne"; and this would have been appropriate in a way that "Elizabeth and Darcy" would not have been, because although Elinor and Marianne have some of both qualities they function as symbolic and permanent opposites as far as their relationships to each other are concerned.

Marianne never has a hostile thought which she forces herself to repress; she openly attacks Edward for his reserve, speaks very rudely to Mrs. Ferrars in defense of Elinor, and is openly indignant at John Dashwood's account of Mrs. Ferrars's disinheriting Edward. In each case, Marianne's anger is justified, but Elinor's obtrusively different behavior brings into question her openness in expressing it.

Whenever Elinor's criticism has ethical foundations and she believes that speaking may be useful or is morally obligatory, she gives her view openly and earnestly. Thus Elinor cautions Mrs. Jenkins against her gossiping about Marianne and Willoughby: "you are doing a very unkind thing"; and she upbraids Miss Steele for listening at a keyhole and reporting what she has overheard. Under other conditions, and if her target is sufficiently dense, Elinor voices her opinion ironically; for example, when John Dashwood complains to her about his financial difficulties, we are told that Elinor, recalling how much cash he has withheld from her family, at first "could only smile." But when John presses his demand for her sympathy, saying, "'You may guess, after all these expenses, how very far we must be from being rich, and how acceptable Mrs. Ferrars' kindness is,'" Elinor responds with adroitly ironic duplicity: "'Certainly,' said Elinor, 'and assisted by her liberality, I hope you may yet live to be in easy circumstances.'" She has read the barometer of complacent self-importance correctly, and her sarcasm goes right over John's head: "'Another year or two may do much towards it,' he gravely replied."

However, when John goes on to tell Elinor of his having pulled down all the walnut trees on the Dashwoods' beloved old property, Elinor in the best tradition of Mrs. Radcliffe's Emily de St. Aubert and Goethe's Werther, is really angry; but, we note, "Elinor kept her concern and her censure to herself; and was very thankful that Marianne was not present, to share the provocation." There is the same reserve when she watches the hopelessly duped Mrs. Ferrars being kind to Lucy Steele: "while (Elinor) smiled at a graciousness so misapplied, she could not but reflect on the mean-spirited folly from which it sprung, nor observe the studied attentions with which the Miss Steeles courted its continuance, without thoroughly despising them all four." As Robyn Housley has observed, "Elinor at her angriest is Elinor at her most silent"; Elinor knows that in her circumstances discretion is the best weapon which sense supplies for the defense of sensibility.

Compared to her behavior in public, Elinor's responses to her sister are much less reserved. From the beginning Elinor teases Marianne about the imprudence and danger of her excessive sensibility. Thus Elinor attempts to caution Marianne against her fast-growing friendship with Willoughby: "'You know what he thinks of Cowper and Scott, you are certain of his estimating their beauties as he ought and you have received every assurance of his admiring Pope no more than is proper. But how is your acquaintance to be long supported, under such extraordinary dispatch of every subject for discourse? You will soon have exhausted each favorite topic. Another meeting will suffice to explain his sentiments on picturesque beauty, and second marriages, and then you can have nothing farther to ask'—." Marianne rejects the warning and counterattacks by asserting her superior sensitivity: "'But I see what you mean. . . . I have erred against every commonplace notion of decorum; I have been open and sincere where I ought to have been reserved, spiritless, dull, and deceitful:—had I talked only of the weather and the roads, and had I spoken only once in ten minutes, this reproach would have been spared.'"

Later, when Marianne has received Willoughby's letter, Elinor's advice becomes passionately serious: "'exert yourself, dear Marianne, if you would not kill yourself and all who love you. Think of your mother; think of her misery while you suffer; for her sake you must exert yourself.'" Marianne remains blind to Elinor's efforts and responds with self-indulgent insult: "'I cannot, I cannot,' cried Marianne; 'leave me, leave me, if I distress you; leave me, hate me, forget me! but do not torture me so. Oh! how easy for those who have no sorrow of their own to talk of exertion!'"

Marianne's willful ignorance would remain invincible but for a combination of further accidents—the discovery of Edward's engagement to Lucy Steele, and Marianne's recovery. On both of these occasions, Marianne certainly voices bitter self-accusation, and her words certainly sound like attempts at self-mortification. But her change of heart surely lacks inwardness and depth.

"Oh! Elinor," she cried, "you have made me hate myself for ever.—How barbarous have I been to you!—you, who have been my only comfort, who have borne with me in all my misery, who have seemed to be only suffering for me!—Is this my gratitude!—Is this the only return I can make you? Because your merit cries out upon myself, I have been trying to do it away."

The ensuing commentary suggests that the narrator, at least, is not wholly persuaded that Marianne's remorse may not be yet another form of high emotional self-indulgence:

In such a frame of mind as she was now in, Elinor had no difficulty in obtaining from her whatever promise she required: and at her request, Marianne engaged never to speak of the affair to any one with the least appearance of bitterness:—to meet Lucy without betraying the smallest increase of dislike to her;—and even to see Edward himself, if chance should bring them together, without any diminution of her usual cordiality.—These were great concessions;—but where Marianne felt that she had injured, no reparation could be too much for her to make.

The listing of Marianne's promises builds up to a climax that is surely one of tolerant irony; and it suggests that there is still a residue of self-dramatizing emotionalism in Marianne; her prime need is still to make herself interesting to herself. Of course, we don't really know if we are dealing with a reliable narrator or not, or what she is reliable about. Is it a prediction, coming out of authorial foreknowledge of the future, that Marianne will never change her ways? Or is it just the persistently ironic tone that everyone except Elinor evokes from the narrator? We do not know, and so, although we are not persuaded that Marianne undergoes the mortification of internal aggression, as we are with Elizabeth and Emma, neither are we persuaded that we know *how* we should see her.

At this point, having tried, in the small hours of the night, to bring my argument to some sort of conclusion, and having failed, I fell asleep. Happily, for the narrator of *Sense and Sensibility* appeared and claimed the right to speak in her own defense. When I woke up, however, I was unfortunately unable to recall her exact words, except for the first sentence:

I see what you would be at, Mr. Watt,—and, yes, I suppose I am in my own way what you would call modern—disgusting word! I first thought about this two generations ago when a copy of *Abinger Harvest* arrived in

Heaven. I noticed that E. M. Forster wrote about T. S. Eliot's "The Love Song of J. Alfred Prufrock": "The author was irritated by tea-parties, and not afraid to say so." It set me thinking: "What's so new about that? And why should people be afraid to say so? But I suppose we are, and I was." Perhaps that's why my family tried to cover up the role of aggression in my novels when they put up that memorial brass to me in Winchester Cathedral, in 1872, that ends with the quotation from Proverbs (31:26): "in her tongue is the law of kindness." Surely they should have noticed from my novels, if they looked nowhere else, that the law of kindness is a very complicated one to obey, especially if you also try to obey the law of truth. I think I did that battle rather well in *Emma*.

Of course it was more difficult, in my day, at least, for a woman: they were supposed to be all kindness, and truth was left to the men, like the right to anger. Men were entitled to have what the psychologists called "pugnacity," as long as most of it was whipped out of them at school; but women weren't supposed to have any, or at least not to show it. It wasn't easy for me when I started writing because I knew I wasn't like that at all. In *Northanger Abbey* I gave the "wrong" side of myself, the one that did not always think nice thoughts, to a man, Henry Tilney: and I'm afraid that later on I did the same thing a good deal in other novels. In a way I wish Emerson's "Self-Reliance" had been written then, at least the beginning, when he says: "In every work of genius we recognize our own rejected thoughts."

I started trying to do more with my "own rejected thoughts" in *Sense and Sensibility*, but I was timid: I hid behind Elinor, and let her hide behind me. Of course, we had a lot of fun together—when we collaborated, for instance, when, after one of Robert Ferrars's interminable vapid pomposities we wrote: "Elinor agreed to it all, for she did not think he deserved the compliment of rational opposition." I do believe that it's no good pretending that society isn't just what we see it is; and I don't think my novels make aggression any commoner or more brutal than it is in ordinary life. That's why I thought that the article by D. W. Harding—"Regulated Hatred: An Aspect of the Work of Jane Austen"—is unfair.[1] He understands my writing very well, I think, and gives me one good clue about why people have been admiring my novels more and more over the years. But why does he use the word "hatred"? That denies the normality of most of the

---

[1] [D. W. Harding's classic article on Jane Austen appeared originally in *Scrutiny* 8 (1940), 346-362. Ian Watt included the essay in his anthology of Austen criticism, *Jane Austen: A Collection of Critical Essays* (Englewood Cliffs, N. J.: Prentice-Hall, 1963), pp. 166-79. There is now a collection of Harding's essays on Austen: *Regulated Hatred and Other Essays on Jane Austen*, ed. Monica Lawlor (London: Athlone Press, 1998)—Ed.]

aggressive feelings and actions which I show in my novels because I observe them in the real world. Does Mr. Harding really think that it would be dangerous to eat the Donwell Abbey strawberries out of fear that Mrs. Elton might have poison hidden away in "all her apparatus of happiness"? Of course, in your century as in mine, the passions take a much less extreme form than those which animated the wars of Troy. But isn't there still, expressed in different manners, the same flux and reflux of aggressive motives as once inspired Homer, and as still animate the crowd when they laugh to see Punch and Judy trying to knock each other's brains out?

It is surely misunderstanding of kindness to think it should blind us to society's lack of it. Shouldn't we attack those who pretend to ignore that lack? Surely that's what comedy is for? After all, when intelligent, sensitive, and principled people meet, what better thing is there for them to do than share their assurance that they are seeing the same world? Isn't it bracing to face together our recognition of irremediable truths? And what better use can there be of our wit and experience than to write novels which make people who understand them laugh in liberated complicity at all the foolish and dangerous manifestations of aggression that are there in the world and in ourselves?

But I've talked too long. You seem quite gentlemanlike, so I'm sure you'll keep this talk as secret as Elinor kept Lucy Steele's about her engagement to Edward Ferrars. Oh, no, thank you, don't get up, I can see myself to the door. In fact, I don't use doors any more. I'm much freer than I was in the old days.

# 12

## ORAL DICKENS

In *A Room of One's Own*, Virginia Woolf asserts that "it is part of the novelist's convention not to mention soup and salmon and ducklings"* when he describes luncheon parties;* the novelists "seldom spare a word for what was eaten."[1]

One knows what she means, but she's wrong. Actually, there are two kinds of novelists: those that do and those that don't. Among the moderns, Joyce, Hemingway, Thomas Wolfe, and Scott Fitzgerald, not to mention Philip Roth, typically activate our tastebuds, while Conrad and Lawrence[2] and Henry James[3] don't, although people occasionally pass the port, meet in the Café Royal, or pour cups of tea. Earlier, there's very little about food and drink in Melville, but lots in the English novelists of the nineteenth century—in Mrs. Gaskell and Meredith as well as in Surtees and Trollope. In the richness and variety of his treatment

---

* "Oral Dickens" appeared originally in *Dickens Studies Annual* 3 (1974), 165-81, and is reprinted here by permission of AMS Press, New York. [For the genesis of this essay and its place in Dickens studies, see John O. Jordan, "The Critic as Host: On Ian Watt's 'Oral Dickens'," *Stanford Humanities Review* 8: 1 (Spring 2000), 197-205—Ed.]. The author is much indebted to those who, at Edmonton or elsewhere, gave him the benefit of their criticism; and especially to Philip Collins, Rowland McMaster, Steven Marcus, Thomas Moser, Robert Polhemus, Bambi Pratt, and Michael Wolff.
[1] *A Room of One's Own* (London: Hogarth Press, 1935), p. 16.
[2] Though food figures vitally and frequently in such travel books as Lawrence's *Sea and Sardinia* (New York: R. M. McBride, 1936), pp. 40-41, 65, 78-79, 98-107, 144-45.
[3] Though a *côtelette de veau à l'oseille* at the Cheval Blanc is specified (*Ambassadors*, XI, iii).

of food and drink Dickens is the indisputable master among the Victorian novelists; as, equally indisputably, he is both the heir of the tradition of Fielding and Smollett, and profoundly original.

I

Dickens's first published work, "Mr. Minns and his Cousin" (1832), was originally entitled "A Dinner at Poplar Walk." Though minimally gastronomic, it does contain, besides the large dinner at the cousin's, a very decent breakfast and an evening brandy-and-soda.[4] Dickens's first published volumes—*Sketches by Boz* in 1836 and *The Pickwick Papers* in 1837—are rich with eating and drinking. Statistically, *Pickwick Papers* probably has the densest alimentary concentration in all Dickens novels: there are apparently thirty-five breakfasts, thirty-two dinners, ten luncheons, ten teas, eight suppers, while drink is mentioned 249 times.[5] One goes through the book with envy, not only at the quality and quantity of the supplies, but at the way that they visit upon gross overindulgence—on that of Messrs. Pickwick, Winkle, Snodgrass, and Tupman, for instance—no worse retributions than permanent obesity, temporary inebriation, or occasional bouts of narcolepsy: those stern natural laws whose mildest sanctions in the real world are dyspepsia and hepatitis surrender to the Napoleonic unreality of Dickensian comedy.

The first gastric phase in Dickens lasts for something like a decade. Accounts of eating and drinking diminish very little, but, although they are normally of a relatively straightforward kind, Dickens also begins to use them to show larger moral and social conflicts. Thus *Oliver Twist* (1838) and *Nicholas Nickleby* (1839) make much of the contrast between grown-up overeating and youthful starvation. The two are memorably juxtaposed in such famous scenes as Oliver Twist in the workhouse asking for more, or Nicholas Nickleby hungering at Dotheboys Hall: in each case, Dickens, by insisting on the choice fare on the tables of the elders, dramatizes the naked intergenerational power play.

---

[4] Cited in William Ross Clark, "The Hungry Mr. Dickens," *Dalhousie Review* 36 (1956), 251. The article's general purport is to use Dickens's "tenacious interest in groceries and the wine list" as evidence of his "good vulgar zest for food" (pp. 256-57).
[5] Margaret Lane, "Dickens on the Hearth," in *Dickens 1970: Centenary Essays,* ed. Michael Slater (London: Chapman & Hall, 1970), p.166.

The climax of this first phase is presumably *A Christmas Carol* in 1843. As with the charmed immunity to gastritis enjoyed by the gourmandizers of *The Pickwick Papers,* it illustrates the extent to which Dickens's attitude toward food can bend not only normal reality but even his own apparent narrative purpose. Thus, in the vision summoned by the Ghost of Christmas Present, Scrooge's utilitarian parsimony would surely best be underlined by making us see how his fifteen-shilling-a-week clerk had a miserable Christmas dinner; but Dickens's own involvement in the happy satisfaction of appetite said no, and consequently both the antiutilitarian economic theme and Scrooge's dramatic change of heart (represented by his later gift of an enormous turkey) are largely undercut when we are invited to observe how the normal Cratchit Christmas fare would in any case have been a splendid triumph over narrow circumstances: "There never was such a goose," and "Oh, a wonderful pudding!"[6]

For Dickens, essential human values are at issue here. The Cratchits cannot really afford their festivities; and if they try, it is simply because good people characteristically place a high value on the good things of existence: conviviality, generosity, the quality of human life, even the truths of religion find their focus in a shared appreciation of the bounty on the festive board. Scrooge, of course, represents the opposite forces of existence—the calculating, the selfish, the isolated, the unspiritual: to him Christmas humbug is an offensive violation of the whole economic code, and of the social and moral attitudes which it dictates. These conflicting attitudes had been given a peculiar importance in the Victorian world by the triumph of industrial capitalism. The most obvious way to accumulate capital is, in general, to spend as little as possible; and so the conflict between the wish to consume and the need to conserve faced Dickens with a real and perpetual political dilemma. Prophetically, he gave literary expression to the only viable solution which Victorian society as a whole was to adopt—the Christmas feast, a temporary moratorium from the Protestant ethic, a few days when, as Claude Lévi-Strauss has pointed out, a burst of ritualized giving matches the wasteful extra-

---

[6] *A Christmas Carol,* in *Christmas Books, New Oxford Illustrated Dickens* (Oxford, 1945), p. 45. Unless otherwise specified, all subsequent quotations from Dickens are from this edition, and are cited by page number in the text.

vagances of the potlatch among primitive people and momentarily re-
stores the principle of reciprocity in social life.[7]

Quite early, then, Dickens expanded the role of food and drink so
that they played a vital part both in the plot structure and in the moral
significance of his novels. In the second phase, in the novels which follow *A Christmas Carol,* those from *Martin Chuzzlewit* (1844) and
*Dombey and Son* (1848) to *Hard Times* (1854) and *Little Dorrit*
(1857), these characteristics continue; there is still a great deal of eating
and drinking, but in keeping with Dickens's new fictional directions,
there is less simple celebration of the pleasures of the table, while the
appetites are presented in a much larger psychological and social perspective.

In *Martin Chuzzlewit,* as is usual in the later Dickens, the attitude of
the characters toward eating and drinking is deeply diagnostic. Thus the
genteel female indifference affected by Mercy and Charity Pecksniff
(shown in their disgust, for instance, at John Westlock whose clothes
smelled "oh it's impossible to say how strong . . . of smoke and punch")
is contrasted with the proper feminine concern for the creature comforts
of their males shown by Mrs. Lupin and especially by Ruth Pinch, with
her fully described, and eventually triumphant, production of a beef-
steak pudding. The good and generous characters—Tom Pinch, that
apologetically "great eater," John Westlock, and Mark Tapley—all have
robust appetites; but their appetite is of a very different kind from the
greed of such people as the inmates of Major Pawkins's boardinghouse
in New York, where "everybody seemed to eat his utmost in self-
defence" (16, 21, 270). As befits its traditional comic nature, the structure of *Martin Chuzzlewit* is very largely organized through scenes of
eating and drinking. The novel begins with supper at the Pecksniffs',
which itself follows the farewell feast of John Westlock offstage, and is
succeeded by the installation banquet for the new aspirant to architecture, young Martin Chuzzlewit. When the novel moves to London the
great contrasts of theme and character are made through the dinner at
Todgers's, the hollow splendor of the entertainment at the Anglo-
Bengalee Disinterested Loan and Life Assurance Company, and the
various marvelous scenes with Sairey Gamp. The conclusion is heralded
by the breakfast at old Mr. Chuzzlewit's, then by the dinner celebrating

---

[7] Claude Lévi-Strauss, *Les Structures élémentaires de la parenté* (Paris: Presses
Universitaires de France, 1949), p.71.

the nuptials of Ruth Pinch and John Westlock, and finally by the appropriately aborted wedding breakfast at Todgers's for Cherry Pecksniff and her Augustus.

*Martin Chuzzlewit* anticipates much of the darker side of the later novels, and in so doing reveals an important advance in Dickens's presentation of the varied pathologies of oral appetite. There are, for instance, the boarders at Major Pawkins': "Dyspeptic individuals bolted their food in wedges; feeding, not themselves, but broods of nightmares" (271); and much the same could be said of Jonas Chuzzlewit's hectic and joyless drunkenness. At the same time the basic theme of the predatory relatives fighting among themselves for old Chuzzlewit's fortune is consistently presented in terms of vampirism, scavenging, and cannibalism. Dickens's comic aim, though, mitigates the consequences of these individual and social perversions of appetite. Dickens cannot save Jonas from death, because he has murdered; but he completely relieves our gloomy foreboding of what sort of fare could be expected at Todgers's. The late Sunday dinner to honor the Pecksniffs is not at all what we might expect from that establishment's seedy environment or from Mrs. Todgers's lifelong mortification at the insatiable appetites of her lodgers for gravy; the meal is princely in substance and genuinely festive in its ceremony: "Oh, Todgers's could do it when it chose! Mind that" (146).

The carnival spirit, in fact, can even humanize hypocrisy and cruelty. When first seen eating, Pecksniff conceals his greed with evangelical rhetoric; but in the dinner scene at Todgers's, by the time Pecksniff has risen in drunken muddlement thirty times from his bed in an attempt to rejoin the company, we can no longer take his villainy seriously; and he becomes almost lovable when he courts Mrs. Todgers, and defying current linguistic prudery, pronounces: "The legs of the human subject, my friends, are a beautiful production." There follows his climactic proposal, whose phallic substitution is child's play to a normally contaminated mind: "I should very much like to see Mrs. Todgers's notion of a wooden leg, if perfectly agreeable to herself!" (152-53). The ancient traditions of feasting and comedy have outwitted Victorian sexual taboos.

Later, Pecksniff, together with that other great, greedy and heartless hypocrite, Sairey Gamp, combine to snap their fingers even at death. For seven nights the corpse of old Anthony Chuzzlewit lies above stairs, and, although its presence haunts his guilty son Jonas, Mrs. Gamp and Mr. Pecksniff, to say nothing of the undertakers, jovially reprove mor-

tality by ordering and devouring whatever their delicate fancies and
Jonas's captive purse can provide.

Mrs. Gamp and Mr. Pecksniff are compulsively oral in another sense.
They exemplify Dickens's characteristic tendency to make greedy people
eloquent—Mr. Chadband in *Bleak House* is another obvious example.
Even when old Martin Chuzzlewit finally unmasks Gamp and Pecksniff,
their oratorical genius rises to the occasion; and we are surely justified
in concluding that the perfunctory nature of their comeuppance in the
story suggests Dickens's sympathetic understanding of how an anxious
and hypocritical preoccupation with food and drink can be the result of
the same loneliness that underlies the individual's basic drive to create
an ideal image of himself through words and to impose this image on
others.

In the later novels Dickens becomes less comic and less forgiving:
witness his relentless treatment of the plethoric and revengeful cruelty of
Major Bagstock in *Dombey and Son* (1848), and of the obscure psychological compensations which lead Mrs. Clennam, in *Little Dorrit*
(1857), to alleviate her bedridden isolation by secretly indulging in par-
tridges and punch, at the cost of compromising her ostentatious Puritanism. On the other hand, Dickens makes no condemnation of the love
of food and drink, even for women; here again he understands very well
how it can become an obsessional compensation for personal sorrow
and frustration: witness the genuine sympathy in his treatment of Flora
Finching, whose frequent recourse to the consolation of brandy in her
tea is the present manifestation of her now permanently frustrated "past
appetite for romantic love" (158).

In *Dombey and Son* the class contrasts in eating, earlier used in
*Chuzzlewit*, function in a much more insistent way. None of the rich
enjoy their plenty, and all their reunions are the reverse of festive. In the
"cold collation" for Paul Dombey's christening, "there was a toothache
in everything"; and the nuptial breakfast for Mr. Dombey's second
wedding freezes the blood. The would-be rich, meanwhile, try to maintain their status by keeping what they have to themselves; Mrs. Pipchin,
for instance, consumes hot mutton chops to strengthen her constitution
from the former ravages of Peruvian mines, while her defenseless little
boarders get dinner "chiefly of the farinaceous and vegetable kind" (57,
101).

But the household servants over whom the rich and the would-be rich
tyrannize contrive to have their appropriate revenges. Below stairs, spe-

cial hot suppers and accompanying beverages, we notice, celebrate Paul's death, the flight of Edith and Florence, and the final crash when Dombey's mansion is put up for sale. There is no community of feeling among social classes even within the same household, at least until the last chapter when the broken father joins his daughter, her husband, and Captain Cuttle to open Sol Gills's long-promised bottle of ancient Madeira.

*David Copperfield* (1850) does not add much that is new to the fictional role of eating and drinking; but Dickens's vivid recall of how the world looks to the hungry child produces several memorable scenes. I still remember my own agonized incredulity as a boy at the way my parents were heartless enough to laugh at the harrowing scene where young David, on his way to Salem House school, is cheated out of his chops, his ale, his potatoes, and even his batter-pudding, by William the waiter. And it was when the well-upholstered and amply provisioned passengers in the coach mocked David Copperfield, even calling him a "boa-constrictor," for his allegedly preternatural gulosity (70) that I first became conscious of what still seems to me the most enduring truth about human affairs: that all power relations, whether between nations, or classes, or age groups, are most directly and yet most hypocritically expressed in the distribution of food and drink.

Many aspects of these relations are illustrated in the novel, from Steerforth's first act in "taking care of" David's seven shillings to purchase "a royal spread,"(54-55) and the conflicts between David and Dora over the grocery bills when they have set up house, to the various ways in which food, more specifically the withholding of food, was used as the major instrument of Victorian paternal tyranny. The most imaginative instance, perhaps, occurs when Mr. Murdstone first baffles David with the dizzy arithmetic of calculating the cost of "five thousand double-Gloucester cheeses at fourpence-halfpenny each, present payment," (84-85) and then punishes him by sending him to bed in disgrace with a dry slice of bread for dinner. The fantasies of parental sadism could hardly go further in elaborate refinement.

In Dickens's last phase—that succeeding *Little Dorrit* in 1857—one can detect some interesting developments in Dickens's own views of food and drink, as well as in the way he uses these concerns in his fiction.

*The Uncommercial Traveller* (1861) may be regarded as a biographical summing-up of the period of the dark novels, as they have come to be called. In vivid contrast to *Sketches by Boz,* two essays, ironically entitled "Refreshments for Travellers" and "A Little Dinner in an Hour," attack the inhospitality, the slowness, and the total culinary bankruptcy of English country inns and railway hotels; Dickens is here, alas! much closer to my own cheerless frequentations than to the jovial gourmandizing celebrated in *Boz* and *Pickwick.* Two other essays, "The Boiled Beef of New England" and "A Plea for Total Abstinence" (again, the title is ironical), take up two of the ways in which the less well-to-do are oppressed: by the usually miserable character of the public eating places for the poor, and by the blind punitive rancor of the temperance movement.

Dickens's last completed novel, *Our Mutual Friend* (1865), is not so much concerned with eating and drinking as most of the earlier novels, but it summarizes Dickens's basic moral and social attitudes. Dickens had rarely achieved anything as brilliantly outrageous as the ceremonial dinners at the Veneerings, fashionable, competitive, wholly unconcerned either with the pleasures of the table or with any adequate human feeling—neither of which would be possible in any case under the frigid tyranny of a butler called the Analytical Chemist. Nor, on the other hand, had Dickens earlier presented anything so close to the hidden yearnings of the human appetite as the total generosity and openness of Mr. Boffin's Bower: a reception room combining the advantages of a larder and taproom, where the ungrateful Silas Wegg, from the comfort of the settle, is permanently offered his choice of fare from the inviting case bottles and pies, cold joints, and other solids drawn up on the shelf in open view.

If *Our Mutual Friend* offers a climactic simplification of one side of Dickens's views on hospitality, *Great Expectations* (1861) offers perhaps the supreme example in Dickens of a comprehensive integration of eating and drinking into every aspect of the novel. Most obviously, food and drink are mentioned hundreds of times; and the attitude of almost every character toward the subject is presented, not only in itself, but as diagnostic of his moral essence and his social role. The rather few characters whom we can think of as good—notably Pip, Joe, Wemmick, Herbert Pocket, Abel Magwitch—are all fond of good food and drink; and in their various ways they express their love and consideration for others through the giving of food. How they do it is the subject of Barbara Hardy's "Food and Ceremony in *Great Expectations,*" the only serious study I know of attitudes to food in Dickens's novels. Her theme, briefly, is that, in *Great Expectations* as in *Bleak House,* "the same moral values are attached to meals—to the giving, receiving, eating, and serving of food. These values might be summed up as good appetite without greed, hospitality without show, and ceremony without pride or condescension."[8]

The novel begins with Magwitch terrifying Pip: "You know what wittles is. . . . You get me wittles." Next morning Pip raids the Christmas larder and smuggles out his haul. When he sees Magwitch wolfing down mincemeat and pork pie and cheese with terrifying animality, Pip's sympathy finally gets the better of his terror and disgust: "Pitying his desolation . . . I made bold to say, 'I am glad you enjoy it.'" At first Magwitch doesn't hear him, but when Pip repeats his civility, Magwitch answers, "Thankee, my boy, I do" (3, 16). "The rudest meal in the novel," Barbara Hardy comments, is thereby turned "into an introductory model of ceremony."[9]

This early reciprocity of compassion and gratitude is immediately rewarded. Magwitch, soon captured, protects Pip by concealing his theft of the food; and Joe easily forgives the theft itself when, in answer to Magwitch's apology, he answers, "God knows you're welcome to it." Later, Magwitch, no longer threatening to eat Pip's "fat checks," determines to provide Pip with his great expectations; in his convict exile, he often imagined: "Here's the boy again, a looking at me whiles I eats and drinks!" (36, 2, 304). But by the time Magwitch returns to England, snobbery has inhibited Pip's natural humanity; when Magwitch visits him in his Temple chambers, Pip at first intends to remain standing and let his guest drink his hot rum-and-water alone; he only changes his mind when, to his uncomprehending amazement, he notices that there are tears in Magwitch's eyes.

In this scene with Magwitch Pip is in a sense only repeating the way Mrs. Joe used to stand over Pip and Joe while she fed them, and the even more contemptuous rejection of Pip by Estella, when she first brought him beer and bread and meat at Satis House, "without looking at me, as insolently as if I were a dog in disgrace." The human importance of these reciprocities, or their damning absence, is expanded in two other episodes of the novel. First, the scene when Joe comes up to London and has breakfast with Pip and Herbert Pocket; Pip, ashamed of

[8] *Essays in Criticism* 13 (1963), 351.
[9] p. 354.

Joe's rough country manners, allows the reunion to become painfully embarrassing. He later blames himself: "I had neither the good sense nor the good feeling to know that this was all my fault." His own memory should really have afforded him a corrective parallel, for when, a country bumpkin himself and also just arrived in London, Pip had dinner with Herbert Pocket, his host so kindly corrected his table manners that "we both laughed and I scarcely blushed." "In London," says Pocket, "it is not the custom to put the knife in the mouth—for fear of accidents—and . . . while the fork is reserved for that use, it is not put further in than necessary" (57, 210, 169).

Magwitch himself, of course, had originally become a criminal out of hunger; he first came to consciousness "down in Essex, a-thieving turnips for my living." So Compeyson only had to tempt him: "What can you do?" he asked, and Magwitch replied, "Eat, drink . . . if you'll find the materials." Magwitch remains, in his own words, "a heavy grubber" (328, 329, 312), and for the same psychological reasons, no doubt, a heavy smoker; but we are obviously meant to see him as a victim of a sick society, not as psychologically maimed himself, as so many of the other characters in *Great Expectations* are.

Outside this quartet of benevolent eaters, Pip, Joe, Magwitch, and Herbert Pocket (and perhaps some of their echoes, like Clara, Wemmick, and his Aged Parent), attitudes to food in *Great Expectations* are diagnostic in quite a different way. Most obviously there is the petty egotistical tyranny of Pumblechook, bringing his Christmas offering of port and sherry to Mrs. Joe, but then dispensing hospitality with it to the sergeant of the search party and claiming all the credit; or Wopsle with his Christmas sermon on the gluttony of swine—the memory haunts Pip, and is only exorcised when he later toasts a sausage made from Wemmick's pig. Mr. Jaggers is tyrannical in a different way: he "cross-examined his very wine," and "seemed to bully his very sandwich as he ate it." Then there is the way that social pressure dictates the mode of eating: Wemmick is a vastly congenial table companion at his Walworth home; but in the official world of Little Britain, he merely "put[s] fish into the post-office" of his mouth. The implication of this gastric mutation is extended when Wemmick and Jaggers, united as proper unfeeling citizens of Little Britain, bully their poor client Mike for insulting them with his tears: "Get out of this office. I'll have no feelings here. Get out," says Jaggers; Mike does, and the two then go back "to work again with an air of refreshment upon them as if they had just had lunch" (229, 159, 396, 394).

As is usual in Dickens, it is the women characters who present the strongest examples or individual and social pathology, and almost without exception their symptoms are manifested through their attitudes to food. Mrs. Joe Gargery, who had married beneath her, even takes out her revenge on the bread and butter; she holds the bread against her "square impregnable bib . . . stuck full of pins and needles," and slaps the butter on "as if she were making a plaister." The vultures around Miss Havisham are all carrion-hungry, waiting until they can "come to feast upon her"; there is Camilla, who claims, "If I could be less affectionate and sensitive, I should have a better digestion and an iron set of nerves"; Georgiana, "an indigestive single woman, who called her rigidity religion and her liver love"; and Miss Sarah Pocket, who, Joe reports, on Miss Havisham's death is left "twenty-five pound per-annium fur to buy pills, on account of being bilious" (6, 8, 82, 193, 441).

Satis House is itself an ironically named symbol of unsatisfied appetite. Once the home of a wealthy brewer who married his cook, it is now the mausoleum of love, betrayed twenty-five years ago and now turned into hatred of others and the self. Miss Havisham lives on, waiting to replace the decaying bride cake on the great table with her own dead body; pretending to herself that she can rise above the humanity that has wounded her, she not only stops the clocks and refuses to see the light of day, but "has never allowed herself to be seen doing either [eating or drinking], since she lived this present life of hers" (228).

All the kinds of frustration and rejection, like all the kinds of satisfaction and acceptance, go together.

## II

There is presumably general agreement that Dickens himself shared the fascination with food and drink exhibited in the novels,[10] that, as Barbara Hardy puts it, Dickens "loves feasts and scorns fasts."[11] The records of the life amply substantiate this view. As soon after his marriage as he could afford it, Dickens made sure that none of Dora Spenlow's

---

[10] The drinking has been studied in Ross Wilson's "The Dickens of a Drink," *The Dickensian* 63 (1966), 46-61.

[11] "Food and Ceremony in *Great Expectations*," p. 351.

underdone mutton appeared on his domestic table. His biography features a virtually endless succession of splendid public banquets and lavish private parties; and the editors of the Pilgrim Edition of the letters even inform us that in the later nineteenth-century versions of Dickens's letters, edited by Georgina Hogarth and Mamie Dickens, "many references to food and drink which might be misunderstood [were] removed."[12]

This is not to say that Dickens personally was given either to overeating or heavy drinking. Dolby, his reading tour manager in America, noted: "Although he so frequently both wrote and talked about eating and drinking, I have never met with a man who partook less freely of the kindly fare placed before him.[13] If, then, Dickens's attentions to the details of the table in real life, or to the ceremony of making punch every evening, seem obsessive, it is as symbolic rather than as physical compulsions. They started, we may surmise, as projections of what Dickens dreamed about rather than of what he had experienced in his own past; and when he began writing, the tendency was probably encouraged by his audience, who loved his domestic hearthside heartiness. In either case we are dealing with wish fulfillments; and so we come, at last, to the cryptic triple pun in my title. What connection, if any, can plausibly or profitably be established between *oral* in the sense of "preoccupied with food and drink," *oral* in the sense of "spoken," and *oral* in the sense of the earliest phase or character formation described by Freud?

A good many biographical connections seem plausible, though also somewhat general and hypothetical. Not that Dickens was an infant starveling; it seems likelier that he had a difficult but not unhappy early childhood, if only because trust of others, success in work, and a great capacity for pleasure feature prominently not only in the novels but in his own character. The crucial biographical episode is more probably the five months or so at Warren's blacking warehouse. Dickens was then twelve; he would be nearing the end of the latency period when infantile sexual attitudes again come to the fore and are shaped into the basic sexual pattern of the future. But Dickens's mother had failed him

[12] *The Letters of Charles Dickens, Volume One 1820-1839*, ed. Madeline House and Graham Storey, The Pilgrim Edition (Oxford, 1965), I, x.

[13] Cited in Alfred H. Holt, "The Drink Question as Viewed by Dickens," *The Dickensian* 27 (1931), 170.

on every count; he was expelled from home and family; he was hungry, and had to find his own food; all his hopes for the future were, it seemed, permanently doomed; and he seems to have laid the blame on his mother—the very mother who, in Dickens's case, had performed not only the usual maternal offices, but had taught him to read. On the other hand, it was his father—the Micawberish grandiloquent spend-thrift—who eventually decided to take him out of Warren's warehouse and send him back to school. It was natural, therefore, that Dickens should have fallen back on the oral patterns of the distant past; that he should set out to achieve his early ambitions through prodigiously hard work; and that these ambitions should be connected with never going hungry, to be sure, but also with finding mother-substitutes rather than sexual experience.

As to the relationship between "oral regression" and Dickens's development as writer and oral performer, some connections seem fairly clear. We don't need Rabelais's Gargantua to teach us that what every baby would like to do at birth is shout: *"A boire! A boire! A boire!"* For most children, though, in this unlike Gargantua, or even John Henry for that matter, words normally come later, after weaning; but when words are finally mastered they provide new ways of obtaining nourishment, approval, and other modes of pleasure. The progression seems biologically natural: sucking, eating, and speaking employ the same organs and reflexes—the lips, the tongue, the jaws, the throat, the breathing appara tus. It is no doubt partly for this reason that writers in general are thought by many psychoanalysts to have strong oral personalities.[14] They are in a special case of people, in Karl Abraham's phrase, whose "longing to experience gratification by way of sucking has changed to a need to *give* by way of the mouth," and who therefore have "a constant need to communicate themselves orally to other people."[15] The contrast between these compulsive talkers, who are often professional actors, preachers, politicians, and professors as well as writers, and their oppo-

---

[14] See especially Edmund Bergler, "On a Clinical Approach to the Psychoanalysis of Writers," *Psychoanalytic Review* 31 (1944), 40-70; Abraham Brill, "Poetry as an Oral Outlet," *Psychoanalytic Review* 18 (1931), 357-78.

[15] In what is still the standard treatment of the subject, "The Influence of Oral Erotism on Character-Formation" (1924), (*Selected Papers of Karl Abraham*, ed. Ernest Jones, trans. Douglas Bryan and Alix Strachey [New York, 1953], I, 401.)

site, the stereotype of the genital character, is tellingly enshrined in the common phrases "the stiff upper lip" and "the strong silent man." Edward Glover amusingly contrasts this stock masculine type, "the stern-jawed hero of romance," with the oral comic performer, "the darling of the music-hall with the slack jaw and loose bibulous lips."[16] Dickens, we know, was a precocious oral performer himself, in storytelling and comic songs; he began to write certainly by his early teens; and his novels, of course, proved highly suitable to oral delivery.

As to the possible connection between speech considered as a mode of erotic satisfaction and the last phase of Dickens's life, the chronology seems almost too neat. In 1857 *Little Dorrit* appeared, the novel where, in Amy Dorrit and Miss Wade, Dickens analyzed the psychic masochism of the rejected child with remarkable insight.[17] It is also in 1857 that Dickens met Ellen Ternan, and stopped playacting. In 1858 he separated from his wife, and began the public readings, of which he gave some 470, beginning on 29 April 1858 and ending a few months before his death.[18] The readings may thus be an example of a syndrome found in such markedly oral writers as Balzac and Thomas Wolfe[19]—an obsessional and self-destructive "overproductivity."

The readings themselves were mainly taken from early works—the latest were from *David Copperfield* (1850); and they mainly feature feast scenes, comic scenes, or scenes where young children die—Nancy and Paul Dombey. In going back to an earlier stage of his development in literary subject matter, Dickens may have been enacting the same regressive impulse as in giving the readings themselves, which can be seen as reviving an earlier and more direct investment in oral satisfaction. He could burn many of the records of the past, cast off Catherine, and defy the world, but the strong oral components in his personality merely diverted their expression into an equally oral outlet in the readings: they would—and in fact did—at last persuade Dickens that he really could

---

[16] "The Significance of the Mouth in Psycho-Analysis," *British Journal of Medical Psychology* 4 (1924), 154.

[17] See Edmund Bergler, "*Little Dorrit* and Dickens' Intuitive Knowledge of Psychic Masochism," *American Imago* 14 (1957), 371-88.

[18] See Philip Collins, "Dickens' Public Readings: the Performer and the Novelist," in *Studies in the Novel* 1 (1969), 118-32.

[19] See Joseph Katz, "Balzac and Wolfe: A Study of Self-Destructive Overproductivity," *Psychoanalysis* 5 (1957), 3-20.

make the whole world hang, visibly and palpitatingly, upon his very lips.

It is not clear to me just what critical advantages would accrue if it could be established that Dickens himself was an oral-erotic character. The demonstration itself would certainly be reductive; it would have to be done most expertly not to be insufferably patronizing; and in the nature of things it would probably be impossible to find adequate evidence. For one thing, the baby's oral phase, being preverbal, is inaccessible to later introspection or analysis; for another, the kind of biographical evidence required is probably unavailable for Dickens. We can only speculate, and in my own view the advantages for literary criticism of so doing rest on rather delicate grounds. Any psychological theory may or may not help us in much the same ways as any other theoretical system may or may not help us understand a literary work more fully. At best it can serve two limited but valuable functions: either to provide a larger context of understanding which suggests possible interrelationships between various literary features that we have already observed or else to make us more sensitive to literary features which we have not previously noticed.

As to the first, the biographical hypothesis about the special nature of the psychological conflict in Dickens's last years, for instance, can provide a general perspective of psychological understanding for our literary sense that the last novels, and especially *Our Mutual Friend,* show a more inward and convincing presentation of adult sexuality; more generally it also helps us to see connections between other literary features of Dickens's work which in themselves have often been observed. For instance, the assumption that speech was itself a basic source of emotional satisfaction to Dickens may supply one reason for understanding why Dickens's whole literary style seems oral. As Robert Garis has observed, our "first impression, and a continuing one, in Dickens' prose is of a voice manipulating language with pleasure and pride in its own skill."[20] Rhetorical analysis also reveals Dickens's great reliance on many of the features of epic style: repetition, apostrophe, stock formulae of

---

[20] Robert Garis, *The Dickens Theatre: A Reassessment of the Novels* (Oxford: Clarendon Press, 1965), p. 16; "the performer is 'there' in the sense that he is displaying his skill" (p. 9); opening a Dickens novel the reader "knows, without consciously defining it as such, that humorous writing is theatrical in nature" (p. 40).

phrase and sound, extended similes, parataxis; and these features are constant in abundance, if not exactly in kind, throughout his writing life.

The same oral context would add a psychological explanation of the commonplace that, in the words of Kathleen Tillotson, Dickens was the first novelist to "put a child at the center of a novel for adults."[21] His novels reveal many of the perspectives of a child. Three obvious instances are: the amazing vividness wherever childhood experience is presented; the segregation of women characters into asexual angels or frustrated witches; and third, the relative lack of any convincing presentation of sexual love. Dickens's imaginative regression to life seen from the child's viewpoint takes many other forms. Thus Freud himself, though a great admirer of Dickens, objected to his characteristic "mannerisms," and singled out the way "all good people immediately become friends as soon as they meet, and work together throughout the whole book."[22] This is surely a youthful dream which later life, alas, rarely supports.

One can even narrow down some of the minor details of the novels to the specific viewpoint of the oral stage of character development. For instance, V. S. Pritchett includes in his anathema of Dickens's women the charge that they are "tiresome in childbirth . . . continuously breeding,"[23] and to this one can add that the only woman in the novels who is a happy mother, morally admirable, and possessed of effective eloquence, happens to be the humble Polly Toodles—Paul Dombey's wetnurse: her understanding is equal to manipulating not only Susan Nipper but even Mr. Dombey, and she consoles Florence with a moral tale that would not be out of place in the mouth of any of the published Victorian matriarchs who provided the reading public with infantile morality.

Many other commonplaces of Dickens criticism can be seen in projections of the psychic politics of the baby. The heroes and heroines are often orphans, or they are only children; or if not, they have no brothers,

---

[21] Kathleen Tillotson, *Novels of the Eighteen-Forties* (Oxford: Clarendon Press, 1954), p. 50.

[22] Ernest Jones, *The Life and Work of Sigmund Freud* (New York: Basic Books, 1963-67), I, 174 (5 October 1883). Another youthful residue, perhaps, was Dickens's "easy toleration of feeblemindedness," which also irritated Freud.

[23] "The Comic World of Dickens," *The Victorian Novel: Modern Essays in Criticism*, ed. Ian Watt (New York: Oxford University Press, 1971), p. 30.

and their sisters die young, like David Copperfield's, or seem to have been born little mothers, like Florence Dombey, Little Dorrit, and Lizzie Hexham: one way of putting all this would be to say that in his novels Dickens permits no threatening sibling rivals at the maternal board or bosom.

The focus on the oral elements in Dickens also seems to me to have a searching power which discovers elements in his characterization and even in his plots which have not been observed before, or at least have received little critical notice. More specifically, it reveals a remarkably detailed anticipation in Dickens's novels of the theories of the oral character initiated much later by Freud and developed by Karl Abraham and Edward Glover.

The psychological concept of the oral character is itself protean and amorphous. Karl Abraham explains the main reason in "The Influences of Oral Erotism on Character-Formation": "The libidinal cathexis of the mouth which characterizes infancy can still be employed in later life," and is not repressed by the adult world, as the later anal and phallic pleasures are. These early oral traits therefore remain as more or less normal ongoing components of the personality, and do "not need to be changed into character formation or sublimated to the same extent as the anal ones."[24]

Karl Abraham, Edward Glover, Freud himself, and various later disciples, such as Erik Erikson, are, however, substantially agreed on the main lasting effects upon individual character which are produced by the particular circumstances of the oral stage. After birth the child develops its sense of pleasure, purpose, and relation to the outside world primarily through suckling. If in its first year or so the experience is gratifying and prolonged, the child is likely to develop an optimistic character. This optimistic and ambitious character can be of two kinds. In favorable circumstances an early self-confidence may later help the child to successfully achieve its aims in life; but a second kind of character may also develop, one in which a vague optimism habituates the individual to passivity, to a life of waiting for the world as mother to give him what he needs. As Edward Glover puts it in "The Significance of the Mouth in Psycho-Analysis," behind the ambition of the oral-erotic there is often "a feeling that the silver spoon is or ought to have been in the mouth." The phrase itself surely recalls many characters in Dickens's

---

[24] *Selected Papers of Karl Abraham* (New York: Basic Books, 1953), I, 394.

novels; when Glover goes on to say that, "if the worst comes to the worst," the frustrated oral character falls back on "the old oral omnipotence" of his earliest experience, and then adds that this character type always assumes that "something is bound to turn up,"—Micawber himself turns up in our minds. Glover explains that such a character "doubtless . . . clings in the secret recesses of his mind to the magic formula, 'Table! Cover thyself.'"[25] Mr. Micawber is ambitious, in his own way, and when catastrophe has become total, we can be sure that a table will soon appear, and cover itself with the ingredients for Mr. Micawber's punch.

Where oral satisfaction has been denied or cut short early, the main tendencies, according to psychoanalytic theory, are toward three related types of character development. First, there are those who are always, whether modestly or aggressively, asking for something from others, the people who "cling like leeches"; secondly, there are the compulsive talkers, those earlier described by Abraham as "having a need to *give* by way of the mouth";[26] and third, we have the oral-sadistic character, where, with the double trauma of the coming of teeth and the end of weaning, biting—or later making biting remarks—becomes the way by which the frustrating world can be held and mastered.

These five oral character types can, of course, only be roughly differentiated, and they are usually found in combination with other traits; nevertheless, I hope that even this brief and simplified outline has been sufficient to transmit some ripples of recognition out into Dickens's fictional world. We surely meet examples of all these character types in the novels of Dickens, and this becomes a more convincing measure of his initial insight when we reflect on how few other novelists even begin to supply the kind of information about physiognomy, gesture, and domestic habits that we need before we can construct such hypotheses about their characters.

The happy but independent optimists no doubt include Mr. Pickwick and Mark Tapley; for the dependent optimists a good many can be added to Mr. Micawber, with Harold Skimpole an extreme example; somewhere in between the two come Dickens's directly autobiographical

---

[25] *British Journal of Medical Psychology* 4 (1924), 154. See also Abraham on the overindulged, whose "whole attitude towards life shows that they expect the mother's breast to flow for them eternally" (p. 399).
[26] *Selected Papers of Karl Abraham*, pp. 400-401.

characters—David Copperfield and Pip—the shy, undersized, and oral-ambitious character, the would-be mother's boy, the "jilted baby," to use Edward Glover's expressive term.[27] Among the leeches Dickens gives a host of clinging, demanding characters, usually women, like Camilla in *Great Expectations*. As for the compulsively verbal characters, they are endless: Pecksniff, Chadband, and Flora Finching, for instance. They are three obvious examples of those multitudes of urban characters of whom Pritchett writes that "Dickens saw they were people whose inner life was hanging out, so to speak, on their tongues."[28] In many cases these talkers tend to oral sadism: Sairey Gamp is presumably the classical example, but there are innumerable variants, from Mrs. Clennam to Uriah Heep. The fully developed pathology of the sadistic biter, physical or verbal, is exhibited in such horrors as Mr. Murdstone, Quilp, Arthur Gride, and Mr. Lammle; its purest manifestation is probably Mr. Carker: at Edith Dombey's wedding he approaches her "with his white teeth glistening . . . more as if he meant to bite her, than to taste the sweets that linger on her lips" (444); and it is significant that it was only because of Lord Jeffrey's objection that Dickens did not, in the event, allow Carker to sink his ever-bared teeth into Edith's white breasts.[29]

Much more could be said on how much of Dickens's characterization fits into the oral categories of psychoanalysis; and one could also make a simpler distinction, that based on the idea that the oral character types may essentially be divided into biters and suckers. Dickens could accept neither as adequate persons, but we might call many of his youthful heroes secret suckers; they are, no doubt, innocent, trusting, and benevolent, but they are also rather simple, passive, and unpracticed with women.

To pass very briefly to how Dickens's plots also reflect the oral perspective, one can say that the job of the typical Dickens plot is to find magic providers for the secret suckers. This narrative direction can be regarded as an exaggerated form of what is probably the tendency of fiction in general. Dickens's novels often begin with the hero in youth,

---

[27] *British Journal of Medical Psychology*, p. 140.

[28] "Histrionic and self-made mythmakers are not simply odd 'characters' but are pretty well the norm in the myth city" (*George Meredith and English Comedy. The Clark Lectures for 1969* [New York: Random House, 1969], p. 21).

[29] Edgar Johnson, *Charles Dickens: His Tragedy and Triumph*, 2 vols. (Boston: Simon and Schuster, 1952), II, 622.

in insecurity and frustration, in the stage, that is, where the neonate has already been separated from his mother; and after endless vicissitudes, we find that the hero ends a step or two back from where the novel began, in a warm little haven, characterized by lots of food and drink, easily available comforts, and total security.[30]

III

That Dickens creates people in his novels who are marked by residues of the oral stage according to Freudian theories of character development, does not, of course, prove anything about Dickens's own personality. On the other hand, if what has been said about the characters in his novels can be demonstrated from the text, it does not require any extraneous biographical and psychological evidence; and we already have the general support we need in the generally accepted view that Dickens's imagination remained rooted in the perceptions of childhood, perceptions which give him an unsurpassed mastery of the internal psychological revelations which are immanent in human physiognomy, gestures, and habits of speech. The present essay could then be viewed primarily as an exploration of one particular aspect of the hallucinated clarity with which the child sees other people as larger-than-life manifestations of his own interests and perspectives.

For Dickens, and indeed for the Victorian child in general, all older people would tend to be seen in two main roles: as eaters, drinkers, and talkers themselves; and as powerful dispensers or withholders of his own oral pleasures. This itself comes close to supplying a perspective for understanding why so many of the basic conflicts in Dickens's novels can be reduced to the simple primitive choice between eating or being eaten. The sociological perspective would reinforce the psychological. We know that Victorian parents habitually used the giving or withholding of food as an instrument of religious, moral, and social discipline.[31] Presumably, therefore, the child not only categorized adults as

---

[30] Dickens's tendency to "miniaturize" the habitations of his good characters is analyzed in an interesting phenomenological study by Lucien Pothet, "Sur quelques images d'intimité chez Dickens," *Études anglaises* 23 (1970), 136-57.

[31] There are many examples in Augustus Hare's autobiography of how not only his mother but his aunt and his grandmother used the withholding of food as moral weapons, treatment varying from being put on "bread and water" to

good or bad according to whether he was being well fed or not. Giving or consuming good food was deeply equated with goodness; and this equation was reinforced by economic and class factors, since there was a much greater difference then than now between the staple diets of different classes.[32]

As for the connection between the three senses of *oral,* a few concluding generalizations seem called for. First, as regards speech, it seems that there is still much to say about the way Dickens makes speaking itself both a directly physical reality in his novels, and also an infinitely symbolic activity; more generally, that there is still much to learn about the physical, physiological, and psychosexual functions of the act of speech.

Secondly, we should surely challenge the adverse judgment on all the oral functions which is implicit in our current terminology. The basic reason for this adverse judgment on oral satisfactions is presumably not so much the puritan objection to gluttony or the pleasures of the physical appetites in general, as it is Freud's biologically based evolutionary model for psychological development: oral satisfactions are "regressive" because they denote a deflection from, or a failure to achieve, "mature genitality," that "psychoanalytic Utopia," as Erik Erikson has called it.[33] Erikson's irony points to the reductive and pejorative connotations of such terms as *oral,* or, for that matter, *anal.* In any case, all surviving biological species have presumably achieved their genital Utopia; and though human civilization has done much with the genital component as a basis—romantic love and the family for instance—it is no more impressive than what man has done with the oral components, and it is certainly not so distinctive of man. All human societies have developed cooking, and no others have; man is indeed, as Boswell defined him, a

---

"break my spirit," to administering a "forcing spoon" of "rhubarb and soda" to punish his "carnal indulgence" in sweets. (Augustus J. C. Hare, *The Years with Mother,* ed. Malcolm Barnes [London: George Allen & Unwin, 1952], pp. 16, 21, 60-62. Hare was born in 1834.)

[32] See John Burnett, *Plenty and Want: A Social History of Diet in England from 1815 to the Present Day* (London: Routledge, 1966), especially the chapters on the food of the town workers and of the rich in the early Victorian period.

[33] Erik Erikson, *Childhood and Society,* 2d ed., (New York: W. W. Norton & Co., 1963), pp. 92, 76.

"Cooking Animal."[34] Among the other oral components of culture which are unique to man one should at least list three that are particularly important for Dickens's novels. First, the invention of fermented beverages, which was no inconsiderable achievement; second, social laughter, which is basic to comedy; and third, of course, speech. *Homo loquens* is a reality, and were it not, we would not even have been able to christen him, however presumptuously, *Homo sapiens.*

The Freudian scheme of libido development also presupposes, primarily for necessary therapeutic purposes, a contradiction between the oral and the genital impulses that is misleading as far as most human, and especially most literary, experience is concerned.[35] There is no doubt considerable truth in V. S. Pritchett's view that oral pleasures were substituted for sexual ones in the Victorian novel: "What replaced the sane eighteenth-century attitude to sex in the comic writings of Dickens? I think probably the stress was put on another hunger—the hunger for food, drink and security, the jollity and good cheer."[36] At a certain point of concentration, interest in food does exclude everything else, as Dick-

---

[34] *Journal of a Tour to the Hebrides with Samuel Johnson, LL.D*, ed. R. W. Chapman (London: Oxford University Press, 1961), pp. 179-80. Burke replied, "Your definition is good, and I now see the full force of the common proverb, 'There is reason in roasting of eggs.'"

[35] The association is manifest, for example, in what is perhaps Dickens's most orgiastic scene, and one which might have been used by Michael Steig in his "Dickens' Excremental Vision," *Victorian Studies* 13 (1970), 339-54. In *A Christmas Carol*, poor anal Scrooge sees his own room transformed, with holly and mistletoe and yule logs and gorgeous groceries: "Heaped up on the floor, to form a kind of throne, were turkeys, geese, game, poultry, brawn, great joints of meat, sucking-pigs, long wreaths of sausages, mince-pies, plum-puddings, barrels of oysters, red-hot chestnuts, cherry-cheeked apples, juicy oranges, luscious pears, immense twelfth-cakes, and seething bowls of punch, that made the chamber dim with their delicious steam. In easy state upon this couch, there sat a jolly Giant, glorious to see; who bore a glowing torch, in shape not unlikely Plenty's horn, and held it up, high up, to shed its light on Scrooge" (p. 39). American idiom, fortunately, makes it superfluous to explicate the symbolism of Plenty's horn.

[36] P. 30. Pritchett continues: "Domestic life means meals. Good food makes people good. To our taste now this doesn't seem very amusing. Half of Victorian England was disgustingly overfed, and since Dickens was an extremist he pushed the note of jollity much too far. The jolly Dickens is the one part of him that has become unreadable."

ens reminds us in his surrealistic vignette of Lady Scadgers in *Hard Times:* "an immensely fat old woman, with an inordinate appetite for butcher's meat, and a mysterious leg which had now refused to get out of bed for fourteen years" (42). But within the more usual ranges of behavior mutual support between the oral and the genital component is the norm. We hardly need reminding of what play kissing is often a prologue to, nor of the traditional cooperation of food, drink, and laughter with Eros. Mr. Bumble understands very well one thing normally leads to another when he remarks to Mrs. Sowerberry, to explain poor Oliver Twist's sudden turning on his tormentors: "It's not Madness, ma'am . . . it's Meat."[37]

As regards literature, we must surely come to terms with the fact that the mouth is the basis for social and intellectual community: beginning with food and drink; going on to talk and laughter; ending in song and story and play. Satire for instance, is supposed to have had its origin in the *lanx satura*, the fertility festival of the full bowl; and comedy, derived from the Greek words for song and social merrymaking, commingles all the oral pleasures, without disdaining the support of whatever anal and genital amusements society allows. As for Dickens, the hypothesis that his own personality was powerfully oral in tendency would only supply another perspective for what we know already; that there is a psychological cost for all achievement—even for the creative achievement which places Dickens among the supreme figures in the pantheon of Western comedy.

---

[37] *Oliver Twist*, ed. Kathleen Tillotson, The Clarendon Dickens (Oxford, 1966), p. 41. Bumble continues: "You've over fed him, ma'am. You've raised an artificial soul and spirit in him, ma'am, unbecoming a person of his condition."

# 13

# THE FIRST PARAGRAPH OF *THE AMBASSADORS*: AN EXPLICATION

When I was asked if I would do a piece of explication at this conference, I was deep in Henry James, and beginning *The Ambassadors*: so the passage chose itself; but just what was explication, and how did one do it to prose? [*1] I take it that whereas explanation, from *explanare*, suggests a mere making plain by spreading out, explication, from *explicare*, implies a progressive unfolding of a series of literary implications, and thus partakes of our modern preference for multiplicity in method and meaning: explanation assumes an ultimate simplicity, explication assumes complexity.

Historically, the most developed tradition of explication is presumably that which developed out of medieval textual exegesis and became the chief method of literary instruction in French secondary and higher education in the late nineteenth century. *Explication de texte* in France reflects the rationalism of nineteenth-century Positivist scholarship. At its worst, the routine application of the method resembles a sort of bayonet drill in which the exposed body of literature is riddled with etymologies and dates before being despatched in a harrowingly insensitive *résumé*. At its best, however, *explication de texte* can be solidly illumi-

---

* "The First Paragraph of *The Ambassadors*: An Explication" appeared originally in *Essays in Criticism* 10:3 (1960), 250-74, and is reprinted here by permission of Oxford University Press.
[1] A paper given at the Ninth Annual Conference of Non-Professorial University Teachers of English, at Oxford on April 5, 1959. I am very grateful for the many criticisms and suggestions made in the course of the subsequent discussion; in preparing the paper for publication I have taken as much account of them as possible, short of drastic expansion or alteration. I also acknowledge my debt to Dorothea Krook, Frederick C. Crews, and Henry Nash Smith.

nating, and it then serves to remind us that a piece of literature is not necessarily violated if we give systematic attention to such matters as its author, its historical setting, and the formal properties of its language.

Practical Criticism, on the other hand, as it was developed at Cambridge by I. A. Richards, continues the tradition of the British Empiricists. Inductive rather than deductive, it makes a point of excluding linguistic and historical considerations, so as to derive—in appearance at least—all the literary values of a work empirically from the words on the page. In the last thirty years, the emphasis of Practical Criticism on the autonomy of the text has revolutionized the approach to literary studies, and has proved itself a technique of supreme value for teaching and examining students; I myself certainly believe that its use should be expanded rather than curtailed. Yet, at least in the form in which I picked it up as a student and have later attempted to pass it on as a teacher, both its pedagogical effects and its basic methodological assumptions seem to me to be open to serious question. For many reasons. Its air of objectivity confers a spurious authority on a process that is often only a rationalization of an unexamined judgment, and that must always be to some extent subjective; its exclusion of historical factors seems to authorize a more general antihistoricism; and—though this objection is perhaps less generally accepted—it contains an inherent critical bias in the assumption that the part is a complete enough reflection of the literary whole to be profitably appreciated and discussed in isolation from its context. How far this is true, or how far it can be made to appear so by a well-primed practitioner, is a matter of opinion; but it is surely demonstrable that Practical Criticism tends to find the most merit in the kind of writing which has virtues that are in some way separable from their larger context; it favors kinds of writing that are richly concrete in themselves, stylistically brilliant, or composed in relatively small units. It is therefore better suited to verse than to prose; and better suited to certain kinds of either than to others where different and less concentrated merits are appropriate, as in the novel.

As for its pedagogical effects—and here again I have mainly my own past experience in mind—Practical Criticism surely tends to sensitize us towards objects only within a certain range of magnitude: below that threshold it becomes subjective and impressionist, paying very little attention to the humble facts of the grammar and syntax of the words on the page; while at the other extreme, it often ignores the larger meaning, and the literary and historical contexts of that meaning.

As a practical matter these restrictions may all be necessary for the pupil and salutary for the teacher; and I mention them mainly to justify my present attempt to develop the empirical and inductive methods of Practical Criticism in such a way as to deal with those elements in a literary text whose vibrations are so high or so low that we Ricardian dogs have not yet been trained to bark at them.

It is mainly in these penumbral areas, of course, that the French *explication de texte* habitually operates; but its analyses of grammar and of the literary and historical background are usually a disconnected series of discrete demonstrations which stop short of the unifying critical synthesis that one hopes for. Until fairly recently the same could have been said, and perhaps with greater emphasis, about the German tradition of literary scholarship, with its almost entirely independent pursuit of philology and philosophy. More recent trends in *Stilforschung* however—of which Wolfgang Clemen's *The Development of Shakespeare's Imagery* (Bonn, 1936) was an early example—come closer to, and indeed partly reflect, the more empirical Anglo-American models of literary criticism; while, even more promising perhaps for the study of prose, though seemingly quite independent of the influence of Practical Criticism, is the development, mainly from Romance philology, of what has come to be called "stylistics."

For my purposes, however, it remains not so much a Method as a small group of isolated, though spectacular, individual triumphs. I yield to no one in my admiration for Leo Spitzer's *Linguistics and Literary History* (Baltimore, 1948), or for the continual excitement and illumination offered in Erich Auerbach's *Mimesis* (1946: trans. Willard Trask, Princeton, N.J., 1963); their achievements, however, strike me mainly as tributes to the historical imagination and philosophical understanding of the German mind at its best; I find their brilliant commentaries on words or phrases or passages essentially subjective; and if I am tempted to emulate the *bravura* with which they take off from the word on the page to leap into the farthest empyreans of *Kulturgeschichte*, I soon discover that the Cambridge east winds have condemned me to less giddy modes of critical transport.

Yet what other models are there to help one to analyze a paragraph of Jamesian prose? Some of the historical studies of prose style could, conceivably, be applied; but I am fearful of ending up with the proposition that James was a Ciceronian—with Senecan elements, of course, like everyone else. As for the new linguistics, the promises as regards lit-

erary analysis seem greater than the present rewards: the most practical
consequence of my exposure to Charles Fries's *The Structure of English:
An Introduction to the Construction of English Sentences* (New York,
1952), for example, was to deprive me of the innocent pleasure that
comes from imagining you know the names of things. Structural linguistics in general is mainly (and rightly) concerned with problems of definition and description at a considerably more basic level of linguistic usage than the analysis of the literary effect of Henry James's grammatical
particularities seems to require.

Perhaps the most promising signs of the gaps being filled have come
from what are—in that particular area—amateurs: from Francis Berry's
*Poets' Grammar* (London, 1958), or Donald Davie's *Articulate Energy*
(London, 1955). But they don't help much with prose, of course, and
they aren't basically concerned with grammatical structure in the ordinary sense; although Davie's notion that the principle of continuity in
poetry is, after all, primarily grammatical and rational at least lessens
the separation between the stylistic domains of poetry and prose, and
suggests some ways of studying how syntax channels expressive force.

Virtually helpless,[2] then, I must face the James passage alone as far as
any fully developed and acceptable technique for explicating prose is
concerned; but there seem to be good reasons why practical criticism
should be supplemented by some of the approaches of French and German scholarship, and by whatever else will lead one from the words on
the page to matters as low as syntax and as high as ideas, or the total
literary structure.

I

Strether's first question, when he reached the hotel, was about his friend;
yet on his learning that Waymarsh was apparently not to arrive till evening
he was not wholly disconcerted. A telegram from him bespeaking a room
'only if not noisy,' reply paid, was produced for the inquirer at the office, so
that the understanding they should meet at Chester rather than at Liverpool
remained to that extent sound. The same secret principle, however, that had

---

[2] This was before the appearance of the English Institute's symposium *Style in
Prose Fiction*, ed. Harold Clark Martin (New York: Columbia University Press,
1959), which offers, besides two general surveys and a valuable bibliography of
the field, stylistic studies of six novelists, including one by Charles R. Crow, of
"The Style of Henry James: *The Wings of the Dove*."

prompted Strether not absolutely to desire Waymarsh's presence at the dock, that had led him thus to postpone for a few hours his enjoyment of it, now operated to make him feel he could still wait without disappointment. They would dine together at the worst, and, with all respect to dear old Waymarsh—if not even, for that matter, to himself—there was little fear that in the sequel they shouldn't see enough of each other. The principle I have just mentioned as operating had been, with the most newly disembarked of the two men, wholly instinctive—the fruit of a sharp sense that, delightful as it would be to find himself looking, after so much separation, into his comrade's face, his business would be a trifle bungled should he simply arrange for this countenance to present itself to the nearing steamer as the first 'note' of Europe. Mixed with everything was the apprehension, already, on Strether's part, that it would, at best, throughout, prove the note of Europe in quite a sufficient degree.[3]

---

[3] Henry James, *The Ambassadors* (Revised Collected Edition, Macmillan: London, 1923). Since there are a few variants that have a bearing on the argument, it seems desirable to give a collation of the main editions; P is the periodical publication (*The North American Review*, clxxvi, 1903); 1A the first American editon (Harper and Brothers, New York, 1903); 1E the first English edition (Methuen and Co., London, 1903); NY, the "New York Edition," New York and London, 1907-9 (the London Macmillan edition used the sheets of the American edition); CR the "Collected Revised Edition," London and New York, 1921-31 (which uses the text of the New York Edition). It should perhaps be explained that the most widely used editions in England and America make misleading claims about their text: the "Everyman" edition claims to use the text "of the revised Collected Edition," but actually follows the first English edition in the last variant; while the "Anchor" edition, claiming to be "a faithful copy of the text of the Methuen first edition," actually follows the first American edition, including the famous misplaced chapters.

ll.4-5.   *reply paid* NY, CR; *with the answer paid* P, 1A, 1E.

l.5.   *inquirer* P, 1A, 1E, CR; *enquirer* NY.

l.6.   *Understanding they* NY, CR; *understanding that they* P, 1A, 1E.

l.11.   *feel he* NY, CR; *feel that he* P, 1A, 1E.

l.15.   *Shouldn't* CR; *shouldn't* NY; *should not* P, 1A, 1E.

l.16.   *Newly disembarked*, all eds. except P: *Newly-disembarked*.

l.20.   *arrange that this countenance to present* NY, CR; *arrange that this countenance should present* P, 1A, 1E.

l.22.   *"note" of Europe* CR; *"note," for him, of Europe*, P, 1A, 1E; *"note," of Europe*, NY.

l.23.   *that it would* P, 1A, NY, CR; *that he would*, 1E.

It seems a fairly ordinary sort of prose, but for its faint air of elaborate portent; and on second reading, its general quality reminds one of what Strether is later to observe—approvingly—in Maria Gostrey: an effect of "expensive, subdued suitability." There's certainly nothing particularly striking in the diction or syntax; none of the immediate drama or rich description that we often get at the beginning of novels; and certainly none of the sensuous concreteness that, until recently, was regarded as a chief criterion of good prose in our long post-imagistic phase: if anything, the passage is conspicuously unsensuous and unconcrete; a little dull perhaps, and certainly not easy reading.

The difficulty isn't one of particularly long or complicated sentences: actually they're of fairly usual length: I make it an average of 41 words; a little, but not very much, longer than James's average of 35 in Book 2, chapter 2 of *The Ambassadors*, according to R. W. Short's count, in his very useful article "The Sentence Structure of Henry James" (*American Literature*, XVIII [March 1946], 71-88).[4] The main cause of difficulty seems rather to come from what may be called the delayed specification of referents: "Strether" and "the hotel" and "his friend" are mentioned before we are told who or where they are. But this difficulty is so intimately connected with James's general narrative technique that it may be better to begin with purely verbal idiosyncrasies, which are more easily isolated. The most distinctive ones in the passage seem to be these: a preference for non-transitive verbs; many abstract nouns; much use of "that"; a certain amount of elegant variation to avoid piling up personal pronouns and adjectives such as "he," "his," and "him"; and the presence of a great many negatives and near-negatives.

By the preference for non-transitive verbs I mean three related habits: a great reliance on copulatives—"Strether's first question *was* about his friend"; "*was* apparently not to arrive": a frequent use of the passive voice—"*was* not wholly *disconcerted*"; "a telegram . . . *was produced*"; "his business *would be* a trifle *bungled*"; and the employment of many intransitive verbs—"the understanding . . . remained . . . sound"; "the. . . principle . . . operated to." My count of all the verbs in the indicative would give a total of 14 passive, copulative, or intransitive uses as opposed to only 6 transitive ones: and there are, in addition, frequent infinitive, participial, or gerundial uses of transitive verbs, in all of which

---

[4] I am also indebted to the same author's "Henry James's World of Images," *PMLA* 68 (Dec. 1953), 943-60.

the active nature of the subject verb-and-object sequence is considerably abated—"on his learning"; "bespeaking a room"; "not absolutely to desire"; "led him thus to postpone."

This relative infrequency of transitive verbal usages in the passage is associated with the even more pronounced tendency towards using abstract nouns as subjects of main or subordinate clauses: "question"; "understanding"; "the same secret principle"; "the principle"; "his business." If one takes only the main clauses, there are four such abstract nouns as subjects, while only three main clauses have concrete and particular subjects ("he," or "they").[5]

I detail these features only to establish that in this passage, at least, there is a clear quantitative basis for the common enough view that James's late prose style is characteristically abstract; more explicitly, that the main grammatical subjects are often nouns for mental ideas, "question," "principle," etc.; and that the verbs—because they are mainly used either non-transitively, or in infinitive, participial, and gerundial forms—tend to express states of being rather than particular finite actions affecting objects.

The main use of abstractions is to deal at the same time with many objects or events rather than single and particular ones: and we use verbs that denote states of being rather than actions for exactly the same reason—their much more general applicability. But in this passage, of course, James isn't in the ordinary sense making abstract or general statements; it's narrative, not expository prose; what need exploring, therefore, are the particular literary imperatives which impose on his style so many of the verbal and syntactical qualities of abstract and general discourse; of expository rather than narrative prose.

Consider the first sentence. The obvious narrative way of making things particular and concrete would presumably be "When Strether reached the hotel, he first asked 'Has Mr. Waymarsh arrived yet?'" Why does James say it the way he does? One effect is surely that, instead of a sheer stated event, we get a very special view of it; the mere fact that actuality has been digested into reported speech—the question "was about his friend"—involves a narrator to do the job, to interpret the action, and also a presumed audience that he does it for: and by implication,

---

[5] Sentences one and four are compound or multiple, but in my count I haven't included the second clause in the latter—"there was little fear": though if we can talk of the clause having a subject it's an abstract one—"fear."

the heat of the action itself must have cooled off somewhat for the translation and analysis of the events into this form of statement to have had time to occur. Lastly, making the subject of the sentence "question" rather than "he," has the effect of subordinating the particular actor, and therefore the particular act, to a much more general perspective: mental rather than physical, and subjective rather than objective; "question" is a word which involves analysis of a physical event into terms of meaning and intention: it involves, in fact, both Strether's mind and the narrator's. The narrator's, because he interprets Strether's act: if James had sought the most concrete method of taking us into Strether's mind—"'Has Mr. Waymarsh come yet?' I at once asked"—he would have obviated the need for the implied external categorizer of Strether's action. But James disliked the "mere platitude of statement" involved in first-person narrative; partly, presumably, because it would merge Strether's consciousness into the narrative, and not isolate it for the reader's inspection. For such isolation, a more expository method is needed: no confusion of subject and object, as in first-person narration, but a narrator forcing the reader to pay attention to James's primary objective Strether's mental and subjective state.

The "multidimensional" quality of the narrative, with its continual implication of a community of three minds—Strether's, James's, and the reader's—isn't signaled very obviously until the fourth sentence—"The principle I have just mentioned as operating . . ."; but it's already been established tacitly in every detail of diction and structure, and it remains pervasive. One reason for the special demand James's fictional prose makes on our attention is surely that there are always at least three levels of development—all of them subjective: the characters' awareness of events: the narrator's seeing of them; and our own trailing perception of the relation between these two.

The primary location of the narrative in a mental rather than a physical continuum gives the narrative a great freedom from the restrictions of particular time and place. Materially, we are, of course, in Chester, at the hotel—characteristically "the hotel" because a fully particularized specification—"The Pied Bull Inn," say—would be an irrelevant brute fact which would distract attention from the mental train of thought we are invited to partake in. But actually we don't have any pressing sense of time and place: we feel ourselves to be spectators, rather specifically, of Strether's thought processes, which easily and imperceptibly range forwards and backwards both in time and space. Sentence three, for example, begins in the past, at the Liverpool dock; sentence four looks forward to the reunion later that day, and to its many sequels: such transitions of time and place are much easier to effect when the main subjects of the sentences are abstract: a "principle" exists independently of its context.

The multiplicity of relations—between narrator and object, and between the ideas in Strether's mind—held in even suspension throughout the narrative, is presumably the main explanation for the number of "thats" in the passage, as well as of the several examples of elegant variation. There are nine "thats"—only two of them demonstrative and the rest relative pronouns (or conjunctions or particles if you prefer those terms); actually there were no less than three more of them in the first edition, which James removed from the somewhat more colloquial and informal New York edition; while there are several other "thats" implied—in "the principle [that] I have just mentioned," for instance.

The number of "thats" follows from two habits already noted in the passage. "That" characteristically introduces relative clauses dealing not with persons but with objects, including abstractions; and it is also used to introduce reported speech—"on his learning that Waymarsh"—not "Mr. Waymarsh isn't here." Both functions are combined in the third sentence where we get a triple definition of a timeless idea based on the report of three chronologically separate events: "the same secret principle that had prompted Strether not absolutely to desire Waymarsh's presence at the dock, that had led him thus to postpone for a few hours his enjoyment of it, now operated to make him feel that he could still wait without disappointment."

Reported rather than direct speech also increases the pressure towards elegant variation: the use, for example, in sentence 1 of "his friend," where in direct speech it would be "Mr. Waymarsh" (and the reply—"*He* hasn't come yet"). In the second sentence—"a telegram . . . was produced for the inquirer"—"inquirer" is needed because "him" has already been used for Waymarsh just above; of course, "the inquirer" is logical enough after the subject of the first sentence has been an abstract noun—"question"; and the epithet also gives James an opportunity for underlining the ironic distance and detachment with which we are invited to view his dedicated "inquirer," Strether. Later, when Strether is "the most newly disembarked of the two men," we see how both elegant variation and the grammatical subordination of physical events are related to the general Jamesian tendency to present characters and actions on a plane of abstract categorization; the mere statement, "Mr. Waymarsh had already been in England for [so many] months," would itself go far to destroy the primarily mental continuum in which the paragraph as a whole exists.

The last general stylistic feature of the passage to be listed above was the use of negative forms. There are six "noes" or "nots" in the first four 4 sentences; four implied negatives—"postpone"; "without disappointment"; "at the worst"; "there was little fear": and two qualifications that modify positiveness of affirmation—"not wholly"; and "to that extent." This abundance of negatives has no doubt several functions: it enacts Strether's tendency to hesitation and qualification; it puts the reader into the right judicial frame of mind; and it has the further effect of subordinating concrete events to their mental reflection; "Waymarsh was not to arrive," for example, is not a concrete statement of a physical event: it is subjective—because it implies an expectation in Strether's mind (which was not fulfilled); and it has an abstract quality—because while Waymarsh's arriving would be particular and physical, his *not* arriving is an idea, a nonaction. More generally, James's great use of negatives or near-negatives may also, perhaps, be regarded as part of his subjective and abstractive tendency: there are no negatives in nature but only in the human consciousness.

## II.

The most obvious grammatical features of what Richard Chase has called Henry James's "infinitely syntactical language" (*The American Novel and its Tradition*, New York, 1957), can, then, be shown to reflect the essential imperatives of his narrative point of view; and they could therefore lead into a discussion of the philosophical qualities of his mind, as they are discussed, for example, by Dorothea Krook in her notable article "The Method of the Later Works of Henry James" (*London Magazine*, I [1954], 55-70); our passage surely exemplifies James's power "to generalize to the limit the particulars of experience," and with it the characteristic way in which both his "perceptions of the world itself, and his perceptions of the logic of the world . . . happen simultaneously, are part of a single comprehensive experience." Another aspect of the connection between James's metaphysic and his method as a novelist has inspired a stimulating stylistic study—Carlo Izzo's "Henry James, Scrittore Sintattico" (*Studi Americani*, II [1956],

127-42). The connection between thought and style finds its historical perspective in John Henry Raleigh's illuminating study "Henry James: The Poetics of Empiricism" (*PMLA*, LXVI [1951], 107-23), which establishes connections between Lockean epistemology and James's extreme, almost anarchic, individualism; while this epistemological preoccupation, which is central to Quentin Anderson's view of how James worked out his father's cosmology in fictional terms (*The American Henry James*, New Brunswick, 1957), also leads towards another large general question, the concern with "point of view," which became a crucial problem in the history and criticism of fiction under the influence of the skeptical relativism of the late nineteenth century.

In James's case, the problem is fairly complicated. He may be classed as an "Impressionist," concerned, that is, to show not so much the events themselves, but the impressions which they make on the characters. But James's continual need to generalize and place and order, combined with his absolute demand for a point of view that would be plastic enough to allow him freedom for the formal "architectonics" of the novelist's craft, eventually involved him in a very idiosyncratic kind of multiple Impressionism: idiosyncratic because the dual presence of Strether's consciousness and of that of the narrator, who translates what he sees there into more general terms, makes the narrative point of view both intensely individual and yet ultimately social.

Another possible direction of investigation would be to show that the abstractness and indirection of James's style are essentially the result of this characteristic multiplicity of his vision. There is, for example, the story reported by Edith Wharton that after his first stroke James told Lady Prothero that "in the very act of falling . . . he heard in the room a voice which was distinctly, it seemed, not his own, saying: 'So here it is at last, the distinguished thing.'" James, apparently, could not but see even his own most fateful personal experience, except as evoked by some other observer's voice in terms of the long historical and literary tradition of death. Carlo Izzo regards this tendency as typical of the Alexandrian style, where there is a marked disparity between the rich inheritance of the means of literary expression, and the meaner creative world which it is used to express; but the defense of the Jamesian habit of mind must surely be that what the human vision shares with that of animals is presumably the perception of concrete images, not the power to conceive universals: such was Aristotle's notion of man's distinguishing capacity. The universals in the present context are presumably the awareness that behind every petty individual circumstance there ramifies an endless network of general moral, social, and historical relations. Henry James's style can therefore be seen as a supremely civilized effort to relate every event and every moment of life to the full complexity of its circumambient conditions.

Obviously James's multiple awareness can go too far; and in the later novels it often poses the special problem that we do not quite know whether the awareness implied in a given passage is the narrator's or that of his character. Most simply, a pronoun referring to the subject of a preceding clause is always liable to give trouble if one hasn't been very much aware of what the grammatical subject of that preceding clause was; in the last sentence of the paragraph, for example, "the apprehension, already, on Strether's part, that . . . it would, at best, . . . prove the 'note' of Europe," "it" refers to Waymarsh's countenance: but this isn't at first obvious; which is no doubt why, in his revision of the periodical version for the English edition James replaced "it" by "he"— simpler, grammatically, but losing some of the ironic visual precision of the original.

More seriously, because the narrator's consciousness and Strether's are both present, we often don't know whose mental operations and evaluative judgments are involved in particular cases. We pass, for instance, from the objective analysis of sentence 3 where the analytic terminology of "the same secret principle" must be the responsibility of the narrator, to what must be a verbatim quotation of Strether's mind in sentence 4: "with all respect to dear old Waymarsh" is obviously Strether's licensed familiarity.

But although the various difficulties of tense, voice, and reference require a vigilance of attention in the reader which some have found too much to give, they are not in themselves very considerable: and what perhaps is much more in need of attention is how the difficulties arising from the multiplicity of points of view don't by any means prevent James from ordering all the elements of his narrative style into an amazingly precise means of expression: and it is this positive, and in the present case, as it seems to me, triumphant, mastery of the difficulties which I want next to consider.

Our passage is not, I think, James either at his most memorable or at his most idiosyncratic: *The Ambassadors* is written with considerable sobriety and has, for example, little of the vivid and direct style of the early part of *The Wings of the Dove*, or of the happy symbolic complexities of *The Golden Bowl*. Still, the passage is fairly typical of the later James; and I think it can be proved that all or at least nearly all the idiosyncrasies of diction or syntax in the present passage are fully justified by the particular emphases they create.

The most flagrant eccentricity of diction is presumably that where James writes "the most newly disembarked of the two men" (lines 16-17). "Most" may very well be a mere slip; and it must certainly seem indefensible to any one who takes it as an absolute rule that the comparative must always be used when only two terms are involved.[6] But a defense is at least possible. "Most newly disembarked" means something rather different from "more nearly disembarked." James, it may be surmised, did not want to compare the recency of the two men's arrival, but to inform us that Strether's arrival was "very" or as we might say, "most" recent; the use of the superlative also had the advantage of suggesting the long and fateful tradition of transatlantic disembarcations in general.

The reasons for the other main syntactical idiosyncrasies in the passage are much clearer. In the first part of the opening sentence, for example, the separation of subject—"question"—from verb—"was"—by the longish temporal clause "when he reached the hotel," is no doubt a dislocation of normal sentence structure; but, of course, "Strether" must be the first word of the novel: while, even more important, the delayed placing of the temporal clause, forces a pause after "question" and thus gives it a very significant resonance. Similarly with the last sentence; it has several peculiarities, of which the placing of "throughout" seems the most obvious. The sentence has three parts: the first and last are comparatively straightforward, but the middle is a massed block of portentous qualifications: "Mixed with everything was the apprehension—already, on Strether's part, that he would, at best, throughout,—prove the note of Europe in quite a sufficient degree." The echoing doom started by the connotation of "apprehension"—reverberates through "already," ("much more to come later") "on Strether's part" ("even he knows") and "at best" ("the worst has been envisaged, too"); but it is the final collapse of the terse rhythm of the parenthesis that isolates the rather awkwardly placed "throughout," and thus enables James to sound the fine full fatal note; there is no limit to the poignant eloquence of

---

[6] Though consider *Rasselas*, ch. xxviii: "Both conditions may be bad, but they cannot both be worst."

"throughout." It was this effect, of course, which dictated the preceding inversion which places "apprehension" not at the start of the sentence, but in the middle where, largely freed from its syntactical nexus, it may be directly exposed to its salvos of qualification.

The mockingly fateful emphasis on "throughout" tells us, if nothing had before, that James's tone is in the last analysis ironic, comic, or better, as I shall try to suggest, humorous. The general reasons for this have already been suggested. To use Maynard Mack's distinction (in his Preface to *Joseph Andrews*, Rinehart Editions, New York, 1948), "the comic artist subordinates the presentation of life as experience, where the relationship between ourselves and the characters experiencing it is a primary one, to the presentation of life as a spectacle, where the primary relation is between himself and us as onlookers." In the James passage, the primacy of the relation between the narrator and the reader has already been noted, as has its connection with the abstraction of the diction, which brings home the distance between the narrator and Strether. Of course, the application of abstract diction to particular persons always tends towards irony,[7] because it imposes a dual way of looking at them: few of us can survive being presented as general representatives of humanity.

The paragraph, of course, is based on one of the classic contradictions in psychological comedy—Strether's reluctance to admit to himself that he has very mixed feelings about his friend: and James develops this with the narrative equivalent of *commedia dell'arte* technique: virtuoso feats of ironic balance, comic exaggeration, and deceptive hesitation conduct us on a complicated progress toward the foreordained illumination.

In structure, to begin with, the six sentences form three groups of two: each pair of them gives one aspect of Strether's delay; and they are arranged in an ascending order of complication so that the fifth sentence—72 words—is almost twice as long as any other, and is succeeded by the final sentence, the punch line, which is noticeably the shortest—26 words. The development of the ideas is as controlled as the sentence structure. Strether is obviously a man with an enormous sense of responsibility about personal relationships; so his first question is about

---

[7] As I have argued in "The Ironic Tradition in Augustan Prose from Swift to Johnson," *Restoration and Augustan Prose* (Los Angeles: University of California Press, 1957).

his friend. That loyal *empressement*, however, is immediately checked by the balanced twin negatives that follow: "on his learning that Waymarsh *was not* to arrive till evening, he *was not* wholly disconcerted": one of the diagnostic elements of irony, surely, is hyperbole qualified with mock-scrupulousness, such as we get in "not wholly disconcerted." Why there are limits to Lambert Strether's consternation is to transpire in the next sentence; Waymarsh's telegram bespeaking a room "only if not noisy" is a laconic suggestion of that inarticulate worthy's habitually gloomy expectations—from his past experiences of the indignities of European hotel noise we adumbrate the notion that the cost of their friendly *rencontre* may be his sleeping in the street. In the second part of the sentence we have another similar, though more muted, hint: "the understanding that they should meet in Chester rather than at Liverpool remained to that extent sound"; "to that extent," no doubt, but to *any other?*—echo seems to answer "No."

In the second group of sentences we are getting into Strether's mind, and we have been prepared to relish the irony of its ambivalences. The negatived hyperbole of "not absolutely to desire," turns out to mean "postpone"; and of course, a voluntarily postponed "enjoyment" itself denotes a very modified rapture, although Strether's own consciousness of the problem is apparently no further advanced than that "he could still wait without disappointment." Comically loyal to what he would like to feel, therefore, we have him putting in the consoling reflection that "they would dine together at the worst"; and the ambiguity of "at the worst" is followed by the equally dubious thought: "there was little fear that in the sequel they shouldn't see enough of each other." That they should, in fact, see too much of each other; but social decorum and Strether's own loyalties demand that the outrage of the open statement be veiled in the obscurity of formal negation.

By the time we arrive at the climactic pair of sentences, we have been told enough for more ambitious effects to be possible. The twice-mentioned "secret principle," it appears, is actually wholly "instinctive" (line 17); but in other ways Strether is almost ludicrously self-conscious. The qualified hyperbole of "his business would be a trifle bungled," underlined as it is by the alliteration, prepares us for a half-realized image which amusingly defines Strether's sense of his role: he sees himself, it appears, as the stage-manager of an enterprise in which his solemn obligations as an implicated friend are counterbalanced by his equally ceremonious sense that due decorums must also be attended to when he comes face-to-face with another friend of long ago—no less a person than Europe. It is, of course, silly of him, as James makes him acknowledge in the characteristic italicizing of "the 'note' of Europe";[8] but still, he does have a comically ponderous sense of protocol which leads him to feel that "his business would be a trifle bungled" should he simply arrange for this countenance to present itself to the nearing steamer as the first "note" of Europe. The steamer, one imagines, would not have turned hard astern at the proximity of Waymarsh's sacred rage; but Strether's fitness for ambassadorial functions is defined by his thinking in terms of "arranging" for a certain countenance at the docks to give just the right symbolic greeting.

Strether's notion of what Europe demands also shows us the force of his aesthetic sense. But in the last sentence the metaphor, though it remains equally self-conscious, changes its mode of operation from the dramatic, aesthetic, and diplomatic, to something more scientific: for, although ten years ago I should not have failed to point out, and my readers would not, I suppose, have failed to applaud, the ambiguity of "prove," it now seems to me that we must choose between its two possible meanings. James may be using "prove" to mean that Waymarsh's face will "turn out to be" the "note of Europe" for Strether. But "prove" in this sense is intransitive, and "to be" would have to be supplied; it therefore seems more likely that James is using "prove" in the older sense of "to test": Waymarsh is indeed suited to the role of being the sourly acid test of the siren songs of Europe "in quite a sufficient degree," as Strether puts it with solemn but arch understanding.

The basic development structure of the passage, then, is one of progressive and yet artfully delayed clarification; and this pattern is also typical of James's general novelistic method. The reasons for this are suggested in the Preface to *The Princess Casamassima*, where James deals with the problem of maintaining a balance between the intelligence a character must have to be interesting, and the bewilderment which is nevertheless an essential condition of the novel's having surprise, development, and tension: "It seems probable that if we were never bewildered there would never be a story to tell about us."

In the first paragraph of *The Ambassadors* James apprises us both of his hero's supreme qualities and of his associated limitations. Strether's

[8] See George Knox, "James's Rhetoric Quotes," *College English*, 17 (1956), 293-97.

delicate critical intelligence is often blinkered by a highly vulnerable mixture of moral generosity towards others combined with an obsessive sense of personal inadequacy; we see the tension in relation to Waymarsh, as later we are to see it in relation to all his other friends; and we understand, long before Strether, how deeply it bewilders him; most poignantly about the true nature of Chad, Madame de Vionnet—and himself.

This counterpoint of intelligence and bewilderment is, of course, another reason for the split narrative point of view we've already noted: we and the narrator are inside Strether's mind, and yet we are also outside it, knowing more about Strether than he knows about himself. This is the classic posture of irony. Yet I think that to insist too exclusively on the ironic function of James's narrative point of view would be mistaken.

Irony has lately been enshrined as the supreme deity in the critical pantheon: but, I wonder, is there really anything so wonderful about being distant and objective? Who wants to see life only or mainly in intellectual terms? In art as in life we no doubt can have need of intellectual distance as well as of emotional commitment; but the uninvolvement of the artist surely doesn't go very far without the total involvement of the person; or, at least, without a deeper human involvement than irony customarily establishes. One could, I suppose, call the aesthetically perfect balance between distance and involvement, open or positive irony: but I'm not sure that humor isn't a better word, especially when the final balance is tipped in favor of involvement, of ultimate commitment to the characters; and I hope that our next critical movement will be the New Gelastics.

At all events, although the first paragraph alone doesn't allow the point to be established fully here, it seems to me that James's attitude to Strether is better described as humorous than ironical; we must learn, like Maria Gostrey, to see him "at last all comically, all tragically." James's later novels in general are most intellectual; but they are also, surely, his most compassionate: and in this particular paragraph Strether's dilemma is developed in such a way that we feel for him even more than we smile at him. This balance of intention, I think, probably explains why James keeps his irony in such a low key: we must be aware of Strether's "secret" ambivalence towards Waymarsh, but not to the point that his unawareness of it would verge on fatuity; and our controlling sympathy for the causes of Strether's ambivalence turns what might have been irony into something closer to what Constance Rourke characterizes as James's typical "low-keyed humor of defeat" (*American Humor*, 1931).

That James's final attitude is humorous rather than ironic is further suggested by the likeness of the basic structural technique of the paragraph to that of the funny story—the incremental involvement in an endemic human perplexity which can only be resolved by laughter's final acceptance of contradiction and absurdity. We don't, in the end, see Strether's probing hesitations mainly as an ironic indication by James of mankind's general muddlement; we find it, increasingly, a touching example of how, despite all their inevitable incongruities and shortcomings, human ties remain only, but still, human.

Here it is perhaps James's very slowness and deliberation throughout the narrative which gives us our best supporting evidence: greater love hath no man than hearing his friend out patiently.

### III

The function of an introductory paragraph in a novel is presumably to introduce: and this paragraph surely has the distinction of being a supremely complex and inclusive introduction to a novel. It introduces the hero, of course, and one of his companions; also the time; the place; something of what's gone before. But James has carefully avoided giving us the usual retrospective beginning, that pile of details which he scornfully termed a "mere seated mass of information." All the details are scrupulously presented as reflections from the novel's essential center— the narrator's patterning of the ideas going forwards and backwards in Strether's mind. Of course, this initially makes the novel more difficult, because what we probably think of as primary—event and its setting—is subordinated to what James thinks is—the mental drama of the hero's consciousness, which, of course, is not told but shown: scenically dramatized. At the same time, by selecting thoughts and events which are representative of the book as a whole, and narrating them with an abstractness which suggests their larger import, James introduces the most general themes of the novel.

James, we saw, carefully arranged to make "Strether's first question" the first three words; and, of course, throughout the novel, Strether is to go on asking questions—and getting increasingly dusty answers. This, it may be added, is stressed by the apparent aposiopesis: for a "first" question when no second is mentioned, is surely an intimation that more are—in a way unknown to us or to Strether—yet to come. The later dislocations of normal word order already noted above emphasize other major themes; the "secret principle" in Strether's mind, and the antithesis Waymarsh-Europe, for instance.

The extent to which these processes were conscious on James's part cannot, of course, be resolved; but it is significant that the meeting with Maria Gostrey was interposed before the meeting with Waymarsh, which James had originally planned as his beginning in the long (20,000) word scenario of the plot which he prepared for *Harper's*. The unexpected meeting had many advantages; not least that James could repeat the first paragraph's pattern of delayed clarification in the structure of the first chapter as a whole. On Strether's mind we get a momentously clear judgment at the end of the second paragraph: "there was detachment in his zeal, and curiosity in his indifference"; but then the meeting with Maria Gostrey, and its gay opportunities for a much fuller presentation of Strether's mind, intervene before Waymarsh himself finally appears at the end of the chapter; only then is the joke behind Strether's uneasy hesitations in the first paragraph brought to its hilariously blunt climax: "It was already upon him even at that distance—Mr. Waymarsh was for *his* part joyless."

One way of evaluating James's achievement in this paragraph, I suppose, would be to compare the opening of James's other novels, and with those of previous writers: but it would take too long to do more than sketch the possibilities of this approach. James's early openings certainly have some of the banality of the "mere seated mass of information": in *Roderick Hudson* (1876), for example: "Rowland Mallet had made his arrangements to sail for Europe on the 5th of September, and having in the interval a fortnight to spare, he determined to spend it with his cousin Cecilia, the widow of a nephew of his father. . . ." Later, James showed a much more comprehensive notion of what the introductory paragraph should attempt: even in the relatively simple and concrete opening of *The Wings of the Dove* (1902): "She waited, Kate Croy, for her father to come in, but he kept her unconscionably, and there were moments at which she showed herself, in the glass over the mantle, a face positively pale with irritation that had brought her to the point of going away without sight of him . . . ." "She waited, Kate Croy"—an odd parenthetic apposition artfully contrived to prefigure her role throughout the novel—to wait.

One could, I suppose, find this sort of symbolic prefiguring in the work of earlier novelists; but never, I imagine, in association with all the other levels of introductory function that James manages to combine in a single paragraph. Jane Austen has her famous thematic irony in the opening of *Pride and Prejudice* (1813): "It is a truth universally acknowledged, that a single man in possession of a good fortune must be in want of a wife"; but pride and prejudice must come later. Dickens can hurl us overpoweringly into *Bleak House* (1852-53), into its time and place and general theme; but characters and opening action have to wait:

London. Michaelmas Term lately over, and the Lord Chancellor sitting in Lincoln's Inn Hall. Implacable November weather. As much mud in the streets, as if the waters had but newly retired from the face of the earth, and it would not be wonderful to meet a Megalosaurus, forty feet long or so, waddling like an elephantine lizard up Holborn Hill. Smoke lowering down from chimney-pots . . .

In Dickens, characteristically, we get a loud note that sets the tone, rather than a polyphonic series of chords that contain all the later melodic developments, as in James. And either the Dickens method, or the "mere seated mass of information," seem to be commonest kinds of opening in nineteenth century novels. For, openings that suggest something of James's ambitious attempt to achieve a prologue that is a synchronic introduction of all the main aspects of the narrative, I think that Conrad is his closest rival. But Conrad, whether in expository or dramatic vein, tends to an arresting initial vigor that has dangers which James's more muted tones avoid. In *An Outcast of the Islands* (1896), for example:

When he stepped off the straight and narrow path of his peculiar honesty, it was with an inward assertion of unflinching resolve to fall back again into the monotonous but safe stride of virtue as soon as his little excursion into the wayside quagmires had produced the desired effect. It was going to be a short episode—a sentence in brackets, so to speak, in the flowing tale of his life. . . .

Conrad's sardonic force has enormous immediate impact; but it surely gives too much away: the character, Willems, has been dissected so vigorously that it takes great effort for Conrad—and the reader—to revivify him later. The danger lurks even in the masterly combination of physical notation and symbolic evaluation at the beginning of *Lord Jim* (1900): 'He was an inch, perhaps two, under six feet . . .": the heroic proportion is forever missed, by an inch, perhaps two; which is perhaps too much, to begin with.

It is not for me to assess how far I have succeeded in carrying out the general intentions with which I began, or how far similar methods of analysis would be applicable to other kinds of prose. As regards the explication of the passage itself, the main argument must by now be sufficiently clear, although a full demonstration would require a much wider sampling both of other novels and of other passages in *The Ambassadors*.[9] The most obvious and demonstrable features of James's prose style, its vocabulary and syntax, are direct reflections of his attitude to life and his conception of the novel; and these features, like the relation of the paragraph to the rest of the novel, and to other novels, make clear that the notorious idiosyncrasies of Jamesian prose are directly related to the imperatives which led him to develop a narrative texture as richly complicated and as highly organized as that of poetry.

No wonder James scorned translation and rejoiced, as he so engagingly confessed to his French translator, Auguste Monod, that his later works were "locked fast in the golden cage of the *intraduisible*." Translation could hardly do justice to a paragraph in which so many levels of meaning and implication are kept in continuous operation; in which the usual introductory exposition of time, place, character, and previous action, are rendered through an immediate immersion in the processes of the hero's mind as he's involved in perplexities which are characteristic of the novel as a whole and which are articulated in a mode of comic development which is essentially that, not only of the following chapter, but of the total structure. To have done all that is to have gone far towards demonstrating the contention which James announced at the end of the Preface to *The Ambassadors*, that "the Novel remains still, under the right persuasion, the most independent, most elastic, most prodigious of literary forms"; and the variety and com-

---

[9] A similar analysis of eight other paragraphs selected at fifty-page intervals revealed that, as would be expected, there is much variation: the tendency to use non-transitive verbs, and abstract nouns as subjects, for instance, seems to be strong throughout the novel, though especially so in analytic rather than narrative passages; but the frequent use of "that" and of negative forms of statement does not recur significantly.

plexity of the functions carried out in the book's quite short first paragraph also suggest that, contrary to some notions, the demonstration is, as James claimed, made with "a splendid particular economy."

# 14

## Winston Smith: The Last Humanist

*Either the future would resemble the present in which case it would not listen to him, or it would be different from it, and his predicament would be meaningless.*

At the beginning of *Nineteen Eighty-Four*, we are given a few facts about Winston Smith.* He's thirty-nine and has "a varicose ulcer above his right ankle"; on the next page we're told he's a small, frail figure with fair hair, and afraid of the Thought Police; and on the next page we learn that he works for the Ministry of Truth in London, the chief city of Airstrip One, the third most populous province of Oceania. The rest of what we are told about him is fairly consistent with this, and makes it clear that there is nothing at all remarkable about Winston Smith except for his unique inner life.

The first thing we learn about it comes when he tries "to squeeze out some childhood memory that should tell him whether London had always been quite like this." The urgency of the word "squeeze" suggests that Winston Smith's interior consciousness is genuinely tormented by what is essentially a historical question. Winston's first significant act tells us a good deal more. He has left his job at thirteen hours, downed a teacupful of nauseating Victory gin, and moved to the alcove which, quite exceptionally, is out of sight of the telescreen, having probably been intended originally "to hold bookshelves." Once there he takes out

* "Winston Smith: The Last Humanist" appeared originally in *On Nineteen Eighty-Four*, ed. Peter Stansky (Stanford: Stanford Alumni Association, 1984), pp. 103-13. Reprinted with permission.

a "peculiarly beautiful book," fits a nib onto an archaic penholder, and begins a diary. Winston Smith's secret life, then, is not merely puzzled by history; it is in love with the products of the past.

Until he started the diary, Winston Smith had imagined that "the actual writing would be easy. All he had to do was to transfer to paper the interminable restless monologue that had been running inside his head, literally for years." But it turns out not to be easy, and the reason for the difficulty is peculiar: "How could you communicate with the future? . . . Either the future would resemble the present in which case it would not listen to him, or it would be different from it, and his predicament would be meaningless." This surely shows that Winston's consciousness in general is dominated by two different kinds of persistent concern: the historical, with its tripartite division of future, present, and past; and the literary, which is more instinctive—he can think of no conceivable reader for his diary but he still writes it.

What first comes out on the page is the date: it is April 4th, 1984, though we've been told he can't be sure that "this *was* 1984." Next, there is a paragraph giving an account of his previous evening at the flicks: the crass patriotic hysteria of the audience and its amusement at the cruel bombing of a shipload of enemy war refugees, an amusement which is interrupted by the protests of an indignant prole woman. Winston's mind then goes back to the Two Minutes Hate ceremony earlier that morning; but when he turns his attention to the diary again he finds that he has written, no longer in his usual "small but childish handwriting" but in large and voluptuous printed capitals, half a page of "DOWN WITH BIG BROTHER."

When he sees what he has written Winston is tempted to tear the page out of the book in terror; but then he reflects that "the Thought Police would get him just the same," whatever he wrote in the diary, or, indeed, whether he wrote in it or not. Next he writes down, in "a hurried untidy scrawl," the words: "theyll shoot me i dont care theyll shoot me in the back of the neck i dont care down with big brother they always shoot you in the back of the neck i dont care down with big brother." What dooms him, he believes, is that, whether he writes down his thoughts or not, he has in any case committed "the essential crime that contained all others in itself. Thoughtcrime they called it."

The essence of Winston's thoughtcrime can be described by saying that he finds nothing in the life of the present that he can bear, and so his sensibility is dominated by the great question: Were things really better now? Some time later he thinks he may get some help on this from a very old man in a pub for the proles, but finds himself defeated by the random but invincible concreteness of what the old man remembers. Yes, the old man says, beer was cheaper in the old days, and it came in pints. Winston attempts to get him to say more; he lists all the alleged horrors of life in the old days, but he gets no reaction until he mentions the top hats worn by the capitalists, and then the old man recalls the last time he himself had worn a rented top hat, for his sister-in-law's funeral some fifty years ago. Winston goes on with his leading questions until he realizes that "the old man's memory was nothing but a rubbish heap of details," and that he can therefore expect no outside help in his quest to discover whether life was or was not "better before the Revolution than it is now."

He realizes, too, that there is a real urgency in his question, for, in "twenty years, at the most . . . the huge and simple question . . . would have ceased once and for all to be answerable" because all the evidence would by then have been altered or suppressed. Winston himself works at the Ministry of Truth doctoring the records whenever there has been a change in policy, or some individual has been disgraced or become an "unperson." For instance, we see him having to remove all mention of a formerly prominent member of the Inner Party, Comrade Withers; and in his place he creates, out of whole cloth, a heroic Comrade Ogilvy in "a few lines of print and a couple of photographs." How can there be history when everything inconsistent with the political needs of the Party today has been sent down the "memory hole," and no book exists in Oceania older than 1960? Even worse, something else is disappearing—the sense that merely knowing the true answer is important. For instance, there is the question of the truth or falsehood of the fact that only four years before Oceania had been a war not with its present enemy, Eurasia, but with its present ally, Eastasia; but this question did not seem important even to his love, Julia. Winston does not feel any temptation to tell lies to Julia, but her love for him is based not on her sense of truth, but on her partisan sense that "I knew you were against them"—the Party. Truth itself is already a casualty as far as other people are concerned; and so Winston is forced to accept the terrible conclusion, "History has stopped. Nothing exists except an endless present in which the Party is always right."

As he listens on the canteen television to the statistics of endless claims of increased productivity, Winston compares their picture of how "year by year and minute by minute, everybody and everything was whizzing rapidly upwards" with the disgusting and degrading realities of actual existence. Could he be "*alone* in the possession of a memory?" he wonders. On the other hand, he cannot see how he should feel the present to be so intolerable "unless one had some kind of ancestral memory that things had once been different."

That mute conviction that he is right is one reason for Winston's love of Oldspeak. Newspeak, he senses, in effect creates a conspiracy of silence about all the horrors of the life that he sees going on around him; it epitomizes, to quote Emmanuel Goldstein's book, *The Theory and Practice of Oligarchical Collectivism*, that "denial of reality which is the special feature of Ingsoc and its rival systems of thought." The denial is not accidental but systematic. For instance, "The empirical method of thought, on which all the scientific achievements of the past were founded," is totally opposed, Goldstein writes, to the most fundamental principles of Ingsoc. As a result, he notes, "in Newspeak there is no word for 'Science'."

Winston's friend Syme, who is working in the research department of the ministry on the eleventh edition of the Newspeak dictionary, sees that Winston lacks a real appreciation of Newspeak, "whose whole aim," he says, is to "narrow the range of thought" that the language permits. When the process has been completed, and "Newspeak is Ingsoc and Ingsoc is Newspeak," thoughtcrime will become "literally impossible." Indeed, in the final revision of Newspeak its vocabulary will have been so drastically controlled and reduced in size that "there will *be* no thought, as we understand it now. Orthodoxy means not thinking—not needing to think. Orthodoxy is unconsciousness."

Syme, Winston realizes, will be "vaporized" because he "sees too clearly and speaks too plainly." Winston is soon proved right in his unspoken prediction; but Syme is also right when he says that Winston Smith in his heart would "prefer to stick to Oldspeak, with all its vagueness and its useless shades of meaning." Winston, of course, here exhibits the preference of the writer to that of the politician: and that opposition is fundamental. For, as Syme says, with the final triumph of Newspeak, "the whole literature of the past will have been destroyed. Chaucer, Shakespeare, Milton, Byron—they'll exist only in Newspeak versions, not merely changed into something different, but actually changed into something contradictory of what they used to be."

The novel does not give us much evidence of Winston's tastes in reading—if only because books of literature, as opposed to pornography and the like turned out collectively by the Fiction Department of the Ministry of Truth, do not seem to exist in the world of *Nineteen Eighty-Four*. Even Goldstein's book, it transpires, was apparently produced collectively. But we are given a good many indications of Winston's literary sensibility. Thus, when Winston dreams of his mother, thirty years missing and probably dead, he sets her and her passionate love for him in a setting of time and place that is very different from the present. It was, he reflects, a time when tragedy was still possible, a time when "there were still privacy, love, and friendship . . . dignity of emotion [and] deep or complex sorrows." Winston also imagines a perfect love encounter, which is set in what he thinks of as "the Golden Country"; it is a symbol of the ancient world of pastoral, and when he suddenly wakes up from the promise of the dream, it is "with the word 'Shakespeare' on his lips." Later he sees the lovely rural setting of his first tryst with Julia as "the Golden Country—almost." Winston's literary sensibility, then, contains the notions both of the tragic and the pastoral genres, and also of Shakespeare; and all three are associated with his notions of death and love.

There are other, and perhaps even more significant, details of Winston's literary tastes in *Nineteen Eighty-Four*. First, there is the diary itself. It is a literary *acte gratuit* of a heroic kind, since endangering his life merely to give an objective testimony to his view of the truth about himself and his time surely bespeaks Winston's deep need for self-expression. Secondly, there is another and almost opposite feature of Winston's sensibility—his characteristic obsession with the folk memories of the past; the most important one is the rhyme "Oranges and lemons, say the bells of St. Clement's,/You owe me three farthings, say the bells of St. Martin's,/When will you pay me? Say the bells of Old Bailey,/When I grow rich, say the bells of Shoreditch." Here one attraction is the idea that the genre represents the literature of the proles; another is that this particular rhyme is a clue to an imaginative reconstitution of the old churches and customs of London as it had once been.

Lastly, there is the way that Winston's love of the past makes him give a symbolic value to the literature, and even to other more physical mementos of history: there is the physical diary itself, a book with cream-laid paper, such as is no longer made; there is the presumably eighteenth-century print of St. Clement's Dane; there is the vast old ma-

hogany bed in which he and Julia make love; and there is the glass pa-
perweight which he buys from old Mr. Charrington and which, Winston
imagines, "was the room he was in, and the coral was Julia's life and his
own, fixed in a sort of eternity at the heart of the crystal."

Winston Smith's sensibility, then, can be seen as representing a constellation of special intellectual, aesthetic, and literary values. There is
the love of what Newspeak calls *oldthink*, that is, the ideas grouped
round the equally outmoded concepts of "objectivity and rationalism"
and of old folk rhymes. There is, further, his love of the particular and
the detailed in other things. It is this love of the particular that makes
Winston remember drawing his wife's attention long ago to the "tufts of
loose-strife growing in the cracks of the cliff beneath them" in which
"one tuft was of two colors, magenta and brick red, apparently growing
on the same root." It is also this love of the particular that causes Winston, just before the Thought Police make their strike, to fall asleep
"murmuring 'Sanity is not statistical,' with the feeling that his remark
contained in it a profound wisdom."

Behind these aspects of Winston's inner sense of values is the larger
idea that individual feeling is the most essential and desirable reality
available. It is this idea that leads Winston, at his first and only real
meeting with O'Brien until his arrest, to propose his toast, "To the
past." The Party has persuaded people that "mere impulses, mere feeling, were of no account"; on the other hand, Winston is loyal to the
values of an earlier generation—like his mother, who had assumed that
"what mattered were individual relationships, and a completely helpless gesture, an embrace, a tear, a word spoken to a dying man, could
have value in itself." It is also the rights of individual feeling which
cause Winston to conclude that he must continue on his present course
to the end; as he puts it, if your "object was not to stay alive but to stay
human, what difference did it ultimately make?" After all, he reflects,
"They could not alter your feelings; for that matter you could not alter
them yourself, even if you wanted to."

II

One term to describe this constellation of private thoughts and feelings in Winston Smith would be Humanism. The term has many diverse
and not wholly clear meanings; but in the inner life of Winston Smith
Orwell certainly describes both some main characteristic features of the

earliest manifestations of Humanism in the history of the West, and some of the essential meanings the term has acquired more recently.

Among the Greeks and the Romans the central doctrine of Humanism was certainly rhetorical, and its first exponents were orators. The nearest Greek equivalent to the Latin *humanitas* was *anthropismos*; and the early development of the notion, like that of its analogue *philanthropia*, had its basis in the close practical relationship in the life of fifth-century Athens among four forces which we would now call freedom of speech, the rule of law, the political freedom of the city, and the individual's right to make his own moral and political decisions. Humanism, then, arose in a society which was radically opposite to that of *Nineteen Eighty-Four*. For Isocrates (436-338 B.C.), who is commonly regarded as the chief precursor of Humanism, persuasion through speech was the key instrument of a free society; as he argued in his long essay "On the Antidosis," it was the power of speech which made man superior to other living creatures: "Because there has been implanted in us the power to persuade each other and the power to make clear to each other whatever we desire, not only have we escaped the life of wild beasts, but we have come together and founded cities and made laws and invented arts; and, generally speaking, there is no institution devised by man which the power of speech has not helped us to establish."

Isocrates, we must remember, held that discourse, or *logos*, is not confined merely to rhetorical arrangement of the words; there is, or there should be, no essential break between form and content, and that content includes the inward qualities of feeling, understanding, and imagination, which can in part be learned from works of literature, history, politics, and philosophy. Still, for Isocrates the master art remains rhetoric; as he wrote in the "Antidosis," "Persuasion is one of the Gods."

It was left to the Romans to develop the idea of *humanitas* in education and to give it a more systematic development. In the second century A.D. the grammarian Aulus Gellius, in his *Attic Nights*, gave a famous description of its aims: "Those who have spoken Latin and have used the language correctly [notably Varro and Cicero] do not give the word *humanitas* the meaning which it is commonly thought to have, namely, what the Greeks call *philanthropia*, signifying a kind of friendly spirit and good feeling toward all men without distinction; but they give to *humanitas* the force of the Greek *paideia*; that is, what we call *eruditionem institutionemque in bonas artes* [education and training in the good arts]."

The word *humanitas* itself was apparently first used, in the sense of good feeling, in an anonymous treatise on rhetoric addressed to one C. Herennius in 81 B.C., a work formerly attributed to Cicero (106-43 B.C.). Cicero, however, certainly has the credit for the first extant use of the phrase "the liberal arts." He used it in his first book, *De Inventione*, and the idea, of course, denotes all the arts which the free men of the society ought to study, as opposed to the mechanical or practical arts learned by slaves and people who work with their hands. Cicero, an admirer of Isocrates, urged that rhetorical skill was valueless unless it was combined with true learning. In his *De Oratore* Cicero stresses the need not only for writing, paraphrase, translation, and imitation, but for the reading of works of oratory, poetry, history, law, and politics. This broader curriculum, or *encyclos paideia*, was worked out in more detail by Quintilian, whose *De Institutione Oratoria* (A.D. 95) supplied the basis of the school curriculum of the West throughout the Middle Ages. The liberal arts were eventually construed as seven, of which the first three, the *trivium*, were Grammar (including literature and criticism), Logic (or dialectic), and Rhetoric. Then there were the more advanced topics of the *quadrivium*—Arithmetic, Geometry, Astronomy, and Music.

In Renaissance Europe, the term Humanism took on a rather new meaning. It is specifically applied, in the *Oxford Dictionary*'s definition, for instance, to the study of "the language, literature, and antiquities of Rome, and afterwards of Greece." Renaissance Humanism began as the educational spearhead of the revival of learning in the fifteenth century, but eventually it acquired the general sense of the classical, and mainly secular, education which was established in high schools and colleges during the sixteenth, seventeenth, and eighteenth centuries. The "good art" became defined as the *litterae humaniores* (more humane letters) of Oxford and other universities on the grounds that the great authors of Latin and Greek literature were more worthy of study than those of other languages.

The final stages in the development of the concept of Humanism came to the fore in the twentieth century. On the one hand, the classical tradition lost much of its power; and on the other, Humanism was colored by the scientific, secular, and empirical attitudes of the period. The idea that man should limit his knowledge to the inquiries, objectives, and limitations of the individual human mind was developed as a specific school of thought by F. C. S. Schiller and William James. The scientific and experimental attitude which they systematized under the name of Humanism no longer survives as a movement, but it has supplied some of the term's secular connotations in its present use.

III

Winston Smith cannot be considered a humanist in any of its earlier senses, if only because he makes no mention of Greek or Latin, and we are told nothing about his schooling. On the other hand, his hostility to Newspeak, his obsession with language, and his need for a free exchange of ideas show him as beginning at exactly the point where the founders of Humanism began. Winston Smith holds fast both to the value of Oldspeak and to the ultimate rationale of the early humanist position—the achievement of individual freedom. This freedom, threatened in the days both of Isocrates and of Cicero, no longer exists at all in the society of *Nineteen Eighty-Four*; but it remains Winston's basic need, and it is essentially that need for free intellectual interchange that explains his obsession with meeting O'Brien, and that had led him to start his diary.

There is a little more to say about the relation of Winston Smith's ideas to Humanism, but first we should, perhaps, consider the question of whether his author, George Orwell, could have had any specifically humanist intention for *Nineteen Eighty-Four*. He would not willingly have affixed any ideological label to himself; but on the other hand, it is an important part of his distinction as a writer that he took nothing for granted, and as a result he was often both well behind the times and well ahead of them.

One example of this concerns his religious position. He had lost his faith in his days at Eton, but in the period when he had returned from Burma and was starting to be a serious writer, Orwell was briefly on fairly intimate terms with a High Anglican curate, Parker, and his wife. He helped Parker in his clerical duties, went to services regularly, and even thought of taking communion. Still, Orwell mocks his "hypocrisy" about this in his letters to an old friend, Eleanor Jaques; and his biographer, Bernard Crick, is no doubt right in saying that it was an accidental and brief religious aberration, and concluding that "George Orwell was to be a clear Humanist, even a rationalist." Nevertheless, Orwell retained "an ironic attachment" to the Church of England and was buried, by his own wish, in a country churchyard.

More directly relevant is how very old-fashioned Orwell was in his attitude to language, and it wasn't just a question of his advocacy of the plain style. It was a lifelong passion. As he revealed in his essay "Why I Write," Orwell, at the age of "about sixteen . . . suddenly discovered the joy of mere words, i.e., the sounds and associations of words," and gave an illustration from *Paradise Lost*. A classmate, Steven Runciman, remembered that at about this time, when Aldous Huxley was for a year supposed to teach a class of Etonians French, he left one very definite positive impression: "Above all it was his use of words that entranced us. Eric Blair . . . would in particular make us note Aldous's phraseology. 'That is a word we must remember,' we used to say to each other. . . . The taste for words and their accurate and significant use remained." And when Eric Blair eventually came to do a little school teaching himself, the "joy of mere words" remained with him. One of his pupils remembered that he "once offered sixpence from his own pocket as a prize for anyone who could spot a ludicrous misspelling in a local laundry window." In his "Why I Write" essay Orwell wrote that he did not wish "completely to abandon the world view that I acquired in childhood"; and the first feature of it that he mentioned was to "continue to feel strongly about prose style."

This attitude to language is old-fashioned because neither the capacity to remember the "accurate and significant" use of words, nor how they are spelled, nor even a genuine concern with "prose style," were much more common then than they are today. For Orwell, however, they remained central; and this was not wholly for literary and stylistic reasons, but because he was also alive, as few other writers have ever been, to the moral and political importance of the notion that, in Keats's words, "English ought to be kept up." In such essays as "Politics vs. Literature: An Examination of *Gulliver's Travels*," "Politics and the English Language," and "Inside the Whale," Orwell demonstrated the necessary connections among literature, language, and the collective life with a fine intensity; and there, as in many other essays, he makes us realize that relatively simple things such as the use of truthful or untruthful language are connected with the greatest issues of social value, political decency, and—ultimately—with the existence of human freedom or of its opposite.

These simple meanings—not unlike the basic views of Isocrates or Cicero—Orwell certainly intended, and indeed consciously and persistently pursued, throughout his life. Especially in *Nineteen Eighty-Four*. One reason for the clarity of this theme in the novel may be that, whatever conflicts may have existed between Orwell the radical and Orwell the traditionalist in his treatment of political problems, there was no conflict in regard to language.

Nor did Orwell's education stop short with his capacity to write. At school, Orwell was something of a social rebel and a political radical, but he was certainly a traditionalist in his studies. At his prep school, and later at Eton, Orwell was a student of the classics, of what amounts to a school version of the *litterae humaniores*; and later he chose Greek, Latin, and Drawing as his three optional subjects for the Civil Service examination that sent him to Burma as a policeman. He paid tribute, later, to the fact that Eton, despite its many faults, had "one great virtue . . . a tolerant and civilized atmosphere which gives each boy a fair chance of developing his own individuality." One wouldn't claim Orwell as a man who read the classics consistently throughout his life; and one must admit that he was bitterly contemptuous of St. Cyprian's, his prep school, and unenthusiastic about many aspects of Eton; nevertheless it was there that he received an education based on the old humanistic classical tradition, a tradition which he never attacked.

It is, therefore, just possible that Orwell, having some conception of the humanist tradition, deliberately used some of its values to inform the positive aspects of Winston's sensibility. This tendency, it must be conceded, goes only as far as is plausible, given the kind of society depicted in the novel and Winston's own lack of educational opportunity; in any case, Winston Smith is not a conscious nor a heroic protagonist of moral and intellectual convictions. One remembers, for instance, his betrayals. They began with his earliest guilty memory of the last moment in which he saw his mother before she disappeared, when, overpowered by desperate childish greed, he had stolen the last quarter of the family's rare and precious two-ounce ration of chocolate from his helpless little sister, and with it fled from his home. At the end Winston betrays Julia—"Do it to Julia," he says, when faced by the rats; and he betrays himself when the novel finishes with Winston's succumbing to the overpowering pressures of the collective ideological machine, and discovering that "He loved Big Brother."

O'Brien affirms that "We"—the Party—"create human nature," and it is, of course, part of Orwell's warning in *Nineteen Eighty-Four* to show that "they" cannot be beaten. Winston learns that he and Julia were wrong when they thought that "They can't get inside you." They can, and, therefore, Winston does not even have the consolation of being able to say, as he once did, "if you can *feel* that staying human is worthwhile, even when it can't have any result whatever, you've beaten them." Orwell's picture of the future defines the villain as the general tendency of modern bureaucratic control to lead to a crippling anti-humanist monolithic collectivism; and so Winston Smith must be ignominiously defeated.

Not much, I believe, has been written about Winston's character; and there is obviously some truth in Irving Howe's concession that "there are no credible or 'three-dimensional' characters in the book." But, as Howe says, Orwell was trying to portray a society in which "the leviathan has swallowed man" and so "the human relationships" that are normally "taken for granted in the novel are here suppressed." Nevertheless, Winston Smith is worth our attention as a crucial test example, and he is in some respects a worthy one. His worth is suggested by his given name, Winston, and perhaps by his sharing Shakespeare's initials of W.S. In any case, Winston Smith has a legitimate love of the traditions of the past, and that love is combined with a genuine concern for the language and literature of Oldspeak, and for the right to independent thought. The critics have not made much of this side of the novel, but Winston Smith is, in the hated jargon of Newspeak, a martyr to the *ownlife*, meaning "individualism and eccentricity." He is even obsessed, in the typical humanist way, with unanswerable questions, and particularly the question of "Why?" As he writes in his diary, "I understand HOW: I do not understand WHY." That he eventually succumbs to the police and O'Brien doesn't weaken the truths of what he thinks and does in the first two parts of the novel. "Truisms are true, hold on to that!" Winston reflects, and writes down in his diary as a credo: "Freedom is the freedom to say that two plus two make four. If that is granted, all else follows."

That is not granted, but we can still say that, however grim his end, Winston Smith is the only person in the novel who makes any sort of stand for the simple intellectual and moral values which, for over two millennia, have had the majority of the literate and the decent on their side. O'Brien three times calls Winston "the last man," with increasing irony at this professed "guardian of the human spirit"; and this is re-flected in the original title for the book, "The Last Man in Europe." Considering how little there is about Europe in the book, "The Last Humanist Man" might have been a more accurate title, although *Nineteen Eighty-Four* is no doubt better for other reasons.

# 15

## THE HUMANITIES ON THE RIVER KWAI

In April 1974 I was present at a meeting in Racine, Wisconsin, at which a small group of scholars, academic administrators, and foundation officials were discussing how to start what has now happily become the National Center for the Humanities in Research Triangle Park, North Carolina.* The discussion was largely concerned with matters of detail— location, money, size, selection of fellows, etc., and at one point Hannah Arendt could bear it no longer and broke out with: "What are we supposed to be talking about? The Humanities. Well, what do we mean by the humanities?" There was an embarrassed silence. Then Hannah Arendt went on, "Well, I will tell you. We mean language and history. That is what man and only man has got: the Humanities mean language and history, and knowing that we have got them."

------

* "The Humanities on the River Kwai" is reprinted here by permission of the Grace A. Tanner Foundation. It derives from the Grace A. Tanner Lecture in Human Values, presented on Thursday, 23 April, 1981, at Southern Utah State College, Cedar City, Utah. [Ed.] The lecture is as delivered except for the omission of references to the slides which were shown, the restoration of various cuts made to save time, and a few clarifications. I am very grateful to Pierre Boulle, John Coast, and the executors of the late Philip Toosey for permission to quote from their letters. Some portions of the lecture first appeared in "The Liberty of the Prison," *Yale Review* 44 (1956), 514-32; "Bridges Over the Kwai," *Partisan Review* 26 (1959), 83-94; "The Myth of the Bridge on the River Kwai," *Observer Magazine,* September 1, 1968, 18-26; "The Real Kwai Bridge Stands Up," *Life,* October 18, 1968, R2, R3; "The Bridge over the River Kwai as Myth," *Berkshire Review 1* (1971), 19-32. For permission to publish here I thank the editors of the periodicals concerned. [IW]

This evening I'm going to explore those themes as I observed them operating in a small fragment of history long ago which later aroused worldwide interest as the result of a novel and a movie about a bridge on the River Kwai. I will begin by saying a little about how the prisoners' lives showed the power of humanistic concerns; and then, at greater length, attempt to apply a humanistic approach to what actually happened, and to how it illuminates the issues raised by the novel and the movie.

## Language and History in the Prison Camps

On February 15, 1942, Singapore capitulated to the Japanese; and some eighty thousand allied soldiers found themselves prisoners of war. They were immediately faced with a new problem: how to be one. Being a prisoner is not an easy task, and it's too long a story to tell here; but I will say a word or two about how the painful process of adapting to our new circumstances revealed the importance of language and history.

Our speech very soon adopted so many loanwords (from the Australians and Dutch, who were our fellow-prisoners, from the countries we lived in—Malaya, Thailand, and Burma—and from our captors, the Japanese) that our talk would soon have been incomprehensible to anyone outside. There was also an extraordinary and imaginative linguistic inventiveness, especially about our main daily preoccupations: food, latrines, news, illness, and the important people in our lives. "Lime and slime" I remember as the name of a hideous dish of tapioca flavored with the leaves of a wild lime tree; and the thin vegetable soup that barely kept us alive was known as "gas-cape stew." Latrines were "benjos" (Japanese for "a convenient place") or "boreholes" (from their mode of construction). Then the word "bore-hole" became more specialised—it meant "news" because we exchanged the latest rumors in our moments of relative intimacy as we squatted perilously on the bamboos above the latrines. Later, new circumstances supplanted "borehole": once we started operating secret radios and smuggling in local papers the direct words—"radio," "newspaper," and so on—would have been dangerous; so "canary," "dicky bird," "birdsong" were used instead; and "no birdseed" meant "trouble with getting car batteries" to operate the radio. For other reasons we needed new abbreviations: "avits" were people—almost everyone—suffering from "avitaminosis," and there were so many amputees from ulcers that we talked of "am-puts" or "stumpies." The most important people in our lives, of course, were our guards: and so—as the Iranian hostages were to do later—we gave them rather imaginative names: the Mad Carpenter, the Undertaker, the Silver Bullet (in allusion to his presumed malady), the Bombay Duck. Our own camp personalities were nicely hit off—I remember especially the Baby Panda, the Whispering Baritone, and two officers whose only recognizable attribute was that they were always together— they got dubbed Null and Void.

There were also more conscious efforts with language: people wrote poems and stories and invented satiric songs about our new life. In the early days we made a fairly successful attempt to build up the system of organized study classes that are a regular feature of most prisoner-of-war camps; but the Changi University, as it was called after the barracks on Singapore Island, was doomed when most of us left for work on the railway in Thailand or Burma. Even there, however, whenever there was a moment of leisure in the jungle camps, some kind of learning seemed to be a common hunger. Many people who had assumed that intellectual pursuits were not for them began to learn foreign languages, to ask about correct English usage, to take an interest in the water economy of plants, or have views about modern poetry. Anyone who could talk about anything would be implored to do it; and every night there were quizzes and discussions and lectures in the dark bamboo huts.

One of the most striking things to me was our fascination with the past. For the first few months, everyone was giving his account of what had happened to him during the disastrous Malayan Campaign; and later this recreation of the past spread more widely. For instance, one man who had been a cricket commentator on the radio was in constant demand; and night after night we listened to a play-by-play account of some famous test match of many years ago. This, incidentally, illustrates another point about our intellectual life on the Kwai: how one's memory improved when the only medium of communication was oral. That cricket commentator really could remember thousands and thousands of details about one three-day match. It made one understand the fixed nature of oral epic and biblical literature; and, conversely, it made one understand how much memory, and the sense of a common history which it keeps alive, have been almost obliterated by our civilization's new machinery for enforcing blindness and forgetfulness, and not only to the life around us but to the past; I mean the perpetual hubbub of the phonograph, the radio, and the television.

My last point about the connection between history and our sense of personal identity happens to belong to a particular place and time; so it needs a few words of explanation.

Once their armies started trying to conquer India, the Japanese realised they needed a railway from Thailand to Burma. In the summer of 1942 many trainloads of prisoners from Singapore were sent up to Thailand, and started to hack a two-hundred-mile trace through the jungle along a river called the Khwae Noi. In Thai, *Khwae* just means "stream"; *Noi* means "small." The "small stream" rises near the Burma border, at the Three Pagodas Pass; and it joins the main tributary of the Me Nam, called the Khwae Yai, or "Big Stream," at the old city of Karnburi, some eighty miles west of Bangkok. It was there that the Japanese faced their biggest engineering task—getting the railway across the river. So, early in October 1942, a large construction camp was set up at a place called Tha Makham, about three miles west of Karnburi.

On August 17, 1945, two days after the war ended, I happened to go to the Tha Makham bridge camp—then derelict; there I saw scores of ex-prisoners circling aimlessly about with their eyes on the ground, like mushroom pickers; as soon as they were free they had set out to find the spot where they had buried their diaries, their letters, and their pictures. The people who had kept those records had done so at the risk of their lives—I did not realise how many had taken that risk until long after the end of the war when I wrote an article about the Kwai; a great many people sent me photos and pictures that had somehow survived, and information about hundreds of others. That need to record and testify is surely an assertion of the individual's sense that his memory of his past, his historical experience, is an essential part of his sense of self; without a past he feels diminished and lost. Our humanity is largely formed by a combination of language and history, as Hannah Arendt said; we renew it through speech, writing, reading, and other forms of shared experience.

### Homo Bifocalis and the Literal Imagination

Before I come to the novel and the movie about the Kwai I want to say a little more about the role of the humanities and their relation to communication and historical interpretation in the modern world. The conflict between the humanities and other kinds of knowledge is an old one, and so are the impulses out of which they arise. One way of approaching the conflict is through E. M. Forster's terms "life by time" and "life by values"; the distinction, roughly between the daily round of our activities and how we think and feel about what we do. Since very early in the history of civilization, one imagines, the individual has been asking himself two different kinds of questions: "Will there be anything for breakfast?" and "Why did I say that last night?"; or, "Have I balanced my cheque book properly?" and "How do I measure up compared to other human beings?" Man, we can say, is essentially an animal with double vision; he's bifocal; he should really be called *homo sapiens bifocalis*.

We can, I think, find evidence of this—unusually unconscious—coexistence of two kinds of value systems, in the 1965 Act which set up the National Foundation for the Humanities:

[T]he humanities include, but are not limited to, the following fields: history, philosophy, languages, literature, linguistics, archaeology, jurisprudence, history and criticism of the arts, ethics, comparative religion, and those aspects of the social sciences employing historical or philosophical approaches. This last category includes cultural anthropology, sociology, political theory, international relations, and other subjects concerned with questions of value.

In this context when our legislators used the term "questions of value" they apparently forgot the tangible and measurable values of the dollar or of the "x" in an equation. The use of "value" in the Act obviously refers to "human values," to the more subjective and yet equally real considerations which are involved most directly in religion and philosophy, but which pervade all our thoughts and actions, since, in the words of the English poet Philip Larkin, "someone will forever be surprising / A hunger in himself to be more serious . . ." ("Church Going").

In a historical perspective it is generally agreed that the division between "life by time" and "life by values" became more conscious and more absolute at the time of the industrial revolution at the end of the eighteenth century. Until then man's life on earth was relatively fixed and stable, and so were the religious and ethical doctrines on which he modeled his scheme of values; there was, therefore, very little intellectual conflict between the assumptions of man's practical and his ideal values. The great triumphs of science and technology in the eighteenth and nineteenth centuries, however, revolutionized the sphere of man's practical life; and the mechanistic and determinist processes of thought which demonstrably produced material change and progress began to dominate not only the sphere of daily life but of "life by values." In the new and more utilitarian systems of thought the concern for language and history and the whole structure of humanistic concerns inevitably lost much of their power;[1] they are not demonstrable, or cumulative, or progressive modes of knowledge, or at least not in the same way; and their rewards for the individual are not as tangible and immediate.

One reaction to this situation was the Romantic one, which made the individual imagination an alternative mode of thought entirely different from rational discourse, entirely independent of demonstrable evidence, and entirely separate from social and traditional considerations. To be an individual was to be different; to be yourself was not to do or think things just because society did; and Wordsworth made people think children were better than grownups because they were spontaneous, unspoiled by conventions and institutions. This summary much oversimplifies the real intentions of the Romantic poets but their antirational and anti-collective attitudes certainly led to the diffusion of an ideology which made people think that fact and reason were things which had to be disregarded if the individual was to be loyal to himself. In particular, imagination was more and more taken to mean fantasy, an ego trip which disregarded reality, and took no account of other people.

The true role of the imagination, I take it, is quite different; it's that on which Coleridge grounded the educational value of literature. He wrote, in the eleventh lecture on Shakespeare, that "the imagination is the distinguishing characteristic of man as a progressive being," and ought therefore "to be carefully guided and strengthened" by education. Coleridge meant the kind of imagination which has for its purpose, as he wrote, "to carry the mind out of self." It was therefore quite different from narcissistic fantasy, or the irresponsible egocentricity that is sometimes complacently called "insight" today. Recently I read that a con-

---

[1] The use of the term "humanities" for the various disciplines concerned with the formal study of values in general (divinity, philosophy), of history, of literature, and of language, arose at about this time, in the middle of the nineteenth century; until then, although the contents of the humanities comprised the major part of the academic curriculum, they were not regarded as a special category of knowledge, in contradistinction to the natural and social sciences. The term "science" itself stood for knowledge in general, until about the same time.

sultant to the Florida Educational Department imagined that the failure
of so many students to pass their tests could be palliated by saying:
"Many kids read things into the problems that were not intended by the
author. . . . Actually . . . they're showing me more insight into the situation—and they're getting penalized for it." What Coleridge wanted, and
what the humanities stand for, isn't that sort of spurious and muddled
self-indulgence, but a way of responding to experience which involves
what I would call "the literal imagination" entering as fully as possible
in all the concrete particularities of a literary work or the lives of others
or the lessons of history. "Sympathy," the great English historian R. H.
Tawney has written, "is a form of knowledge."

### Colonel Nicholson and Colonel Toosey

I come now to my main theme. What really happened on the Kwai is
very far from the public notion of it which the fantasies projected by the
novel and the movie created; and I will try to show this in two central
instances: in the character of the British officer who was in charge of the
prisoners at the main camp; and in the ultimate fate of the bridge—or
rather bridges—that were built there.

The novel and the movie are essentially works of fiction—the novel of
an individual fantasy, the movie of a collective one; but there is some
slight historical basis for two essential components of their narratives.
The first of these is the historical basis which may underlie Colonel
Nicholson's decision in the story that the bridge which the Japanese had
begun must be abandoned, and that a better bridge must be built in a
more suitable place. The Japanese did in fact build two bridges at Tha
Makham: a wooden structure, which no longer survives; and another
begun at the same time and finished in May 1943, a permanent iron-
trestle bridge on concrete piers, which, though not in its original form,
still stands. But the fact that there were two bridges is the only parallel,
and for obvious reasons.

When, as often happens, people ask me if the movie gave a true picture of my experiences on the Kwai, I sometimes reply: "Come on. What
makes you think the Japanese can't build their own bridges?" It's only
then, I notice, that people remember the obvious fact that the Japanese
beat the Allies in a campaign which, among other things, showed a remarkable command of enormously difficult engineering and transport
problems. That people seeing the movie hardly noticed this contradic-

tion with their own knowledge surely illustrates the force of fantasies of the collective ego; to present the Japanese as comically inept bridge-builders gratified the self-flattering myth of white superiority whose results we have seen most recently in Vietnam.

In the movie the bridge, with the beauty of its two giant cantilevers, was itself a symbol of Western engineering mastery; the real bridges over the Kwai were, of course, designed by the Japanese; they were much duller structures; and so, as we shall see, was their story.

The second historical basis of the novel and the movie is the exceptional nature of our prison camps. When, early in 1942, Singapore, the Dutch East Indies, and the Philippines surrendered, Japan was suddenly left with the task of looking after more than two hundred thousand prisoners of war. The normal military procedure is to separate the officers from the enlisted men and put them into different camps; but the Japanese hadn't got the manpower to spare, and so they left the job of organizing the prison camps almost entirely to the prisoners themselves. Prisoners of war, of course, like other prisoners, don't usually command anyone; they don't have anything to negotiate about with their captors, as Colonel Nicholson does in the novel and the film; and so—though in a very different way—did the actual British commander at the real bridge camp.

All the Far Eastern prison camps had a very small and incompetent Japanese staff. Most of the officers were men who for one reason or another were unfit for combat duty: too old, perhaps, in disgrace, or just drunks. What was special about the camps on the Kwai was that they were also partly under the control of the Japanese military engineers who were building the railway. These engineers were active and efficient; and they usually despised the Japanese camp staff almost as much as they did the prisoners. This played an important part in the frictions that beset the camps during the early days of building the railway.

Daily routine in the railway camps normally went like this: up at dawn; tea and rice for breakfast; and then on parade for the day's work. We might wait anything from ten minutes to half an hour for the Korean guard to count the whole parade and split the work parties into groups. Then we marched to a small bamboo shed where the picks, shovels, and so on were kept. Under any circumstances it would take a long time for one or two guards to issue tools for thousands of men out of one small shed; the delay was made worse because the tools usually belonged to the engineers, so two organizations were involved merely in issuing and checking picks and shovels. That might take another half hour, and then we would be reassembled and counted all over again before finally marching off to work.

When we had finally got out on the line, and found the right work site, the Japanese engineer officer in charge might be there to explain the day's task; but more probably not. He had a very long section of embankment or bridge to look after, and perhaps thirty separate working parties in different places to supervise. He had usually given some previous instructions to the particular guard at each site; but these orders might not be clear, or, even worse, they might be clear to us, but not to the guard.

There were many other organizational problems. For instance, in the early days of the railway the total amount of work each man was supposed to do—moving a cubic meter of earth or driving in so many piles—was quite reasonable under normal circumstances. But some groups might have to carry their earth much further than others, or drive their teak piles into much rockier ground. So, as the day wore on, someone in a group with a very difficult, or impossible, assignment would get beaten up: the guard knew that he'd probably be beaten up himself if the work on the section wasn't finished on time, so he struck out blindly at the nearest target.

Meanwhile, many other prisoners would already have finished their task, and would be sitting around waiting, or—even worse—pretending to work. The rule was that the whole day's task had to be finished before any single work party could leave the construction site. So some more prisoners would be beaten up for lying down in the shade when they were supposed to look as though there was still work to do in the sun.

At the end of the day's work an individual prisoner might well have been on his feet under the tropical sun from 7 in the morning until 7 or 8, even 9 at night, even though he'd only done three or four hours' work. He would come back exhausted, and late for the evening meal; there would be no lights in the huts; and as most of the camp guards went off duty at six, he probably wouldn't be allowed to go down to the river to bathe, or to wash his clothes.

So our lives were poisoned and our health worn down, not by calculated Japanese brutality, but merely by the familiar trade-union issues of long portal-to-portal hours of work, and the various tensions arising from failures of communication between the technical specialists, the personnel managers, and the on-site foremen—in our case the Japanese engineers, the higher prisoner administration, and the guards.

At first there was the same lack of understanding and communication at the Bridge Camp of Tha Makham, which I've mentioned already. But in a month or so this began to change, mainly because of the senior British officer in charge there.

Colonel Philip Toosey was a tall, rather young, man with one of those special English faces like a genial but skeptical bulldog. Unlike Boulle's Colonel Nicholson, he was not a career officer, but a cotton merchant and banker; he had experienced the decline of the Lancashire cotton industry, strikes, unemployment, the Depression; he'd even gone bankrupt. All this past experience helped him to see that the problem confronting him wasn't a standard military problem at all: it had an engineering side, a labor-organization side, and above all, a very complicated psychological side affecting both the prisoners and their captors.

Toosey, then, decided that refusing to work would only mean some men killed, and all the rest punished; a token resistance would make things worse; what remained was the possibility that his imagination could discover whether some other maneuver wouldn't be more effective. Toosey was a brave man, but he never forced the issue so as to make the Japanese lose face; instead he first awed them with an impressive display of military swagger; and then proceeded to charm them with his apparently immovable assumption that no serious difficulty could arise between honorable soldiers whose only thought was to do the right thing. The right thing, he persuaded the Japanese, was to let him handle things like issuing tools and allocating the day's tasks to each working party. He also persuaded the Japanese that output would be much improved if the duties of the guards were limited entirely to preventing the prisoners from escaping. We would be responsible for our own organization and discipline. The prisoner-officer in charge of outside working parties would supervise the construction work; while back at camp headquarters, if the Japanese engineers would assign the next day's work to Colonel Toosey, he and his staff would plan how best to carry it out.

There was another different kind of problem. The bridge—indeed the whole railway—was a vital part of the enemy's war effort; and so the Japanese were flouting the international convention which forbids the use of prisoners for military work. In yielding to duress, we prisoners, of course, were disobeying our own military code by helping the enemy's war effort. But we had tried protesting against the violations of the Geneva convention; and the results had been grim. For instance, it is the duty of prisoners of war to try to escape; but when some captured escapees had been ceremonially shot by the Japanese in front of the British senior officers, we had signed an "oath" not to escape.

There were some protests against being forced to work on a military railway; but they were purely formal. At Tha Makham Colonel Toosey noted in his diary:

It had now become clear to me that whether we liked it or not this work had to be done. I therefore addressed the troops giving them my views and told them that good discipline was essential and that they should work cheerfully to keep their spirits up, and that we (the officers) on our part would do our best to ensure they got good food and fair treatment. They responded as usual cheerfully.

The next notation records that he had succeeded in persuading Sergeant Major Saito that:

1 day's holiday a week plus better rations would (a) get the necessary work done more simply, and (b) keep them in good health. This was achieved when the troops were suffering very [badly] from debility, malaria, dysentery, and various avitaminoses.[2]

When the issues arose of officers doing manual work—again contrary to Geneva convention—Toosey reacted in a similarly pragmatic fashion.

I explained to all Officers [he wrote], that 2 courses were open to them—firstly, to refuse flatly to obey this order and to continue to refuse until, if necessary, someone was shot; secondly to work willingly. I pointed out that a compromise would only cause the Japanese to put the screw on harder than before and the Officers thereupon decided unanimously to work. Lieut. Bridge was released from the Guard Room and on the following day all Officers went out prepared to work with the men. In actual fact, once having shown this willingness, the Japanese generally lost their wish to make the Officers work and in many cases stopped them from doing so. In other Camps, we knew that Officers had already been forced to work, shots having been fired over their heads to coerce them.

I was an officer in the Chung Kai camp on the other side of the bridge at that time; what happened there was a bit closer to the token resistance shown in the movie. The Japanese colonel went on holiday, to

---

[2] From a transcript kindly supplied by John Coast.

leave the dirty job to his subordinates. We were called on parade, re-fused to work, and stood immobile while machine guns were posted around us; when the order to load was given, our commanding officer yielded; detachments of officers were formed, and went off to work.

I myself think Toosey's judgment was sounder; but I suspect that his dislike of histrionics, of a face-saving charade, was not without influ-ence. At all events the new organisation he had set up suffered no set-back, and it transformed the conditions of life in Tha Makham. There was much less waste of time; daily tasks were often finished early in the afternoon; weeks passed without any prisoner being beaten; and the camp became almost happy.

Looked at from outside, Toosey's remarkable success obviously in-volved an increase in the degree of our collaboration with the enemy; and it is on the interpretation of this fact that the main divergencies later occurred in the novel and the movie: was it right or wrong? Was it un-patriotic? Was it treason?

The author of the novel, *Le Pont de la Rivière Kwai,* Pierre Boulle, was a Free-French officer, who had never been to Thailand or been a prisoner of the Japanese. His book, as he wrote to me, was "pure fic-tion"; he took the river's real name merely because, "I picked up the name of Kwai on an atlas . . . when I was looking out for a suitable place to locate the story I imagined."[3] He did in fact intend his novel to raise the issue of collaboration, but not in terms which apply to the bridge or the Japanese at all. For, as Boulle recounted in his fascinating but—on this topic—not very explicit autobiographical memoir, *The Sources of the River Kwai* (1966), his Colonel Nicholson was based on two French colonels he had known in Indochina. Having been Boulle's comrades in arms until the collapse of France in 1940, they then sided with Vichy, and eventually punished Boulle's activities on behalf of the Free French as treason, quite blind to the notion that it was they, and not Boulle, who had changed sides. Then, when it appeared that de Gaulle and the Allies would win, they again changed sides, and without any apparent awareness that they had done so.

Boulle, then, intended his Colonel Nicholson to be a satiric embodi-ment of the total reversals of attitude which occur—constantly and yet hardly noticed—in our strange world of changing ideological alliances

---

[3] Letter from Pierre Boulle to Ian Watt, August 11, 1976.

among nations. Boulle's Colonel Nicholson also embodies a larger paradox of collective life in general; how the military—like any other institutional—mind will tend to generate its own objectives, objectives which often develop until they are quite different from, and may even be contrary to, the original purposes of the institution.

I have observed the operation of these paradoxes myself; and I think any reader of the novel would see that the character and the plot were intended to be self-evidently absurd, and therefore recognizably satiric, in their purpose. Boulle's novel, in fact, belongs to the general intellectual and political context of the immediate postwar world. His first collection of short stories was called *Tales of the Absurd,* and it expressed the Existential perspective of the period; and so, essentially, did the Kwai novel. Its epigraph is taken from Joseph Conrad's *Victory:* "No, it was not funny; it was, rather, pathetic; he was so representative of all the past victims of the Great joke. But it is by folly alone that the world moves, and, so it is a respectable thing on the whole. And besides, he was what one would call a good man."

Boulle's book was published in 1952 and sold about 6,000 copies annually in France until 1958. That year sales leaped to 122,000—the film had come out in 1957. Its great success caused the book to be translated into more than twenty languages, and to sell millions of copies; it was the movie which made a little river in Thailand that is not marked in most atlases into a household word.

The tremendous worldwide popularity of the movie obviously presupposes a very complete adaptation to the tastes of the international cinema public: and this process of flattering popular wishes can be seen in the main differences between the book and the movie, which is much further from what really happened on the railway. Of course, the movie was under no obligation to show the real life of the prisoner-of-war camps, if only because that life was boring even to those who lived it. In any case, David Lean was primarily out for entertainment, and he succeeded brilliantly. I am concerned only with some quite incidental results of that success, results which are based on the very nature and conditions of the movie business, and the mass media generally.

First of all, using the name of an actual river suggested an element of authenticity; and since the history of the Kwai railway was very well known, especially in England, it was inevitable that the public would assume that they were seeing the real thing. To the survivors of the real Kwai story the movie version naturally seemed a gross insult to their in-

telligence and to that of their commander. When news of the film's being made came out, the association of Far Eastern prisoners of war protested against the movie's distortion of what had actually happened. But
history had given the producer, Sam Spiegel, a lot of free publicity, and
he refused to change even the mention of the river Kwai in the film's title. Retaining the name was vital for the box office.

The pseudo-reality of the movie was as such inevitably reinforced by
its medium. You can't photograph fantasies as such; but if they are embodied in a script and acted out, the camera can't help giving these embodied fantasies an air of total visual authenticity. The effect of this
technical authenticity tends to spread beyond the visual image to the
substance of what is portrayed. We all know that—whenever we can
check against our own experiences—life isn't really like what we see in
the movies; but when we're watching we forget it most of the time, especially when the substance of what we see conforms to our own psychological or political wishes.

This pseudo-realism inevitably affected the portrayal of Colonel Nicholson. Boulle had made him conform to the French stereotype of the
English character: an amiable fellow in his way, but egocentric; admirable but ridiculous; intelligent, but not really grown-up. This infantile
and egocentric side of Nicholson's character is essential to Boulle's plot:
it is after all a fantasy about carrying out a boy's hobby in the real
world: he builds a bridge but not with an Erector set; he plays with a
train, but his isn't a toy one.

The movie made that game seem very real; and it also gave a pseudo-
reality to another universal infantile fantasy, the schoolboy's perennial
dream of defying the adult world. Young Nicholson cheeks the mean
old headmaster, called Saito: he gets a terrible beating, but the other
students kick up such a row about it that Saito just has to give in; Nicholson is released and carried back in triumph across the playground. In
the end, of course, he becomes the best student-body president Kwai
High ever had.

Total rebellion combined with total acceptance is common enough in
dreams; I don't believe it has ever occurred in any educational institution; and I am forced to report that nothing like it ever happened in the
prison camps along the Kwai. There, all our circumstances were hostile
to individual fantasies; surviving meant accepting the intractable realities which surrounded us, and making sure that our fellow prisoners accepted them too.

No one would even guess from the novel or the film that there were any wholly intractable realities on the Kwai. The essential theme of the novel, and especially of the movie, is really a simple syllogism: war is madness; war is fought by soldiers; therefore, soldiers are mad. It's a flattering notion, no doubt, to non-soldiers, but it happens not to be true; it's really much too easy a way out to think that wars and follies and injustices are caused only by lunatics, by people who don't see things as we think they ought to.

The movie was not alone in refusing to accept the possibility that certain rational distinctions remain important even under the most difficult or confusing circumstances. Much recent literature seems to derive a peculiar satisfaction from asserting that in a world of madness the weakness of our collective life can find its salvation only from the acts of madmen. There is no need to insist on the authoritarian nature of this idea; but it does seem necessary to inquire why these last two decades should have created this and so many other myths which totally undermine our experience of the stubbornness of facts.

The basic cause is presumably the widespread belief that all institutions are bad either because they frustrate our individual fantasies, or because they fail to live up to our ideal picture of what they should be. A prisoner-of-war camp is an exaggerated version of our modern world in one basic respect: both offer the individual a very limited range of practical choices. No wonder the public acclaimed a film where both its heroes—Colonel Nicholson and Shears—did just what they wanted. Nicholson built his bridge, and Shears—the part played by William Holden—managed to escape. Bill Holden has no counterpart in Boulle; but the movie needed an American hero in the cast. So he was given a key role in the collective fantasy. No one wants to be a prisoner; the movie suggested you don't have to be one; just blow the joint and heroic Thai villagers and allied submarines will somehow happen along. On the Kwai, hundreds tried to escape; most of them were killed; not one succeeded; but for Bill Holden it was a breeze. Obviously, if our circumstances on the Kwai had been as pliable as those of the movie, there would have been no reason whatever for Toosey or anybody else to make all the compromises which their actual circumstances forced on them.

There is, of course, another side to the question. In 1968 I wrote an article about the movie which was published in the London *Observer*. In it I argued that anybody on the spot knew that the real issue facing

Toosey was not between building or not building the bridge; it was merely how many prisoners would die, be beaten up, or break down, in the process. At the same time Toosey had never been accused by his fellow prisoners—as Colonel Nicholson certainly would have been—of collaborating, of being, as we said, "Jap-happy." Some prisoners regarded Toosey as a bit too regimental for their taste; but, unanswerably, he delivered the goods. Eventually, in all the dozens of camps up and down the River Kwai, Toosey became a legend: he was the man who could "handle the Nips," and his general strategy of taking over as much responsibility as possible was gradually put into practice by the most successful British, American, Australian, and Dutch commanders in scores of other camps along the river. Even more convincingly, early in 1945, when the Japanese saw defeat ahead, and finally concentrated all their officer prisoners in one camp, the vast majority of the three thousand or so allied officers agitated until various senior commanding officers were successively removed and Colonel Toosey was put in charge. He remained in command until the end of the war in August 1945, when, to general consternation, various ancient military characters precipitately emerged from the woodwork to reclaim the privileges and rewards of seniority.

My attack on the treatment of Nicholson, and the general ideological implications of the movie, evoked a strong letter of protest to *The Observer* from Carl Foreman, the celebrated movie writer, director, and producer, perhaps best known for the screenplay of *High Noon* (1952). Foreman had been cited by the Un-American Activities Committee in 1951, and driven into exile in London. He bought the film rights of Boulle's novel in 1954 (for £3,000), and later wrote most of the scenario. His letter (dated 3 September 1968) was not published by *The Observer,* probably because it was very long (six single-spaced pages) and he insisted that it only be published complete and unchanged; hardly anybody gets that treatment from the press, and I confess I was much amused that someone who was after all in the mass-media business should have been hoist with his own petard. Still, Foreman's letter—even though I cannot quote it—seems to me to be worth considering as a fascinatingly revelatory statement of the perspective of a highly intelligent moviemaker.

On the question of Colonel Nicholson, Foreman indicated, no doubt justly, that one difference of interpretation between him and Mr. David Lean arose from the question of nationality. As a British subject David

Lean was naturally more concerned than Foreman was about a British subject whose collaboration with the Japanese had been so close as to be treasonable; on the other hand Foreman was much more concerned that accepting the reasons for that collaboration would in effect dismiss the sacrifices of those who did not collaborate with the Nazis in Europe. But this argument really missed my point, which was essentially that the film was trying to have it both ways; the audience had to be made to think that the movie, though fiction, was somehow about the real bridge over the Kwai. Carl Foreman didn't seem at all aware of that confusion, presumably because he shared it; and he showed this by not seeing that I was merely comparing Colonel Nicholson's "collaboration" with the historical realities on the River Kwai. If one knew all the actual circumstances there, one could understand the actions of Colonel Toosey better, and at the same time one would know that in the real world the Colonel Nicholson of the movie would not have been able to act in the way he did. For instance, the prisoners wouldn't really have let themselves be commanded by a man who genuinely shared the Japanese objectives. In fact when, as occasionally happened on the Kwai, our commanding officers broke down under the strain of their impossible task, or even when they were suspected of not resisting Japanese orders as strongly as possible, they were quietly removed from their positions; this actually happened at the Chung Kai camp nearby, and in one case it was done by threatening a medical finding of insanity if the colonel concerned didn't voluntarily resign.

On the Kwai, Toosey may reasonably be said to have employed the two basic methods of how literary and historical scholarship attempt to dispel fantasy and discover the truth: a careful and unprejudiced collection of all the relevant facts; and an imaginative awareness of the human meaning of those facts. He began with a full sense of the realities of the situation, and then he applied his imagination to them, not to avoid reality, but to discover its meaning. He was also, I later discovered in correspondence, very aware of his situation, and—incidentally—of how his values and motives could never be presented, or even understood, by the mass media.

Our correspondence began when I wrote to him for permission to use his name in an article. He agreed, and wrote:

You do describe, as far as I am concerned, exactly what I was trying to do. To put it in other words—which I do not want you to repeat to anyone—I felt I had a mission not only to save as many lives as possible but also to maintain human dignity in those ghastly circumstances, and it is nice to know that at any rate you feel I had a measure of success.

I saw the film once and heartily disliked it, except that it had an effect on me in almost the same way that it affected you.

Thank you for sending me this fascinatingly interesting document. I will be extremely interested to know if it is published. It is not easy to destroy a myth. You may or may not know that we tried very hard to get the film altered before it was produced, but failed utterly because so much money had already been spent and the public had to be satisfied at the cost of the truth.[4]

In a second letter Toosey refers to his refusal to take part in a planned TV program about the Kwai, in which he and Alec Guinness were going to discuss their respective roles; it is dated 15 August 1967:

I have always been very frightened of publicity and particularly films since my experience has been that in order to sell the thing they have to appeal to the public and this is rarely done by telling the truth. In addition to that, personal publicity always makes me feel exceedingly uncomfortable. Perhaps this also is an aftermath of being a prisoner when I did a number of things which, if found out, would have had disastrous results for me and maybe I have an inbred wish to keep everything to myself.[5]

One of the activities which might have had "disastrous results" rose from the fact that Toosey, unlike the Nicholson of the book and the movie, not only saw both sides of the problem but played a double game. There was, for example, his prominent part in what was called "V" Organization, a secret underground group of people—Thai and Allied people both inside and outside the prison camps—who smuggled in what money, medicine, and food they could. All of those who took part were risking their lives every day, and—unlike the commandos in the novel and the movie—they operated, undramatically, for over two years, saved thousands of lives, and lost none.[6]

---

[4] Letter, Philip Toosey to Ian Watt, June 14, 1967. Toosey died in 1975, and I believe that there is good reason why his testimony should now be published.

[5] Philip Toosey to Ian Watt, August 15, 1967.

[6] Most people in the camps knew nothing about this operation; I myself, though friendly with its chief Thai member, the late Boon Pong, knew nothing at the time of the vast scale of "V's" operations.

A passage from a third letter concerns the attempts of *The Observer* to get Colonel Toosey to give a published interview about my article (October 25, 1967):

It may interest you to know that I had a long interview with the *Observer*, who tried to make me give my views. I flatly refused, and said I would not continue the interview, unless they promised me no[t] to personalise your article, and to reproduce it as written. I believe they got the point, and maybe we have together struck a blow for truer reporting—a newspaper's job anyway—and less of this stupid building up of ordinary human beings for some ulterior motive.

The last extract I shall quote is from a letter of January 23, 1969; it gives a glimpse of how Toosey looked at himself:

Having been lucky enough to rub shoulders with a few really great men, I have always found them simple and, in a way, humble and certainly realising that they are held in place by those below them.

I have just read a life of Gordon of Khartoum by Nutting. He was an odd and complex character, but, in one letter to his sister he wrote as follows: "The fact is that if one analyses human glory it is composed of 9/10ths twaddle, perhaps 99/100ths twaddle."

I will not comment on the psychology of these letters except to suggest that they reveal a degree of skeptical self-understanding which comple ments Toosey's realism and tenacity; the letters surely take us into the real world where unwelcome and often insoluble complexities and contradictions cannot be avoided.

## The Fate of the Bridge

The main differences between the way the novel and the movie treated the bridge reinforce what I have already said about how the movie flattered the fantasies and muddled the thoughts of the audience in a way that Boulle did not.

In the novel Boulle drove home his point about the absurd contradictions in institutional and ideological politics by sending the Allied commandos to blow up the bridge with exactly the same patient technological expertise as had been used by their former comrades in arms to build it. We watch the equally impressive though oppositely directed efforts of the commandos and the prisoners; we marvel at how well both are doing their jobs; and only at the end do we wake up and realize that all this marvelous technological proficiency harnessed to admirable collective effort has been leading to nothing except cross-purposes, failure and death. Nicholson sabotages the saboteurs, and then dies under the fire of Warden's mortar. But the bridge remains, so that, finally, we are forced to confront what Boulle's novel is really about: how the vast scale and complication of the operations which are rendered possible, and are even in a sense required, by modern technology, are under no rational or responsible control; the West is the master of its means, but not of its ends.

We can say, then, that Boulle used fantasy to convey a real and salutary truth; while the movie used realistic means to convey a false and —I think dangerous—collective contemporary fantasy. What is that fantasy?

The movie credits read "Screenplay by Pierre Boulle, Based on His Novel." Actually, though Boulle got an Oscar for the screenplay, he took only a "modest" part in the preliminary discussions of the screenplay with Sam Spiegel and David Lean. The main writer, as we have seen, was Carl Foreman; and then, over the question of Nicholson's attitude to the blowing up of the bridge, a new writer, Michael Wilson, was brought in to redeem Nicholson from treason and madness. Pierre Boulle eventually approved their final version; but only after he'd objected to many of their changes—especially to the movie's climax, in which the bridge was blown up. Boulle was told, he says, that the audience would have watched the screen "for more than two hours . . . in the hope and expectation" of just that big bang; if it didn't happen "they would feel frustrated"; and anyway it was quite impossible to pass up "such a sensational bit of action."[7] So, on March 12, 1957, a beautiful bridge that had cost a quarter of a million dollars to build was blown up with a real train crossing it.

Building a bridge just to blow it up again so that the movie public won't feel frustrated is an unbelievably apt illustration of Boulle's point about how contemporary society employs its awesome technological means in the pursuit of derisory and often destructive ends. Boulle had made his readers think about that; the movie didn't. It's true that our pacifist consciences were kept quiet by the movie's well-intentioned anti-war message—the killing of the terrified young Japanese soldier, for ex-

---

[7] Pierre Boulle, "Le Pont de la rivière Kwai," *La Nef* 13 (January 1958), p. 90. My translation.

ample. But, as we all ought to know, you can't turn an exotic adventure-comedy into a true film about war just by dunking bits of it in blood. Very typically, the film only *seemed* to take up real problems; at the end a big explosion blew up the bridge, thus compensating for the Allied lives lost by the deaths of hundreds of Japanese soldiers; so the final message was clear: when things will work out nicely by accident, why bother to think ?

Here again the moviemakers seemed to want to have it both ways, while denying that there was any contradiction. Thus Carl Foreman on the one hand denies my saying that Pierre Boulle protested against the changes which were made in the movie (which, as we have seen, he had done in print), and affirms that the movie was unprecedentedly truthful to the novel; on the other hand Foreman claims that he and Spiegel figured out a way in which the main artistic flaw of the book—the fact that the bridge was not completely blown up—could be rectified. So pleased, indeed, was Spiegel with this "improvement," that he invited Pierre Boulle to London for him to admire this and other changes from the novel which were contemplated for the movie.

There is surely a wonderfully zany confusion in the suggestion that the movie deserves praise for actually destroying the bridge whereas in the book poor Boulle had only succeeded in damaging it. Daddy knows best, and these authors really must learn to recognize their blindness to the spirit of their own work.

Foreman does allow that there was one exception to the movie's faithfulness to the book. It concerns Nicholson's fanatic devotion to the bridge, which goes to the point of betraying the Allied commandos who are trying to destroy it. So finally Carl Foreman was replaced by Michael Wilson, who worked out a compromise whereby Colonel Nicholson both accidentally caused the death of the commandos and then, when he'd discovered what was really going on, blew the bridge up with his own hand as his last act. It was a move which confused a good many viewers; but at least they were thereby spared from shedding all their illusions about the uniform sanity of British colonels. But on the main issue—the blowing up of the bridge—David Lean and Carl Foreman were equally responsible for betraying Boulle's intentions; and they were therefore equally responsible for promoting the notion that however muddled we may be about our political aims, advanced high-explosive technology will always do the right thing—the very illusion which Boulle wanted to destroy.

The history of the actual bridges on the Kwai tends to support Boulle's position, as against the movie's.

In the summer of 1944 the new American long-range bombers, the B-29's, started bombing the bridges. To anyone who knows any military history, the results were predictable. A lot of people, mainly prisoners, were killed or injured; but eventually the bombers got some direct hits, and two spans of the steel bridge fell into the river. While it was being repaired, the low wooden bridge was put back into use; when that, too, was damaged, it was restored by the labor of the prisoners in the nearby camps; and Japanese military supplies weren't substantially delayed. The historical lesson is obvious: if you can build a bridge, you can repair it; and in the long run, bombing military targets yields significant military advantages only if the targets can later be captured and held by ground forces.

## Concluding Reflections

Since 1866 and Nobel's invention of dynamite, popular credulity has attributed magical power to this particular miracle of science; all kinds of individuals and groups have refused to see that the most you can reasonably expect from explosives is an explosion. By accepting that delusion, the movie in effect promoted an attitude which is totally opposite to the movie's ostensible antiwar message.

The Big Bang theory of war is essentially one form of what Freud called the omnipotence of thought. The ending of the movie of *The Bridge On the River Kwai* reflects that infantile delusion, and, no doubt unconsciously, shapes it according to the values of contemporary culture. In this it reflects the common tendency of Hollywood, the advertising industry, Existentialism, and what is left of the counterculture; they are alike in their unconscious acceptance of their unthinking exploitation of the omnipotence of thought. From this delusion—and its rejection of all realities except the demands of the self—come many of their other similarities: that they are egocentric, romantic, anti-historical; that they all show a belief in rapid and absolute solutions of military, political, and social problems; they are all, in the last analysis, ego-centered institutional patterns disguised as anti-institutionalism.

Here again, the lessons of experience on the real Kwai may be worth attending to.

It's probably true that at the beginning of our captivity many of us prisoners thought that at last the moment had arrived for revolt, if not against the Japanese, at least against our own military discipline and anything else that interfered with our individual liberty. But then circumstances forced us to see that this would be suicidal. We were terribly short of food, clothes, and medicine; theft soon became a real threat to everyone; and so we had to organize our own police. When cholera broke out the demonstration was horrifyingly clear: whole camps of indentured laborers, lacking any form of social organization, because their guards had fled, were completely wiped out; whereas in our own camps nearby, with an effective policing system to make sure everyone used the latrines and ate or drank only what had been boiled, we often had no deaths, even though we had no vaccine and no medical services worth the name.

The actual circumstances of our experience on the Kwai were not, of course, reflected in the novel or the movie; there is no reason why they should have been. But it is surely the deep blindness of our culture and its media, both to the obdurate stubbornness of reality and to the stubborn continuities of history, which allowed the public to accept the plausibility of Nicholson's triumphs over his Japanese captors; and that blindness reflects the same romantic egoism, the same fantasy that the individual will has limitless power, as the big bang theory of war.

When I leafed through the Visitor's Book at one of the military cemeteries on the Kwai in 1967 one entry caught my eye. An American private from Apple Creek, Wisconsin, then stationed at Da Nang, had been moved to write a protest that made all the other banal pieties look pale: "People are STUPID."

Stupid, among other things, because they are mainly led by what they want to believe, not by what they know. For almost a decade it seemed easier to go along with the implication of the movie, and believe that a big bang will somehow end the world's confusion and our own fatigue; no doubt it would, but only in larger cemeteries for the victims of what Boulle called the Great Joke.

Now that the sky is black with chickens coming home to roost, perhaps we should try to accept the dull fact that from the hour of his birth, and even before, the individual can only survive through the existence of a number of institutions; the continuity of human affairs will not happen of itself.

The three versions of the story of the Kwai enforce that truth, for we can hardly look at them fairly without coming to terms with a habituation to complexity and compromise that denies our hunger for the romantic absolutes. That denial is perhaps one of the most humbling lessons of the humanities—that one must not expect certain progress or a permanent resolution of conflicting opinions; the best that one can do is to look at the whole picture, try to see what it means, and act accordingly.

In this I think I am lucky, over nearly forty years, to have been able to increase my understanding of what happened on the Kwai. It is certainly a piece of historical luck that circumstances should have provided so wonderfully representative a pair of opposites to give us an inside commentary on the history of the Kwai as Carl Foreman and Philip Toosey: the radical absolutist versus the conservative skeptic; romantic fantasy versus pedestrian responsibility.

Along the Kwai, Colonel Toosey was almost universally recognized for what he was—as near a hero as we could afford then and there. For he was led, not by what he wanted to believe, but by what he knew: he observed all the circumstances of the life around him, and then used his imagination to see how the experience of the past, of history, could help the present and prepare for the future. He knew that the world would not do his bidding; that he could not beat the Japanese; that on the Kwai—even more obviously than at home—we had to accept the role of being, in most matters, the prisoners of coercive circumstances. But he also knew that the only thing worth working for was the possibility that tenacity and imagination could find a way by which the chances of decent survival could be increased. It was, no doubt, a very modest objective; but in our circumstances then on the Kwai, the objective was quite enough to be getting on with; as it is here, now.

# INDEX

# INDEX